BETWEEN REDEMPTION AND DOOM

TEXTS AND CONTEXTS

•

General Editor: Sander L. Gilman, *University of Chicago*

•

Editorial Board: David Bathrick, *Cornell University*

•

J. Edward Chamberlin, *University of Toronto*

•

Michael Fried, *The Johns Hopkins University*

•

Anton Kaes, *University of California, Berkeley*

•

Robert Nye, *University of Oklahoma*

•

Nancy Leys Stepan, *Welcome Unit History of Medicine, Oxford*

NOAH ISENBERG

# Between Redemption and Doom

*The Strains
of German-Jewish
Modernism*

UNIVERSITY OF NEBRASKA PRESS

LINCOLN AND LONDON

This volume was published with
the support of a generous grant
from the Cleveland Foundation to the
Department of Religion at Case
Western Reserve University, as part
of a project on Jewish-Christian
relations directed by Professors
Susannah Heschel and Eldon Jay Epp.

Acknowledgments for the use of
previously published material
appear on pages xii–xiii
© 1999 by the University
of Nebraska Press
All rights reserved
Manufactured in the United States
of America

⊗

Library of Congress Cataloging-
in-Publication Data
Isenberg, Noah William.
Between redemption and doom :
the strains of German-Jewish
modernism / Noah Isenberg.
p.   cm. – (Texts and
contexts (Unnumbered))
Includes bibliographical
references and index.
ISBN 0-8032-2502-4 (cl.: alk. paper)
1. Jews – Germany – Intellectual life.
2. German literature – Jewish
authors – History and criticism.
3. Jews in literature.   4. Kafka,
Franz, 1883–1924 – Criticism and
interpretation.   5. Zweig, Arnold,
1887–1968 – Criticism and interpretation.
6. Golem (Motion picture)
7. Benjamin, Walter, 1892–1940 – Criticism
and interpretation.
8. Germany – Civilization – 20th century.
9. Germany – Ethnic relations.
I. Title.   II. Series.
DS135.G33I74   1999
305.892'4043'09041 – dc21        98-36813        CIP

To my family

# Contents

# Illustrations

# Preface

Several years ago, when I was invited to give my first public lecture, I titled the paper "Between Redemption and Doom." It was an investigation of Walter Benjamin's theory of memory and his musings on Jewish identity in *Berliner Kindheit um Neunzehnhundert* (*A Berlin Childhood around 1900*, 1932–38). Not only did the focus of that paper set the parameters for my discussion of Benjamin in the present study, but it has also helped to conceptualize the general framework for my analysis of German-Jewish modernism. For my selections as exemplary case studies of German-Jewish modernism are figures, texts, and debates that, to varying degrees, position themselves between "redemption" – renewal, revitalization, repair – and "doom" – dissolution, death, destruction. Far from being simple binary oppositions or altogether mutually exclusive, these markers work dialectically to shape each of the cases and their attendant strains. "Redemption," sought alternately in language, culture, memory, and representation, runs along a parallel trajectory to "doom," that is, the limitations of the quest.

As an exploration of distinct moments within an expansive history, the present study does not pretend to offer a complete overview of German-Jewish modernism; the partial, episodic, and fragmentary nature of the project precludes such aims. Instead, what I wish to present is a critique of related cases that I consider to be characteristic junctures in the larger history. I situate my project in the uniquely tumultuous period that spans from the eve of the First World War to the rise of National Socialism, precisely when the debates on German-Jewish modernism reach their ripest and most critical expression.

Academic inquiry almost invariably faces the requisite task of selecting – and thereby neglecting – texts for analysis. In choosing case studies, I am fully aware of the fact that not *all* facets of German-Jewish modernism can be included within my angle of interpretation. For example, although there are otherwise no set geographic limits to my undertaking, I do not examine at any great length the Viennese variety of German-Jewish modernism (a rich, complex, and certainly related history, whose peak, however, predates the main focus of my study). Similarly, there remain numerous figures from the greater scene (e.g., Alfred Döblin, Else Lasker-Schüler, and Kurt Tucholsky) who are addressed only nominally if at all. The cases I have chosen were selected with the hope that they would shed as much light as possible onto the most vital dimensions of this history. It is as case studies, and case studies alone, that both the possibilities and limitations should shine through.

When possible I have used standard translations, in some instances revising them slightly (indicated by "trans. rev."). If no reference is given for a translation, it is my own.

In the time since I first delivered the lecture of the same title, I have presented portions of the book manuscript at various conferences and symposia in Europe and in the United States as well as in reading groups at the University of California at Berkeley and Wesleyan University. I am especially indebted to my mentors at Berkeley who carefully read and commented on the original manuscript: to Anton Kaes, my ever supportive adviser who guided the project from the beginning and whose input both in and out of the classroom always provided new insights into the larger concerns I faced; to Hinrich Seeba, a tireless critic and one of the most painstaking readers one could ask for; and to Martin Jay, whose wisdom, intellectual rigor, and generosity were invaluable at every stage. I am also grateful to the friends and colleagues who have offered comments and criticism on individual chapters: Nina Caputo, Mitchell Hart, Paul Reitter, and Kathryn Starkey at Berkeley; Natasha Korda, Sean McCann, Ellen Nerenberg, and David Weisberg at Wesleyan. Complete drafts of the revised manuscript were read by David Schorr and Michael Brenner, both of whom offered useful suggestions. Brett Wheeler, my main collaborator and dear friend, has critiqued nearly every draft from beginning to end. I would also like to express my deep gratitude for the detailed and instructive reports by Sander Gilman and a second reader whose identity remains unknown, and for the shrewd advice of my editor, Douglas Clayton at the University of Nebraska Press.

During the years of research and writing, I have accumulated numerous debts to institutions, funding sources, and individuals who have offered support for the project. In this vein, I'd like to thank the Fulbright Commission for a one-year fellowship as well as a subsequent summer grant; the German Academic Exchange Service for a short-term research grant and a sur place grant; Wesleyan University for a project grant; and the American Institute for Contemporary German Studies in Washington DC for a summer humanities fellowship. At the Leo Baeck Institute, I wish to thank Diane Spielmann and Renata Stein; at the Stiftung Deutsche Kinemathek in Berlin, the staff of the library and archives; at the American Institute for Contemporary German Studies, Susanne Dieper, Jackson Janes, Carl Lankowski, and Frank Trommler; and at the Museum of Modern Art Film Stills Archive, Mary Corliss. I would like to express many thanks to Wesleyan's Department of German Studies: to Annemarie and Herbert Arnold, Peter Frenzel, Vera Grant, Leo Lensing, Diane Snyder, Arthur Wensinger, and Krishna Winston; and to the numerous outstanding students from whom I have benefited in my classes.

Throughout the entire process, my parents, Jon and Laury, my sisters, Nancy and Rebecca, and my extended family have given me enormous support. I am forever grateful for all their intellectual and emotional encouragement. Finally, I want to thank one person who has helped with every phase of editing, revising, and preparing the final manuscript, Melanie Rehak. Her contribution has been truly immeasurable.

A highly condensed early version of chapter 3 has appeared in *The Yale Companion to Jewish Writing and Thought in German Culture, 1096–1996*, eds. Sander L. Gilman and Jack Zipes (New Haven: Yale University Press, 1997).

BETWEEN REDEMPTION AND DOOM

# Introduction:
# Community in Crisis

As even the most cursory glimpse into recent German literary and cultural history attests, the position of the Jew – the definition and self-definition of Jewishness – has remained a point of contention. Both as storytellers (authors) and as story-dwellers (figures), Jews have occupied a liminal space in the modern German world, one where competing currents, ideas, fantasies, and realities have been played out.[1] Never has this cultural world experienced more tension, at once productive and destructive, than during the brief era that extended from the eve of the First World War to Hitler's rise to power. During this period, national identity was fiercely challenged, cultural and aesthetic movements were introduced, and the predominant notions of community were reassessed.

Although modernism is a highly elusive term that resists any short-hand classification, in the German context as elsewhere it has much to do with redefining a sense of community (national, cultural, social, and racial) and, by extension, with forging a new identity. Aesthetically, modernism has commonly been construed as a self-conscious movement, radically innovative, critically self-reflexive, and paradoxical.[2] These stock features, sometimes at the expense of others, have tended to shape the definitive underpinnings of the "modern" and its bearing on community formation. Certainly the various trends in German modernism – Bauhaus, expressionism, symbolism, *Neue Sachlichkeit*, and dada, to name but a small selection – were not equally preoccupied with the notion of community. And yet all of them, to varying degrees, were concerned with fashioning a new identity. While modernism encompasses many divergent and contradictory strains, from the "avant-garde" to what has been called "nativist modernism" or "reactionary modernism," its cultural logic, as Zygmunt Bauman has argued, "is about identity: about the truth of existence being not-yet-here, being a task, a mission, a responsibility."[3] As a pivotal axis along which identity was constructed, the widely used concept of *Gemeinschaft* (community) became both a romantic ideal and a source of wistful reflection among many modern thinkers. In Germany of the 1920s, at the high point of modernism, the philosopher and critic Helmuth Plessner proclaimed that *Gemeinschaft* had become "das Idol unseres Zeitalters" ("the idol of our times").[4] For more than a generation, *Gemeinschaft* was to symbolize what was absent for some in the modern *Gesellschaft* (society) and an ideal that could be recultivated for the future.

The search for community was, in great measure, a search for lost tradition and a search for belonging. Despite the fact that many emerging trends set themselves against tradition, the rejection was often based on a form of modernist antimodernism.[5] German modernism, as Peter Gay has suggested in his study of Weimar culture, represented a "hunger for wholeness," a desire for a "communally defined" world; it was a feeling, moreover, that transcended political and cultural lines.[6] In the case of German-Jewish modernism, we may alternately observe the impulse of aesthetic innovation (à la high modernism) and the equally profound antimodern turn toward tradition and a perceived purity and authenticity.[7] Jews, however, much to their chagrin, were viewed by society at large as agents of modernity (of urbanism, cosmopolitanism, mass society, etc.). They were stigmatized with the mark of the "modern" even if their own leanings were in part antimodern. During the first decades of this century, after modernization had taken hold, they were thus seen both on the margins and at the center of German society, as outsiders and insiders, pariahs and parvenus.

In the wake of the Enlightenment, Jews in German-speaking Central Europe had largely assimilated their ways to those of their gentile "hosts." As so-called "Deutsche Staatsbürger jüdischen Glaubens" ("German citizens of the Jewish faith") and as members of the German and Austro-Hungarian bourgeoisie, they had gained certain rights and privileges, mastered the German language and education (*Bildung*), and increasingly learned to identify with the dominant culture.[8] However, two factors challenged the growing complacency among post-emancipation Jews toward the end of the nineteenth century: the spread of political and racial antisemitism, and the concomitant rise of Zionism.[9] Two additional factors that accentuated the complexity of German-Jewish modernism must also be considered: the acute generational conflict (played out in the homes of Jews and gentiles alike and widely portrayed in the literature of the period) separating children born during the last decades of the nineteenth century from their parents; and the migrations of large numbers of nonassimilated, unmodernized East European Jews (*Ostjuden*), both prior to and during the First World War.[10] Taken together, these factors may help to explain some of the vicissitudes of modern German-Jewish identity as it came to be understood during the second and third decades of this century.

Like German modernism, German-Jewish identity had its share of diverse strains. There were Jews who participated in the cultural and political sphere of German modernism and for whom Jewishness remained, by and large, a secondary concern. There were also those Jews who chose altogether to avoid addressing their Jewishness. Yet there was a growing cross section of Jews who rejected the paltry Jewish traditions of their parents, turning instead toward something (Zionism, Socialism, Eastern Jewish culture and lore, mysticism) that might revitalize their sense of Jewishness. The question of Jewish identity, as it was raised at the time, produced a wide array of competing responses. Consider two prominent examples from the vast body of writings. In 1916, the future German-Jewish statesman Walther Rathenau expressed his deep-felt ties to his Germanness: "I have, and know no other blood [*Blut*] than German blood, no other tribe [*Stamm*], no other people [*Volk*] than the German. Expel me from my German soil [*Boden*], I still remain German, and nothing changes."[11] Ten years later, speaking to the B'nai B'rith in Vienna, Sigmund Freud, perhaps the most famous German-speaking Jewish modernist, declared his bond to his Jewishness as built upon "many obscure emotional forces [*viele dunkle Gefühlsmächte*], which were the more powerful the less they could be expressed in words, as well as a clear consciousness of inner identity,

3

the safe privacy of a *common* mental construction [*die Heimlichkeit der gleichen seelischen Identität*]."[12]

Clearly, the competing currents of the rational and emotional, the individual and communal, the national and cultural in the modern discourse on Jewish identity are many. It is thus my chief aim not to provide an exhaustive survey of the variations of German-Jewish modernism, but rather to focus on several distinct, paradigmatic moments within this broader context. While the figures and texts addressed in each of the following four critical interpretations may be viewed as exceptional in their own right, the resonance that they strike helps give further definition to the sweep of German-Jewish literary and cultural history. "The Jew," writes Hungarian author George Konrad in his recent reflections on the impact of modernity on Jewish culture, "has a hard time working free of his ambivalence and multivalence, being more at home in the territory of paradox and irony" (579). In German-Jewish modernism, the variegated responses, particularly to the main social, cultural, and aesthetic trends, converge around the discourse on community: its renaissance, its crisis, and its dissolution. Here, the complex and often contradictory perspectives emerge as indicators of the underlying questions of Jewish and German self-understanding.

### SYMPTOMS OF A MODERN IDENTITY CRISIS

Ferdinand Tönnies's pioneering study *Gemeinschaft und Gesellschaft* (*Community and Society*) was first published in 1887. It was perceived as "the foundation of a new science of sociology," blending English empiricism with German rationalism, while providing rationally ordered empirical data from Tönnies's investigations of the experiences and patterns of social life.[13] According to his retrospective view of the project, conveyed in 1931, the concepts he used to examine societal foundations (e.g., *Gemeinschaft*, *Gesellschaft*, *Wesenwille*, and *Kürwille*) were "ideal types . . . and should serve as standards by which reality may be recognized and described" (C&S, 248).[14] For Tönnies, "reality" and "identity" can be seen as methodologically interchangeable. Like "reality," "identity" can be recognized and described according to specific social and cultural categories.

Tönnies divides social relations and human will into two interconnected spheres: *Gemeinschaft* (community), based on *Wesenwille* (natural will) and the essential foundation of human beings as they are defined according to such cultural markers as kinship, language, and religion; *Gesellschaft* (society), based on *Kürwille* (rational or unconstrained will) and the foundation of reason, scientific progress, and economic exchange. In their relationship to each other, the two "ideal types" characterize not only specific periods and stages of development, but also the trappings of personal and collective identity. As Tönnies suggests, "The relationship itself, and also the resulting association, is [generally] conceived of either as real and organic life – this is the essential characteristic of the Gemeinschaft (community); or as imaginary and mechanical structure – this is the concept of Gesellschaft (society)" (C&S, 33). In its most rudimentary form, *Gemeinschaft* may be understood as an authentic "living organism," a unified body of practices that maintains its essential features, whereas *Gesellschaft*, by contrast, bears the mixed composition of a nonorganic "mechanical aggregate and artifact," assimilating divergent, heterogeneous practices (C&S, 35). As has often been noted in the Tönnies reception, *Gemeinschaft* seems to invoke a pre- or even anti-modern wholeness, while *Gesellschaft* speaks more to the conditions of modernity, to the rupture in unity, to alienation, atomization, and the so-called "realm of inauthentic experience."[15]

For the sake of the present study, what is most remarkable about Tönnies's work is the great popularity and radically diverse appropriation it enjoyed during the rise of German modernism. When Tönnies died in 1936, seven editions of *Gemeinschaft und Gesellschaft* had been published and critical debate on his model had proliferated throughout the first three decades of the century.[16] As Peter Gay has remarked, *Gemeinschaft und Gesellschaft* "made its fortune in the Weimar Republic, with its invidious contrast between the authentic, organic harmony of community and the materialistic fragmentation of business society."[17] Gay pinpoints the primary distinction of Tönnies's work, recognizing the sharp bearing it had on modernist debates. Though the two concepts should not be seen as mutually exclusive or in strict opposition to each other – indeed, Tönnies himself later emphasized their "interwoven" character (C&S, 249) – it is important to note the polarized relationship that crystallized around these concepts and that in the discourse of German modernism found its counterparts in *Zivilisation* and *Kultur*, *Großstadt* and *Land*, and *Geist* and *Blut*.[18] It was from within this tension that the modern necessity of self-definition and the reassessment of individual, cultural, and national identity found some of its most prominent expression.

In German-speaking Central Europe, beginning with the years immediately preceding the First World War and extending into the Third Reich, these concepts helped to define insiders and outsiders, Germans and non-Germans, gentiles and Jews. Tönnies's terms were widely used as markers of newly invented or reinvented identities: for example, the ideal of *Gemeinschaft* was instructive for self-fashioning groups such as German Zionists. While the main focus of this study lies in the various modes of Jewish identity formation during this time – precisely in the crisis of community as it concerned the Jews – the framework of discussion is the persistence of these debates and the vast questions surrounding German modernism and national identity formation in general. The specific discourse on Jewish identity must therefore be seen as symptomatic of the larger discourse of German modernism.

Germany's leading sociologist, Max Weber, himself indebted to the critical legacy of Tönnies, understood the fate of modern times in terms of "rationalization," "intellectualization," and what in 1919 he famously dubbed the "disenchantment of the world."[19] It was during the time that Weber speculated on the impact of the "modern" that he also studied the culture of Mediterranean antiquity and its religions, culminating in his *Das Antike Judentum* (*Ancient Judaism*, 1917–19). Here, the Jew as pariah – an idea that Hannah Arendt would continue to investigate in her work some two and one-half decades later – received due consideration: "Sociologically speaking the Jews were a Pariah people (*Pariavolk*), which means, as we know from India, that they were a guest people (*Gastvolk*) who were ritually separated, formally or *de facto*, from their social surroundings. All the essential traits of Jewry's attitude toward the environment can be deduced from this pariah existence" (3). Although Weber does not speak directly to the modern condition of German Jewry, focusing instead on ancient and premodern times, it remains an obvious subtext of his discussion. For

Weber, modernity had produced a heightened sense of alienation, a fragmented society, a world in which the Jew would once more be cast as a pariah figure. Yet his concept of the Jewish *Pariavolk*, on the margins of society, clearly had much larger implications.

Hannah Arendt thus undertook to broaden the scope of Weber's model in her essay of 1944, "The Jew as Pariah: A Hidden Tradition." Juxtaposing the pariah ("social outcast") and parvenu (the Jew who attempts "to ape the gentiles"), and finally showing their interconnections, Arendt sought to account for a certain disposition she attributed to modern European Jewish writers, artists, and thinkers from Heine to Kafka, Bernard Lazare to the cultural and ethnic exception Charlie Chaplin.[20] In passing reference to Weber, Arendt pronounces the pariah a "human type" that developed in the wake of Jewish emancipation leading up to the twentieth century, evolving from centuries of interaction between Jews as a "guest people" and their gentile "hosts."[21] The strength of the pariah as a concept for understanding modern European Jewry lay in its potential for outlining the modern bind of assimilation. "However slender the basis out of which the concept was created," suggests Arendt, "and out of which it was progressively developed, it has nevertheless loomed larger in the thinking of assimilated Jews than might be inferred from standard Jewish histories" (69).

If we recognize Arendt's account as a type of counterhistory – and a history comprised of contradictory affinities at that – it is no wonder that the figure who exemplifies this tradition most dramatically is Franz Kafka. In Kafka's work and life, as Arendt claims, we encounter "the entire dilemma of the modern would-be assimilationist Jew":

What Kafka depicts is the real drama of assimilation, not its distorted counterpart. He speaks for the average small-time Jew who really wants no more than his rights as a human being: home, work, family and citizenship. He is portrayed as if he were alone on earth, the only Jew in the the whole wide world – completely, desolutely alone. Here, too, Kafka paints a picture true to reality and to the basic human problem which assimilation involves, if taken seriously. For insofar as the Jew seeks to become "indistinguishable" from his gentile neighbors he has to behave as if he were indeed utterly alone; he has to part company, once and for all, with all who are like him. (84–85)

Along with his vivid fictional portrayals of shattered dreams of assimilation – Arendt takes *The Castle* as her main example – Kafka's own personal reaction to the predicament in which he found himself as a self-conscious Jew unable to declare a clear allegiance to either German letters or Jewish Zionism was also endemic to the world Arendt observed. Kafka was what Gershom Scholem would later call (albeit in reference to himself) a "post-assimilatory Jew"; as such his art and life represent the conflicting impulses of German-Jewish modernism.[22] Chief among these concerns was the disenchantment that assimilation had brought to an increasingly large number of Jews of his generation.

### ASSIMILATION AND ITS DISCONTENTS

Arguably the sharpest invective ever launched against German-Jewish assimilation appeared in the spring of 1912. Known as the *Kunstwart-Debatte*, and discussed widely among Germans and Jews alike, an article – a "documentary confession," as it would later be disparagingly referred to – by a rebellious young German Jew named Moritz Goldstein sparked enormous controversy when it was published in Ferdinand Avenarius's conservative journal, *Der Kunstwart* (*The Art Guardian*).[23] Entitled "Deutsch-jüdischer Parnaß" ("German-Jewish Parnassus"), Goldstein's essay expressed intense dissatisfaction with the dilemma that German-Jewish authors of his age had to face: "Suddenly, Jews are to be found in all the positions from which they are not deliberately excluded; they have made the tasks of the Germans their own; German cultural life seems to pass increasingly into Jewish hands. This, however, the Christians had neither foreseen nor intended when they granted the Pariahs in their midst a stake in European civilization. They began to resist, again they began to call us foreigners, to consider us dangerous in the temple of their civilization."[24] Goldstein's argument, which was understood variously as a Zionist case for cultural separatism and an antisemitic tract against the *Verjudung* (Jewification) of German culture, was revolutionary insofar as it attacked head-on what Jews of previous generations had so passionately been aspiring to achieve, namely, a complete and harmonious German-Jewish symbiosis.[25] Goldstein was truly unabashed in his critique of assimilation and the one-sided love affair that he saw in the modern German-Jewish condition. Even the German *völkisch* ideologues, Goldstein claimed, would need to recognize that "German culture in no small measure is Jewish culture" (*Berliner Jahre*, 221). He made his case most forcefully with the provocative and oft-cited hypothesis: "We Jews are administering the spiritual property of a nation which denies our right and ability to do so" ("German Jewry's Dilemma," 237).

Calling for "German-Jewish cultural disengagement," Goldstein suggests, if only polemically, that Germany's Jews should found their own culture.[26] They must recognize the fact that their "unrequited love" for Germany will continue to go unappreciated and, instead, should reorient their spiritual energy toward the establishment of a stronger Jewish literary and cultural sphere within Germany. For Goldstein, the "oversensitive" issue of the "Jew in German literature" is merely a window into the larger Jewish Question. The point at which his critical reading arrives is, for Jews and gentiles alike, an alarming one: "among ourselves, we Jews may care to have the impression that we speak as Germans to Germans – and we have this impression. Yet even if we care to consider ourselves entirely German (*ganz deutsch*), the others consider us entirely un-German (*ganz undeutsch*)" (*Berliner Jahre*, 217).

As was to be expected, Goldstein's article was met with heated debate. Among the Jews, as Goldstein himself noted retrospectively, "the Zionists applauded enthusiastically, the assimilationists were furious" ("German Jewry's Dilemma," 246). The German-Jewish patriot Ernst Lissauer wrote a vociferous reply to Goldstein in which he refuted the very idea that a Jewish *Volk* existed. For Lissauer, it was all a matter of assimilation into the "German-European spiritual community." He conclusively added that the Jew had only two opposing choices to make: "emigrate or become German" ("German Jewry's Dilemma," 246). On the other side of the Jewish political spectrum, Ludwig Strauß, future brother-in-law of Martin Buber and loyal correspondent of Walter Benjamin on the subject of German Zionism, replied in predictably affirmative terms. In his view, Goldstein had alerted Jews to the importance of recognizing their own distinct cultural particularities. There was, he argued, such a thing as a Jewish *Volk* whose "Jewish mind differed funtamentally from the German mind" ("German Jewry's Dilemma," 248). The dangers of ethnic and racial essentialism were readily apparent in the debate. And the easy shift from German-Jewish acculturation to a type of Jewish anti-assimilationist tribalism – in tandem with its German *völkisch* counterpart – was made possible. "It is tribalism," suggests Zygmunt Bauman, "miraculously reborn, that injects juice and vigour into the eulogy of community, the acclaim of belonging, and the passionate search for tradition"(79).

In this regard, the debate drew attention to another key issue: a viable segment of German Jewry was now ready to consider alternative modes of self-fashioning, to go beyond the uncritical embrace of German culture. With this, in contradistinction to the aping of German and European culture by the Jewish parvenus, came the search for a Jewish authenticity.[27] In his subsequent critique of assimilation, published in the Berlin-based Zionist journal *Die Freistatt*, Ludwig Strauß defined the terms of the debate as follows: "We think: not because the German-Jewish writers are Jews, but because they have already abandoned much too much of their Jewishness (*Judentum*), there appear among them so disproportionately high imitative rather than original creative talents . . . [These conditions] need to teach us to search for a milieu in which we can freely develop our kind (*Art*) and our entirely special capabilities"(14). The turn toward an ostensibly more authentic realm of Jewish expression was something that affected not only young Zionists such as Strauß, but Jews who, like Kafka, Arnold Zweig, Benjamin, Scholem, and countless others, rejected total assimilation without embracing the principles of Jewish nationalism. Around the years 1911–13, which were marked by several historical turning points (e.g., the conclusion of Buber's lectures at the *Bar Kochba* Academy in Prague, the *Kunstwart* debate, and the publication of the monumental collection *Vom Judentum* [*On Judaism*, 1913]), many Jews began to cultivate what Anson Rabinbach has termed a "new Jewish sensibility."[28] As the socialist revolutionary Gustav Landauer, otherwise not known for his "Jewish" writings, put it in an essay of 1913, "For all of us, when we began to be Jews with a full consciousness, it was an enrichment, an elevation, and a strengthening of our true existence."[29] Even more liberal Jews had to confess that a palpable, broad-scale transformation had taken place among Western Jews of the period.[30] And although this transformation of Jewish self-awareness can be traced back to the turn of the century, its clearest and most radical formulation did not appear until the 1910s and 1920s.[31] By this point, the Jewish populations of major German-speaking Central European cities, from Budapest and Vienna to Prague and Berlin, had grown significantly and the attention that the Jewish Question, in its various incarnations, received had similarly increased. The rise of the big city, as German modernism would amply document, and the position of the Jew therein had become prominent concerns.

### TRANSFORMATIONS OF GERMAN MODERNISM

While Tönnies saw the city as "the most complex form of social life" and the condition towards which all nations were tending (C&S, 227), responses to the city among German modernists were anything but uniform. One of Weimar's most noted and controversial thinkers, Ernst Jünger, maintained a highly unusual stance vis-à-vis urban modernity, yet one that also exemplifies the widely felt ambivalence toward the modern city and community. Unlike Oswald Spengler, who only a few years earlier had emphatically warned against the decline of German national and cultural identity in the big city, Jünger rejected the romantic visions of a harmonious, pure, unified, pastoral landscape.[32] Influenced by his wartime experiences, Jünger attempted to construct a "new community" within the metropolitan setting. Unapologetically, he perceived the city as the place for a "new nationalism"; he envisioned a revitalized national identity brought about by the big-city feeling, or "großstädtisches Gefühl," as he called it.[33] In his essay of 1926, "Großstadt und Land" ("Big City and Countryside"), Jünger remarks, "The city is the brain through which the fundamental will [cf. Tönnies's *Wesenwille*] of our time thinks, the arms with which it creates and strikes, and the mediating consciousness through which the finite comprehends what the infinite has to say to it."[34] As if to turn Tönnies's concepts on their heads, Jünger regarded the city not as the consum-

mate expression of *Gesellschaft*, but rather as the fertile ground for a re-
defined, renewed *Gemeinschaft*, albeit one with the heightened mental
sensibilities of the metropolitan *Gesellschaft*. According to Jünger, the
city offered the energy and force for national renewal. In this regard,
his conception speaks most powerfully against the *völkisch* notions of a
degenerate, rootless mass devoid of national identity that was seen as a
chief cause of cultural decline.[35]

Instead, Jünger argued that Germany "must come to terms with the
following necessity: We must penetrate and enter into the power of the
metropolis, into the *forces of our time – the machine, the masses, and the
worker*. For it is in them that the potential energy so crucial for tomor-
row's national spectacle resides. . . . We will try to put aside the objec-
tions of a *misguided romanticism which views the machine as in conflict
with Kultur*. . . . If our era does possess a culture, it will be through the
use of machines alone that it will be in a position to either expand or
defend its living space [*Lebensraum*]."[36] Such rhetoric is consonant
with the reverence for technology expressed in other modern German
aesthetic and political movements – for example, Bauhaus and *Neue
Sachlichkeit*, Weimar film productions such as Fritz Lang's *Metropolis*
(1927) and Walther Ruttmann's *Berlin: Die Sinfonie der Großstadt* (1927),
and the German reception of Italian Futurism. Neither does it seem far
removed from the future cries for the unity of technology and human
emotion made by Adolf Hitler. Unique to Jünger, however, are his
embrace of urban power and his dreams of founding a unified national
community within this realm. Jünger envisioned politics in the aesthetic sphere of which Goebbels would later speak as "steel-like romanticism" (*stählernde Romantik*).[37] Jünger's brand of national identity
therefore confronts what George Mosse has called "the dilemma of
*community* in the modern age," an acute crisis of identity that all modern nationalist movements must attempt to resolve.[38] In Jünger's case,
the overwhelming pervasiveness of this dilemma was affected by a climate in which the discussion of *Gemeinschaft* and the role of the emerging *Gesellschaft*, regardless of ideological stance and critical position,
figured prominently in the process of self-definition. Thus, the dichotomy of big city and countryside posited by Jünger also finds expression, though at an inverted angle, in the writings of another national

movement passionately concerned with the fashioning of a new identity: German Zionism.[39]

In 1920 greater Berlin had already grown to 4.3 million inhabitants, making it the third largest city in the world behind New York and London; by 1925, approximately one-third of all Germans were city-dwellers.[40] Just as Tönnies had concluded his *Gemeinschaft und Gesellschaft* by pointing to the potential diluting process of the city, particularly to the transformation into "a civilization of state and Gesellschaft" and thus the need for "fostering a new culture amidst a decaying one" (C&S, 231), German Zionists were likewise alert to such dangers they observed in an increasing need for cultural and spiritual renewal. In the second edition of *Der Untergang der deutschen Juden* (*The Decline of the German Jews*, 1921), the Zionist social scientist Felix Theilhaber warned of the cultural decline of the city and the deleterious effects that an assimilated, urban capitalist society might have on Judaism.[41] According to Theilhaber, by 1920 three-quarters of all Jews lived in urban centers, resulting in a severe loss of cultural identity due to intermarriage, conversion, urban nervous disorders, and the abandonment of Jewish beliefs and practices; the very structure of Jewish *Gemeinschaft*, as it were, was being undermined by the city's forces of fragmentation. It is no wonder that Zionist rhetoric shared a great deal with that of other nationalist, anti-assimilationist, and antimodern ideologies. As Mosse puts it: "Zionism, like all modern national liberation movements, was hostile to the modern city, the 'whore of Babylon,' which encouraged rootlessness. Here, once more, Zionism felt a special urgency, as most Jews were indeed city dwellers and therefore exposed to temptations which would lead to shattered nerves and the destruction of strength and beauty."[42]

Although Theilhaber's work should not be considered mainstream, having itself set off a series of debates, his fears of urban assimilation were not especially unusual among young German (mostly Zionist) Jews influenced by the early speeches of Martin Buber, the writings of such Zionist luminaries as Theodor Herzl, Ahad Ha'am, and Max Nordau, and such institutional bases as the *Bar Kochba* Academy in Prague. Buber's plea for Jewish renewal in 1911, imploring all Jews to "free [themselves] from the designing hustle and bustle of modern society [*moderne Gesellschaft*] and begin to transform our existence into true life," was championed among the newly awakened German Jews.[43] Jewish antipathy toward the modern *Gesellschaft* became a focal point of numerous writings during the Weimar period.

In his essay of 1925 entitled "Kulturzusammenhänge" ("Cultural Connections"),the Berlin rabbi and philosopher Leo Baeck expressed a great sense of urgency to combat what he perceived to be signs of cultural disintegration. Tracing recent socio-political and cultural developments in Jewish history, Baeck pointed to the profound impact of Jewish emancipation from the ghetto. Movement from the ghetto into dominant civilization, he argued, had brought about a crisis in Jewish life, namely, "the Jewish individualist without culture" (*der kulturlose jüdische Individualist*).[44] Pitting *Zivilisation* against *Kultur*, Baeck claimed that the Jew had moved into civilization at the expense of his cultural identity; only when culture had been revitalized could *Gemeinschaft* flourish again.[45] "It is the task of the present," he wrote, "in these new days to secure this personal and spiritual connection in Jewish life [i.e., between *Gemeinschaft* and *Kultur*]" (81). Unlike political Zionists, who advocated emigrating to Palestine, Baeck expressed the desire to preserve a Jewish *Gemeinschaft* amidst the pressures of *Zivilisation* and mass society. In view of Tönnies's conceptual framework, what is most illuminating in Baeck's position on society and the city is the fact that nearly half a century earlier, in the final pages of *Gemeinschaft und Gesellschaft*, Tönnies himself offered a similar reading of society's developments: "The entire culture has been transformed into a civilization of state and Gesellschaft, and this transformation means the doom of culture itself if none of its scattered seeds remain alive" (C&S, 231).

The following study explores four characteristic responses to the discourse on the rise of modernism and the crisis of community. The first part, comprising chapters 1 and 2, investigates the search for community in the works of Franz Kafka and Arnold Zweig. In Kafka, the notion of a *Sprachgemeinschaft* (community of language) in Yiddish language and culture illustrates a tension – between Yiddish and German, between the past and the present, the intimate and the official – that figures prominently in his writings of 1911–12. His private reflections on language and identity, their relation to his literary production, and the greater concerns of the surrounding historical moment in which he lived and worked receive critical attention.

In the case of Arnold Zweig, discussion is limited to his treatment of the *Shtetl-Gemeinschaft* in his work of 1920, *Das ostjüdische Antlitz* (*The Face of Eastern Jewry*). Zweig serves as a paradigmatic case of the assimilated German Jew searching for "authentic" Jewish life in the East. Like other writers such as Alfred Döblin and Joseph Roth, whose respective works *Reise in Poland* (*Journey to Poland*, 1926) and *Juden auf Wanderschaft* (*Wandering Jews*, 1927) similarly chronicle the German-Jewish search for community among the *Ostjuden*, Zweig reacted against the tendencies of modernity. Perhaps prefiguring his emigration to Palestine and later reemigration to the German Democratic Republic, Zweig envisioned a utopian, agrarian, Socialist community where identity could be preserved and sheltered from the corrupting forces of Western society. The sentiments he expressed in *Das ostjüdische Antlitz* incorporate facets of reactionary modernism, a modernism that attempts to undo *Zivilisation* in favor of *Kultur*.

The second part of the study, comprising chapters 3 and 4, investigates the responses among modernist filmmakers, philosophers, critics, and writers to the rise of *Gesellschaft*. Chapter 3 examines Paul Wegener's *Der Golem: Wie er in die Welt kam* (*The Golem: How He Came into the World*, 1920) in terms of the iconography of the Jew: the ghetto images, the incongruous inflections of industrialism and medieval alchemy, of German mass society and (Eastern) Jewish community. Wegener's film is situated within the historical context in which it was produced, thereby highlighting the rich commentary that it offers on the widely discussed Jewish Question. Although reference to contemporary social and political issues remained buried in the sixteenth-century legend, the *Golem* spoke directly to Weimar fears, fantasies, and illusions of the Jew and his/her identity. Rather than attempting to prove any complicity with the rampant antisemitism of the age, chapter 3 seeks to uncover the rich layers of cultural stereotyping that helped constitute Jewish identity as it was perceived around 1920.

*Introduction*

The final chapter, an examination of Walter Benjamin's theory of memory and its relation to his sense of Jewish identity, explores Benjamin's ambivalent confrontation with modernity as a response to *Gesellschaft*. Benjamin's fragmentary notes on memory are read in conjunction with his reflections on Judaism in order to outline the relationship between these two fields of interest. Finally, a critical excursus on his *Berliner Kindheit um Neunzehnhundert* (*A Berlin Childhood around 1900*, 1932–38) explores Benjamin's observations on the shattering of the community from which he and many other German (Jewish) modernists came. Implicitly, then, in its focus on the elegiac quality of Benjamin's writings, this chapter also traces the "death" of German modernism, a death which may be seen symbolically reflected in Benjamin's suicide in 1940.

The book aims to demonstrate how community (*Gemeinschaft*) and society (*Gesellschaft*) emerged as cultural concepts by which to measure the variegated responses to modernity. These categories, popularized in Weimar, do not merely represent the "invidious contrast between the authentic, organic harmony of community and the materialistic fragmentation of business society" (Gay, *Weimar Culture*, 80), but reflect even more the complexity of destabilized, rapidly evolving, and perpetually reconfigured identities. Just as Tönnies's concepts remain "interwoven," as he reminds us, demanding repeated revision among those who appropriate them, so, too, do the markers of identity formation cross the boundaries of political, social, and cultural distinctions. Rather than viewing identity as something fixed in a stable community – defined by the limits of "natural will" – Tönnies's model suggests new ways of examining the malleable nature of self-understanding.[46]

What is "modern" in Kafka is certainly not the same as the portrayal of the "modern" in Wegener's *Golem*. To be sure, the contradictions rendered in a comparison of Arnold Zweig and Walter Benjamin yield equally dramatic results. Yet these contradictions, as they take shape in the following case studies, define the deep complexity of the cultural world and the task that the respective authors and texts set for themselves. By employing disparate cases as revealing examples, it is my hope that the strains of German-Jewish modernism will be demonstrated in all of their distinctiveness. While various patterns can be charted from within this literary and cultural constellation, the unique nature of these cases should also become clear. To approach German-Jewish modernism is ultimately to approach a landscape riddled with idiosyncracy and contradiction. It is this aspect, above all, that makes the world it represented so engaging.

# ONE

# In Search of Language: Kafka on Yiddish, Eastern Jewry, and Himself

*Kafka wanted to be a Jew, but he didn't know how.* – I. B. Singer, "A Friend of Kafka"

In his 1990 speech delivered at the Hebrew University in Jerusalem, Czech President Václav Havel dedicated the auspicious occasion of receiving an honorary doctoral degree to the discussion of his "long and intimate affinity with one of the great sons of the Jewish people, the Prague writer Franz Kafka."[1] Although at the outset of his lecture Havel admits he is neither an expert nor even a truly thorough reader of Kafka, he insists that he *knows* Kafka. In fact, as Havel provocatively suggests, were he a better writer himself and had Kafka never lived, he might have been capable of producing Kafka's works. The Czech head of state then goes on to announce that "in Kafka I have found a portion of my own experience of the world, of myself, and of my way of being in the world."[2] Complementing the opening of Kafka's early short story, "Der Fahrgast" ("On the Tram," 1907) – "I stand on the end platform of the tram and am completely unsure of my footing in this world, in this town, in my family" – Havel locates his identification with Kafka in their shared anxiety about human existence in the modern world.[3] Accordingly, in his somewhat cursory outline of the "Kafkaesque" – the "vague sensation of culpability," the "powerful feeling of general alienation," the "experience of unbearable oppressiveness" – it becomes clear that Havel's conception of Kafka invokes the stock attributes of the Prague writer, which to this day have served to distinguish him as a preeminent modernist. To be sure, Kafka is still largely recognized for his angst-ridden portraits of modern life, for his tales of familial and communal crisis, and for his depictions of the contingent horrors of a brutally administered society. In Kafka, as Havel and many others would attest, we sense an acute state of "non-belonging," of complete and utter alienation, perhaps the quintessential modernist state of being. Havel's lecture succeeds in calling our attention to this critical aspect of Kafka's work. Yet it fails to acknowledge the flip side – the side that conveys his unfulfilled yearnings for "belonging" and the acutely felt exigencies of community. For in Kafka's work we see not only the dark visions of modernity – with which he has arguably achieved his international fame – but also the hopeful gestures of founding a place within an otherwise alienating modern society. Kafka highlighted these yearnings throughout his writing, and in late October 1921, less than three years before his death, he regrets in his diary that during his lifetime he had only rarely "crossed over the borderland between alienation [*Einsamkeit*] and community [*Gemeinschaft*]" (T 401; D 396 – trans. rev.). Caught as he was in this "borderland," in this dialectic between *Einsamkeit* and *Gemeinschaft*, Kafka had long sought to overcome his enigmatic position. Readers of his diaries will recall that ten years earlier it was precisely because of this longing that Kafka became intensely preoccupied with Jewish culture and lore, particularly with the Eastern European variant – that is, the Yiddish language in which he hoped, albeit temporarily, to discover refuge from modern Western society in Prague. Along with the general sense of alienation and "non-belonging," the passionate search for *Gemeinschaft*, indeed for a *Sprachgemeinschaft* (community in language), can be viewed as a vital undercurrent in Kafka's spiritual and literary world.

As early as the autumn of 1911, at the age of twenty-eight, Kafka extensively documented his encounters with a Yiddish theater troupe at Prague's Café Savoy in his diaries and letters. Among the countless pages of notes, Kafka jotted down plot summaries of some twenty plays he saw, character analyses of the individual players, and comparative cultural critiques. Focusing on Kafka's sustained support of the Yiddish Theater, Evelyn Torten Beck has argued that this deeply felt commitment instigated in Kafka a "radical shift in feeling" towards Judaism, a major "breakthrough" in his writing (especially around September 1912, when he composed "Das Urteil" ["The Judgment"]), and to a large extent determined the structural foundation for much of his literary repertoire.[4] Even more important, however, Kafka's liaison to the Yiddish Theater and its players represents his first encounter with an authentic *Gemeinschaft* of Jews, a community that was believed to maintain its own language, customs, and traditions while living a pure life devoid of the identity problems from which the Western (Prague) Jews suffered. Indeed, as the Czech Germanist Eduard Goldstücker has observed, Kafka's experiences with the Yiddish Theater and East European Jewish culture from the autumn of 1911 to the winter of 1912 are not only relevant for understanding the influence of Yiddish literature on Kafka and his religious transformation (*Konversion*); they are also significant for what Goldstücker considers the "Entdeckung der Gemeinschaft" ("discovery of community").[5] Nowhere else, to be sure, does Kafka find such "a sense of belonging to a national community" (i.e., a community that exists beyond the geographic and political realm) as in his encounters with the Yiddish Theater, with its cherished actors and, above all, its language.[6]

As representatives of a perceived Jewish authenticity, the Yiddish actors embodied for Kafka the romanticized world of *Ostjudentum* (Eastern Jewry), a foil against which increasing numbers of young, assimilated Western Jews of Kafka's generation were beginning to compare themselves. Kafka's confrontation with the *Yiddishkeit* of the actors serves as an impetus for reflection on his own impoverished sense of Jewishness, and thus, in turn, provides him with inspiration for his writing. During the years 1911 to 1913 – precisely the period in which Kafka first encounters the Yiddish Theater and begins to struggle with defining his Jewish identity – he fills the first half of his diaries with hundreds of pages of material for both his fictional output and for his ongoing catalog of personal reflections (T 29-253; D 34-250). Although Kafka's published works never make overt reference to the influence of Yiddish, his attention to the *Sprachgemeinschaft* he observes and the dilemma he sees in German-Jewish cultural and linguistic assimilation are readily apparent. A particularly poignant example of Kafka's views on the community of language manifested in Yiddish appears in his "Rede über die jiddische Sprache" ("Talk on the Yiddish Language," 1912) which, when examined in the context of a greater Jewish awakening, reveals the special features Kafka attributes to the language. "This often overlooked lecture," notes Harmut Binder, "is the most important and most comprehensive testimony to Kafka's Jewishness."[7] The following discussion focuses on the period in which Kafka acquaints himself with the Yiddish actors, the socially and politically turbulent time immediately preceding the First World War and the grand-scale cultural migrations of East European Jews, which later initiated widespread encounters with *Ostjudentum* among Western Jewry at large. Of particular interest is the sharp contrast between Kafka's conception of an authentic Yiddish-speaking *Sprachgemeinschaft* and his understanding of its German-speaking counterpart. Here we see how Kafka's yearnings for "belonging" – though ultimately unfulfilled and no doubt amplified during this period – can be considered as much an integral component of his modernist writings as are his portraits of alienation and "non-belonging."

KAFKA'S PRAGUE

*I am a memory come alive.* – Franz Kafka

The environment in which Kafka grew up was of a curiously mixed cultural and political composition. Indeed, Prague at the turn of the century was among the most culturally heterogeneous capitals of Europe; within the city limits there lived Czechs and Prague Germans, as well as German- and Czech-speaking Jews.[8] In the year 1900, when Kafka was seventeen years old, Prague's population consisted of approximately 415,000 Czechs, 25,000 Jews, and 10,000 Prague Germans, all living in what Hans Tramer has fittingly called a "city of three peoples."[9] While there was a growing Czech-speaking Jewish community, comprising more than half of the Jewish population in 1900, the Jews of Prague generally saw themselves, at least culturally, as members of the German-speaking Hapsburg Empire. And like their coreligionists in Germany and Austria, they too had increasingly assimilated themselves to German culture. "The strange fate of this city," writes Felix Weltsch, "where Germans and Czechs had confronted each other since time immemorial, had made the Germans aggressive and nationally conscious. Oddly enough, the same historical evolution had, for the most part, made the Jews of the city into nationally conscious – Germans."[10] The

Jews of Prague, according to Weltsch, had been thoroughly affected by the reform policies of the Hapsburg Empire, first instituted under Joseph II in 1782, to "Germanize" the Jews. They dutifully sent their children to German schools, became members and even leaders of German clubs and associations, and zealously contributed to the German cultural life of the city. By the beginning of this century they had become loyal "national allies of the Prague Germans in their struggle against the Czechs" ("Rise and Fall," 256) and, by extension, self-appointed representatives of the minority German culture within the dominant Czech population. In consideration of this unique situation, Weltsch goes on to affirm the existence, albeit short-lived, of a "cultural symbiosis" between Prague Germans and Jews. Such liberal institutions as the *Lese- und Redehalle* (Reading and Debating Club) at the German University of Prague, the German Theater, the *Deutsches Haus*, as well as numerous literary clubs, cafés, journals, and newspapers offered Jews places for full cultural participation.[11]

Inevitably, along with this spirit of liberalism and openness toward Jewish participation, there came a time when the Jews of Prague began to feel a "loss of Jewish consciousness," an unequivocal Germanization of their cultural heritage in which, as Weltsch puts it, "Schiller had ousted Rashi" and Judaism "was condemned to lead a pseudo-existence."[12] Especially the younger Jews of Prague — Kafka's generation — began to notice the absence of Jewish culture and tradition in their lives. In 1908, the Jewish writer and future leader of Prague's Zionist student association, Hans Kohn, wrote, "Judaism was foreign to us, almost a faraway legend. . . . Assimilation [on the other hand] was for us all a reality."[13] The awareness of this loss became so acute that in January of the same year "the time was ripe," asserted Kafka's contemporary Robert Weltsch, for Martin Buber to deliver the first of his famous *Drei Reden über das Judentum* (*Three Addresses on Judaism*, 1909–1911) at the *Bar Kochba Verein* in Prague.[14] In his letter inviting Martin Buber to speak in Prague, the leader of *Bar Kochba*, Leo Hermann, describes the Jewish milieu of Prague circa 1908:

> We live in Prague under totally unique circumstances. A large, old Jewish community — for a long time now absorbed in German cul-

23

ture, and supposedly German itself. Meanwhile, however, all the Aryan Germans have been subjected to "Czechization" [*Cechisierung*], [a process] which is also beginning to assail many Jews. Only the Jews continue to believe that it is necessary to defend German culture [*Deutschtum*]. Since they live without any contact with national Germans, their character remains predominantly Jewish. But no Prague-dweller [*Prager*] notices this. And almost everyone guards against conscious Jewishness.[15]

Sparking heated discussions among the members of the young Jewish community, Buber's first lecture, entitled "Das Judentum und die Juden" ("Judaism and the Jews"), implored the Jews of Prague to question themselves about their Jewishness, to probe the depths of their identities as Jews, and to assess their ties to past Jewish traditions, the Jewish people (*Volk*), and the Jewish community in general:

> The people [*das Volk*] are for him [the Jew] a community [*Gemeinschaft*] of human beings who were, are, and will be – a community [*Gemeinschaft*] of the dead, the living, and the yet unborn – who, together, constitute a unity. It is this unity that, to him [the Jew], is the ground of his I [*Ich*], this I which is fitted as a link into the great chain. . . . Whatever all the men in this great chain have created and will create he conceives to be the work of his own unique being; whatever they have experienced and will experience he conceives to be his own destiny. The past of his people is his personal memory [*Gedächtnis*], the future of his people his personal task. The way of his people teaches him to understand himself, and to will himself.[16]

Needless to say, Buber's call to transcend the elements of the environment in which the Diaspora Jews lived, and to recognize the deeper connection to the *Blutgemeinschaft* (racial, or biological, community) of all Jews was at once frightening and liberating. Many of the young Jews who attended the lectures – it is quite likely that Kafka was present at least for the last two lectures – began for the first time to consider the possibilities of inner Jewish renewal.[17] It was for them a matter of rejecting the hollow, or "empirical," Judaism of their parents for something more substantial, something vital that combined the authenticity of the ancient past and the youthful spirit of the modern present.[18] In this transformation of Jewish life in fin-de-siècle Prague and the ensuing "Jewish awakening" among young Jews there were several key events, figures, movements, and institutions that facilitated changes over the years. Kafka's world, likewise, was significantly shaped by these socio-political and cultural events.

In the wake of the 1897 First Zionist Congress in Basel, Switzerland, and the riots sparked by the Hilsner affair (a modern blood libel trial in Austro-Hungary) of the same year, the fledgling Zionist organization *Jüdischer Volksverein "Zion"* (Jewish People's Association "Zion") was founded in 1899. *"Zion"* was known as one of the earliest organizations to awaken Jewish sensibilities among Bohemian Jews. Also in 1899, the previously declining Prague-based Zionist student association, originally called *Maccabäa* and then simply *Verein der jüdischen Hochschüler* (Association of Jewish Students), achieved wider recognition under its new, glorified name *Bar Kochba*.[19] In the following years, several additional Zionist student groups were founded, among them the more radical *schlagende Verbindungen*, or dueling fraternities, *Barissia* and *Jordania*. Although Kafka was never an official member of any of the Zionist associations, opting instead to join the more liberal *Rede- und Lesehalle*, where he first came into contact with Max Brod, he often attended lectures at the *Bar Kochba Verein* and collaborated with its members while organizing the Yiddish lecture evening at the Jewish Town Hall. He was also an avid reader of Zionist publications (e.g., *Die Selbstwehr*) and generally maintained favorable ties to numerous friends and colleagues who were more actively involved in building Prague Zionism.

The brand of cultural Zionism promoted by the *Bar Kochba Verein* enjoyed a certain prominence in Kafka's Prague, hosting Martin Buber's three lectures in 1909 and 1910 and shortly thereafter producing its renowned volume of essays *Vom Judentem* (*On Judaism*, 1913). When Buber came to Prague in 1909, he had long been considered a spiritual guide among Prague Zionists, having already earned a name with the publication of his earlier speeches and his Hasidic works, *Die Geschichten des Rabbi Nachman* (*The Tales of Rabbi Nachman*, 1906) and *Die Legende des Baalschem* (*The Legend of the Baal-Shem*, 1908). Especially appealing to the Jews of Prague was the idea, first propagated by

Ahad Ha'am, of inner renewal of Judaism, that is, a spiritual and culturally oriented Zionism without the programmatic goal of *aliyah*, or Palestinian migration.[20] For Buber, the active spiritual life of the East European Hasidic shtetls became a romantic model for the return to an organic *Gemeinschaft*; Jews of the West were thus asked to consider new ways of revitalizing their ties to Judaism. Buber, who had first visited the *Bar Kochba* Academy in 1903, ultimately assumed the task of reminding Prague's Zionists of their Jewishness. There he found that he could help the young Jews to realize "a new beginning and new hope," as Maurice Friedman suggests, "to find their way back to Jewishness."[21]

At the core of the new wave of Prague-based cultural Zionism that culminated in the publication of *Vom Judentum* lies a central idea articulated by Hans Kohn in the introduction to the volume, namely, that the collective and communal project was to recognize the "necessity of expression among a generation, which lives with the conscious awareness that *in* its life and *through* its life Judaism will experience a vital transformation."[22] The organizers were Jews who considered themselves, at least on some level, members of the Jewish *Volksgemeinschaft* (community of people), a connection that Buber's lectures had affirmed. It is also important to note that contributors to *Vom Judentum* were not limited to Prague Zionists, nor to the young members of the *Bar Kochba*. Rather, the collection also contains articles by such established literary figures as Karl Wolfskehl, Jakob Wassermann, Max Brod, and Arnold Zweig, as well as Jewish spiritual revivalists such as Nathan Birnbaum, Moses Calvary, and Buber himself, and radicals such as Gustav Landauer, Moritz Goldstein, and Moritz Heimann. Although Kafka did not contribute to the volume, he knew its credo firsthand. He not only acquired a copy of *Vom Judentum* for his library but was also closely acquainted with the volume's organizers and contributors, particularly Hugo Bergmann and Max Brod.

At the other end of the spectrum of Prague Zionism, *Barissia*'s more aggressively political bent inspired the founding of the important Zionist weekly newspaper *Die Selbstwehr* (*The Self-Defense*) in 1907. As has been amply documented by Hartmut Binder, Kafka held the *Selbstwehr* in high regard, subscribing to it in his later years and referring to it in his diaries and letters more frequently than to any other newspaper or journal.[23] Until the First World War, and again after the war's end, the *Selbstwehr* published a variety of news, literary, and cultural pieces, most of which upheld the Zionist principle of invigorating the idea of Jewishness (*Belebung der jüdischen Idee*). From 1907 until the outbreak of the war, the editorship of the paper came under such renowned figures from the Prague Zionist establishment as Leo Hermann, Hans Kohn, Robert Weltsch, and Siegmund Kaznelson (all friends or acquaintances of Kafka's).[24]

All in all, Kafka's ties to the paper span more than a decade. In the late autumn of 1911, during the height of his support for the Yiddish theater, he solicited the help of the *Selbstwehr* to publicize the attractions of the Eastern Jewish acting troupe. Between September 1915 and September 1921, Kafka published four of his stories in the *Selbstwehr*: "Vor dem Gesetz" ("Before the Law") in 1915, "Eine kaiserliche Botschaft" ("A Message from the Emperor") and "Die Sorge des Hausvaters" ("The Cares of a Family Man") in 1919, and "Ein altes Blatt" ("An Old Manuscript") in 1921. During this period, while the *Selbstwehr* was under the editorship of Felix Weltsch, Kafka's work also received critical reviews by Max Brod and Weltsch himself. Finally, it is worth noting that on 6 June 1924, three days after Kafka's death, an entire page paid tribute to the memory of Franz Kafka, "an honor which," as Binder points out, "had not been paid to anybody before, apart from Theodor Herzl" ("Wochenschrift," 300).

A significant collective effort on the part of the *Selbstwehr*, the *Bar Kochba* circle, and the Prague Zionist scene at large came to fruition in the 1917 publication of *Das jüdische Prag* (*The Jewish Prague*), a multifaceted anthology that included Kafka's short story "Ein Traum" ("A Dream") alongside works by Herzl, Buber, Birnbaum, and Brod in one section, Paul Kornfeld, Ernst Weiß, and Oskar Baum in another. While Kafka's own contribution bears few traces of "Jewishness" — save the sheer alienation and lack of spiritual direction in his figure of Josef K. — it is worth noting that the contribution by Max Brod, "Zum Problem der Gemeinschaft" ("On the Problem of Community"), uncannily prefigures an essential line of inquiry in Brod's later Kafka criticism. Not only the talmudic dictum with which Brod opens his essay, "Schließe dich nicht aus der Gemeinschaft aus" ("Do not exclude yourself from the community"), but also his concern with the tension between *Einsamkeit* and *Gemeinschaft* in Kafka, anticipates his study of 1948, *Franz Kafkas Glauben und Lehre* (*Franz Kafka's Faith and Doctrine*). Brod, who in 1917 considered *Gemeinschaft* to be the "essence of our Zionism," would argue some thirty years later that Kafka passionately sought a "lebendige jüdische Gemeinschaft" ("living Jewish community") and that his quest increasingly became a central goal for his life's pursuits.[25] In what is perhaps an overemphatic assessment of the writer's Jewishness, Brod views Kafka within a noble lineage of Jewish spiritual revivalists of his age. "Although the word 'Jew' never appears in his [Kafka's] works," insists Brod, "they are among the most Jewish documents of our time. . . . He has created wonderfully vivid symbols of the repentant consciousness of exclusion [i.e., non-belonging] that rages through the soul of the modern Jew."[26] Whether Kafka was in fact a part of the Jewish cultural revivalist trend, or even a true Zionist for that matter – as Brod, Bergmann, Weltsch, and others would have us believe – is not of the utmost concern here.[27] Yet the close proximity of the Prague Zionist sensibilities, aspirations, and ideals to those of Franz Kafka cannot be ignored.

What significance do the few initial issues addressed up until now have for the understanding of Franz Kafka's life and work? Where did he stand in relation to these developments? How was he affected by the unique socio-political and cultural climate that characterized his city? And what are the historical underpinnings that informed his views of the Yiddish Theater, Eastern Jewry, and the *Gemeinschaft* that these people were seen to enjoy?

Having observed Kafka's experiences with such Zionist institutions as the *Bar Kochba Verein*, the *Selbstwehr*, and the general network of Prague Zionism, there are a few important summary distinctions that might serve to distinguish him from these groups. First, Kafka never formally associated himself with any of Prague's Zionist clubs. In fact, he consistently maintained the role of honored guest and privileged outsider, a position that offered him access without commitment. Indeed, the recurrent ambivalence and equivocation – the solid refusal to express commitment – in Kafka's stance vis-à-vis Prague Zionism must be emphasized. Second, although Kafka certainly admired some of the communal aspects of the Zionist movement, he had little patience for its politics. While in Vienna on business in 1913, he paid a visit to the Eleventh World Zionist Congress. In a letter to Max Brod written shortly after his visit, he elaborates on his feelings of detachment and irreverence experienced at the Congress: "It is hard to imagine anything more useless than such a congress. I sat in the Zionist Congress as if it were an event *totally alien* to me, felt myself cramped and distracted . . . and if I didn't quite throw spitballs at the delegates . . . I was bored enough to" (B 120; L 100; emphasis added). Such gestures of disassociation, while quite extreme in this instance, are not limited exclusively to political engagements. In a somewhat pithy and caustic remark recorded in his diary of January 1914, Kafka expresses his deep-seated ambivalence: "What do I have in common with the Jews?" he asks. "I barely have anything in common with myself" (T 255; D 252 – trans. rev.).[28] Mirroring to some degree the competing cultural developments of fin-de-siècle Prague itself, Kafka's own development was similarly fraught with paradox and contradiction, as he straddled the so-called "borderland between alienation (*Einsamkeit*) and community (*Gemeinschaft*)," exerting great resistance from both directions.

A deeper consideration of Kafka's biography and the paths his life followed, especially those which led him through the inner corridors of the urban center, might shed some light onto the broader constellation of Kafka's Prague. Born on 3 July 1883 to assimilated parents – both Herrmann and Julie Kafka (*née* Löwy) had moved to Prague from the countryside, abandoning the traditions of orthodox Judaism – Kafka was the product of the Prague liberalism of his parents' generation and the rising Jewish self-awareness among his own generation. As much as Kafka expressed his unfulfilled desire to leave Prague, declaring early in life that this "old crone [*Mütterchen*] has claws" (B 12; L 5), he remained in his home city throughout his lifetime, breathing its air and speaking its vernacular with such authority that Kafka's contemporary Johannes Urzidil once remarked, "Kafka was Prague and Prague was Kafka."[29] Apart from vacations, his travels to Italy, France, Switzerland, and elsewhere, as well as the time spent in various sanatoriums and the final months spent with his last love, Dora Diamant, in Berlin in 1923 and 1924, Kafka lived and worked within an unusually restricted space in Prague: he never seemed to move farther than a few blocks from the house where he was born. An examination of a map of Prague during Kafka's life-time (figure 1) reveals the intimacy of the urban network of apartments, employers, cafés, schools, and other institutions he inhabited.

The elementary school Kafka attended, the *Deutsche Knabenschule in Prag-Altstadt*, was a short walk across town. The Gymnasium he at-tended and the university where he studied law were both literally around the corner. His various workplaces from 1906 to 1922 – the jobs he held at the courts, the insurance offices, and eventually the *Arbeiter-Unfall-Versicherungsanstalt* (Workmen's Accident Insurance Institute) – were never far from his living quarters. During 1911 and 1912, he walked three blocks from his family's apartment to the Café Savoy to watch the performances of the Yiddish Theater troupe; it was only two blocks to the *Jüdisches Rathaus* (Jewish Town Hall), where he delivered his lec-ture on Yiddish in February 1912. Max Brod's apartment was also quite close to where Kafka lived, as were the many theaters, cafés, and other locales that he frequented. Considering the intimate quality of Kafka's Prague, it is no wonder that he so often expressed strong feelings about his hometown – feelings that, while in some regards discomforting, con-nected him inextricably to the history of a particular quarter of the city.

The sector of Prague in which Kafka lived, the *Altstadt*, or Old City, was predominantly Jewish, and, although he worked and was educated in the German world of Prague, the circles in which he traveled were largely made up of German-speaking Jews. The *Altstadt* also encom-passed the historically Jewish quarter known as *Josefov* or the *Josefstadt*, an area where the Jewish ghetto of past centuries had been located. Un-like Berlin and Vienna, where the Jewish quarters, the *Scheunenviertel* and the *Leopoldstadt* respectively, were populated almost exclusively with newly arrived *Ostjuden*, during Kafka's time the *Josefstadt* was oc-cupied by assimilated bourgeois Jews of Herrmann Kafka's genera-tion.[30] The Eastern Jewish migrations (mainly from Galicia and other regions in Poland) did not reach Prague until the middle of the First World War. Nonetheless, despite the absence of a large Eastern Jewish population, the *Altstadt* and former *Josefstadt* remained a ghetto-like community, continuing even in Kafka's time to bear discernible signs of the past. Kafka once remarked to a friend:

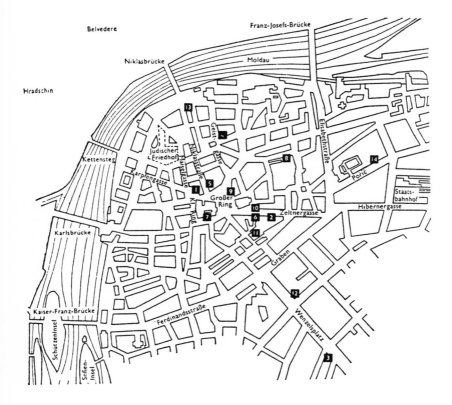

Map of the Old City in Prague During Kafka's Lifetime

1. Kafka's birth house (1883–1885).
2. Father's shop, 12 Zeltnergasse (from 1882).
3. Residence, 56 Wenzelsplatz (1885).
4. Residence, Geistgasse (1885–1887).
5. Residence, 6 Niklasstrasse (1887–1888).
6. Residence, 2 Zeltnergasse (1888–1889).
7. Residence, 2 Altstädter Ring, "Minuta" House (1889–1896).
8. Kafka's Elementary School, Fleischmarkt (1889–1893).
9. Kafka's Gymnasium, in Kinsky Palace (1893–1901). The father's shop was later located in the same building.
10. Residence, 3 Zeltnergasse (1896–1907).
11. Karolinum. Kafka attended law school here (1901–1906).
12. Building of Assicurazioni Generali, where Kafka worked briefly after receiving his degree (1907–1908).
13. Residence, 36 Niklasstrasse (from 1907).
14. Building of Workmen's Accident Insurance Institute, where Kafka was employed until retirement (from 1908).

In us all it [the ghetto] still lives – the dark corners, the secret alleys, shuttered windows, squalid courtyards, rowdy pubs, and sinister inns. We walk through the broad streets of the newly built town. But our steps and our glances are uncertain. Inside we tremble just as before in the ancient streets of our misery. Our heart knows nothing of the slum clearance which has been achieved. The unhealthy old Jewish town within us is far more real than the new hygienic town around us. With our eyes open we walk through a dream: ourselves only a ghost of a vanished age. (J 80)[31]

In spite of the gentrification that took place in Prague's *Altstadt* around the turn of the century, for Kafka the legacy of the ghetto lived on. He seems to have been keenly aware of the complicated relationship between the collective, ancient, and even more recent cultural past of the ghetto and the individual, modern present. Considering himself at one point "a memory come alive," Kafka concludes his remarks on the ghetto by stating that he, together with other assimilated Prague Jews, is "a ghost of a vanished age."[32]

Kafka's claim appears strikingly similar to a statement made by Buber in his first *Bar Kochba* lecture, emphasizing the connection between the collective Jewish past and the personal memory of the individual Jew ("the past of his people is his personal memory"). His conception of the present is clearly linked to the past of the Prague ghetto, infusing his sense of self with the larger cultural history of the Jewish people. Hence, it is memory that continues to define his present, to remind him of what has been irretrievably lost in history's wake, and what, in his eyes, has been transformed into a ghost. The Czech writer and Kafka critic Gustav Janouch has asserted, "The past was for him [Kafka] not some historically dead collector's piece, but a supple instrument of knowledge, a bridge to today" (J 48). Among the vast landscape of ruins, Kafka recognized the spectral legacy of Judaism that his father's generation had passed on. He maintained an awareness of the mythical foundations of the ghetto, the traditions of Rabbi Loew and the golem, kabbalah and alchemy.[33] Furthermore, Kafka's remarks on the Prague ghetto implicitly underscore the stark contrast between the disappointingly sparse traditions passed down to him by his father and the more substantial, living traditions that he observed among the East

European Jews.[34] Despite its former slum status, the ghetto – in particular, Kafka's memory of it – serves as a trope for the shtetl and the "authentic" lifestyle that Kafka attributed to such a community. "The unhealthy old Jewish town within us," as Kafka puts it, can thus be interpreted as the Eastern shtetl which, as he adds, "is far more real than the new hygienic town [the modern city] around us" (J 80).

This critique of the city and tribute to the "real life" of the shtetl *Gemeinschaft* finds its most poignant expression in Kafka's famed *Brief an den Vater* (*Letter to His Father*, 1919). Considered in the context of Kafka's admiration for the Yiddish actors and the untainted Jewish life they represent for him, Kafka's *Letter* exhibits an acute awareness of the contrast between Eastern and Western Judaism. The son of a kosher butcher, Kafka's father had moved from the Bohemian countryside to Prague in the latter half of the nineteenth century, leaving behind the orthodox tradition with which he had grown up for the more modern ways of life in the city.[35] After three years of military service, having proven his loyalty to the Hapsburg monarchy, Herrmann Kafka was, as his son tells us, even less interested in his Jewish background than before. In his discussion of the role of Judaism in his relationship to his father, Kafka explains the process of Western assimilation that took place during his father's lifetime:

> You really had brought some traces of Judaism with you from the ghetto-like village community; it was not much and it dwindled a little more in the city and during your military service; but still, the impressions and memories of your youth did just about suffice for some sort of Jewish life. . . . Even in this there was still Judaism enough, but it was too little to be handed on to the child; it all dribbled away while you were passing it on. . . . It was also impossible to make a child, overacutely observant from sheer nervousness, understand that the few flimsy gestures you performed in the name of Judaism, and with an indifference in keeping with their flimsiness, could have any higher meaning. (LF 78–81; H 145–46)

Such movements toward assimilation, and the accompanying migrations from the (Eastern) countryside to the (Western) city, were of course not limited to Kafka's father. "It was much the same," Kafka goes on to remark in his *Letter*, "with a large section of this transitional generation of Jews, which had migrated from the still comparatively devout countryside to the cities. It happened automatically" (LF 81–83; H 146).

Although Judaism and Herrmann Kafka's abandoned traditions may have been, as Kafka claims, an arena where the young Kafka had hoped to find a common ground for communication, this clearly never became possible. As Max Brod has observed, the figure of the father generally represented for the son a perceived "religious decadence" that had already taken its toll on Western Judaism.[36] Kafka himself discusses the hollow ritualism of Western Judaism in his diaries. Following the circumcision ceremony of his nephew in December 1911, he states, "I saw Western European Judaism before me in a transition whose end is clearly unpredictable and about which those most closely affected are not concerned" (T 150; D 147). And in 1912, when Kafka heard a lecture on the pitfalls of German-Jewish assimilation by the Zionist social scientist Felix Theilaber (most likely lecturing from his *Der Untergang der deutschen Juden* [*The Decline of the German Jews*, 1911]), he notes: "It [the decline of German Jewry] is unavoidable, for . . . if the Jews collect in the cities, the Jewish communities in the country disappear" (T 180; D 177). The past communities of the fathers, in other words, were believed to have vanished in the hustle and bustle of the modern city; all that remained were the memories and ghosts of this past. Since the young Jews of Kafka's generation could no longer turn to their fathers for the real Judaism and the living Jewish *Gemeinschaft* they desired, they had to search elsewhere.[37] In Kafka's case, this search was first and foremost directed toward the Yiddish acting troupe from Lemberg (Lvov) that he encountered in autumn and winter of 1911–12.

### EASTERN JEWRY AND THE TROPES OF AUTHENTICITY

*Eastern and Western Jews, a meeting. The Eastern Jews' contempt for the Jews here [in Prague]. Justification for this contempt. The way the Eastern Jews know the reason for their contempt, but the Western Jews do not.* — Franz Kafka

Early in October 1911, Kafka began to chronicle in his diary a series of observations on the Yiddish actors. He frequently kept notes on the performances he saw, compared the actor's roles, and rated the works themselves. Interspersed among these diary entries, Kafka also includes extensive reflections on two of the developing relationships he maintained to the actors: on his intense love for the Yiddish actress Frau Tschissik, and on his friendship with the troupe's leader, the much-admired Yitzhak Löwy. In Tschissik, Kafka appears to have seen a natural, almost mythical grace: "The beautifully founded, moderately strong, large body did not belong with her face . . . , and she reminded me vaguely of hybrid beings like mermaids, sirens, centaurs" (T 144; D 142). Kafka intricately describes her acting, her supple gestures, and the awesome beauty she radiates in the various Yiddish plays. In response to her spirited singing in a work by the modern Yiddish playwright Abraham Goldfaden entitled *Bar Kokhba* [sic], for instance, Kafka claims that Tschissik has a mouth "like a twinkling eye" and, still further, that she virtually "led the whole performance like the mother of a family" (T 107; D 107). Needless to say, Kafka idealizes Tschissik, projecting onto her qualities that he had never before observed in the Western European world. These qualities are of course largely imagined – mythical and even literary in essence – and deeply romanticized.

Kafka's perception of Frau Tschissik – part human, part animal; part reality, part legend – prefigures one of the most magnificent players in Kafka's fictional repertoire, Josephine the Singer, from his very last story, "Josephine die Sängerin oder das Volk der Mäuse" ("Josephine the Singer, or the Mouse Folk," 1924). In light of Kafka's encounter with Yiddish, we may read this tale as a critique of (Western) Jewish assimilation and the struggle for an authentic language. Like Frau Tschissik, Josephine appears as a symbol of beauty, purity, and truth in the face of an increasingly disenchanted modern world. Among the members of the assimilated mouse folk, who have lost their ties to tradition, "Josephine is the sole exception; she has a love for music and knows too how to transmit it; she is the only one; when she dies, music – who knows for how long – will vanish from our lives" (E 200–201; CS, 360). Kafka writes of a certain "purity of . . . song," and "power of life" conveyed in Josephine's rich gestures and heightened "mouse vernacular" – or, better, in her *mauscheln*.[38]

As the the receptive assimilated German-speaking Jews are affected by Yiddish, so the mice in Kafka's story "admire in her [Josephine] what we do not at all admire in ourselves" (E 202; CS, 362). In an almost elegiac tone, mourning the loss of memory and tradition, the narrator of "Josephine" remarks: "Although we are unmusical we have a tradition of singing; in the old days our people did sing; this is mentioned in legends and some songs have actually survived, which, it is true, no one can now sing" (E 201; CS 361). The distinction between "singing" (the language of tradition) and everyday "piping" ("our people's daily speech") that Kafka draws in this story parallels the distinction between his own romanticized notion of an authentic Jewish language (i.e., Yiddish and later Hebrew) and the everyday German he speaks and writes.[39] Moreover, the captivating quality that Kafka notes in Frau Tschissik's performance in the Yiddish Theater is transferred quite directly to Josephine: "At her concerts, especially in times of stress, it is only the very young who are interested in her singing as singing, they alone gaze in astonishment as she purses her lips, expels the air between her pretty front teeth, half dies in sheer wonderment at the sounds she herself is producing and after such a swooning swells her performance to new and more incredible heights, whereas the real mass of the people – this is plain to see – are quite withdrawn into themselves" (E 209–10; CS 370).[40] Regarding Frau Tschissik's performance in *Bar Kokhba*, Kafka notes that she leads the play, singing "the song in which she proclaims the appearance of the Messiah." Elevated to the next level, Josephine's performance is taken to resemble the maternal "saviour of our people." And like Frau Tschissik, Josephine draws the attention of her audience to the language and gesture she conveys.[41]

Kafka's perceptions of Löwy are not altogether different from his view of Frau Tschissik, at least in the intellectual and cultural sense. Like Frau Tschissik, Löwy helps to familiarize Kafka with the Jewish world of Eastern Europe. He tells him stories of his days as a Talmud student at the yeshiva in Poland and discusses with him the great Yiddish writers and poets, describing for him everyday life of the *Ostjuden*. When Kafka first observed Löwy reading excerpts from the masters of the Yiddish tradition, Sholom Aleichem, I. L. Peretz, and Morris Rosenfeld, he wrote in his diary: "A recurrent widening of the eyes, natural to the actor, which are then left so for awhile, framed by the arched eyebrows. Complete truth in all the reading" (T 78; D 81 – trans. rev.). If Frau Tschissik symbolized to Kafka the embodiment of Eastern-Jewish beauty, then Löwy was her counterpart in Eastern-Jewish lore. For Kafka, who in 1920 confessed to Milena Jesenská that he considered himself "the most Western-Jewish" of all Jews (M 247; LM 217), Löwy surely represented "the most Eastern-Jewish" of all Jews he had yet to know. He was "a hot Jew" (*ein heißer Jude*), as Kafka once called him, a passionate man who conveyed great spiritual intensity. As Kafka's extensive diary entries attest, his knowledge of the Eastern Jewish community and his desire to learn about their living heritage and traditions were greatly augmented by his relationship to Löwy.[42]

Upon being introduced to Löwy for the first time, Kafka's father is said to have warned his son, "Whoever lies down with dogs gets up with fleas" (T 103; D 103). For Herrmann Kafka, an upwardly mobile assimilated Jew of Prague, the sight of an Eastern Jew in the figure of Löwy was an unwelcome and indeed haunting lapse into the past, into the world of the abandoned shtetl. The fact that he chooses to use such an unflattering expression, likening Löwy to a dog and suggesting further the link between dogs and vermin, is not insignificant. For many years, Jews, in particular Eastern Jews, had been referred to as animals in German idiomatic expressions – used by Jews and Gentiles alike.[43] With specific regard to their language, the nineteenth-century Jewish historian Heinrich Graetz, whose *Geschichte des Judentums* (*History of the Jews*, 1888–89) Kafka read and cited in his diaries, was noted for calling Yiddish "semi-animalistic" (*eine halb-tierische Sprache*).[44] Because Yiddish was so commonly viewed as "animalistic" and (Eastern) Jews were compared to animals, it is no wonder that Kafka himself employs such metaphors in his stories. It is likely no coincidence that at the dramatic close of *The Trial* (1915), K. dies "like a dog," or that Kafka's only literary work with overt reference to Judaism, the fragment "In unserer Synagogue" ("The Animal in the Synagogue"), deals with a prophetic little beast who seems to know more about Judaism than the three generations of Jews that have gathered in the synagogue. Kafka's animal stories, many of which convey traces of a perceived authenticity in contrast to the world beyond the animals, emerge from within the same cultural context as his personal struggles to conceive of an authentic Jewishness. "To Kafka," writes Walter Benjamin, "the world of his ancestors was as unfathomable as the world of realities was important to him, and we may be sure that, like the totem poles of primitive peoples, the world of ancestors took him down to the animals."[45] Kafka's animals, in other words, might be viewed as literary envoys from the world of his ancestors, the "animal family," as he would call them many years later in a letter to his sister Elli (LF 294).

In view of the ostensibly "Jewish" metaphor of the dog, Kafka's posthumously published "Forschungen eines Hundes" ("Investigations of a Dog," ca. 1922) offers an allegorical base quite close to that of "Josephine." Commentators have argued that the story offers a Zionist critique (where the *Lufthunde* are nothing more than Jewish *Luftmentshen*, devoid of any national ties, and where the "congress of all dogs" symbolizes the Zionist Congress) and that, in terms of literary convention, it is Yiddish-inspired.[46] Like "Josephine," this story pits tradition against modernity, community against alienation (society), and, on a more subterranean level, the Yiddish culture of Eastern Jewry against assimilated Western Jewry. The first-person narrator tells of the tragic fate of the "dog" diaspora:

> No creatures to my knowledge live in such wide dispersion as we dogs, none have so many distinctions of class, of kind, of occupation, distinctions too numerous to review at a glance; we, whose one desire is to stick together – and again and again we succeed at transcendent moments in spite of everything – we above all others live so widely separated from one another, engaged in strange vocations that are often incomprehensible even to our canine neighbors, holding firmly to laws that are not those of the dog world [*Hundschaft*], but are actually directed against it. How baffling these questions are, questions on which we would prefer not to touch – I understand that standpoint too, even better than my own – and yet questions to which I have completely capitulated. Why do I not do as others: live in harmony with my people [*Volk*] and accept in silence whatever disturbs the harmony, ignoring it as a small error in the great account, always keeping in mind the

things that bind us happily together, not those that drive us again and again, as though by sheer force, out of our ethnic circle [*Volkskreis*]? (E 49–50; CS 279–80 – trans. rev.)

The "dog world" portrayed in the story – dispersed, severely conflicted, and undeniably isolated – invokes the modern Jewish world of Kafka's Prague. Although a nostalgic memory of the first-person narrator recalls a time when he was a "member of the canine community, sharing in all its preoccupations, a dog among dogs" (CS 278), he goes on to announce the "other side of the picture," the side that seemingly mirrors the modern Jewish condition.

Having observed in Löwy and the Yiddish actors precisely what he never saw in his family or in Prague Jewry at large (i.e., a vital community of Jews), Kafka continued to ponder the distinctions between Eastern and Western Jewry throughout his life. In his now famous letter of 1921 to Max Brod, he writes: "Most young Jews who began to write German wanted to leave Jewishness behind them, and their fathers approved of this, but vaguely (this vagueness was what was outrageous to them). But with their posterior legs [*Vorderbeinchen*] they were still glued to their father's Jewishness and with their wavering anterior legs [*Hinterbeinchen*] they found no new ground. The ensuing despair became their inspiration" (B 337; L 289). According to Kafka, the modern Western Jew, writing in German, reveals himself to be a different "animal" than the Eastern Jew. Dialectically caught between the past of the fathers and the present of the sons (and, to some extent, daughters), the Western-Jewish author, as Kafka attests, was faced with a form of modern disenchantment, or "despair," that shaped his writing.

From the beginning, Kafka's observations on the Yiddish Theater players focus on the salient characteristics of the traditions that separate their sense of *Yiddishkeit* from the Western Jewish life of Kafka's Prague. In an entry that begins simply "Last night Café Savoy. Yiddish troupe," Kafka proceeds self-reflexively to examine the uniqueness of the Yiddish actors. He expresses his uncertainty in categorizing the Yiddish players, speculating that they might be "sextons [*shamashim*],

39

employees of the temple . . . privileged shnorrers for some religious reason, people who, precisely as a result of their being set apart, are very close to the center of the community's life." As Kafka adds, however, they might also be considered people who "see clearly to the core the relationship of all members of the community, . . . people who are Jews in an especially pure form because they live only in the religion, but live in it without effort, understanding, or distress" (T 60–61; D 64 – trans. rev.). More than anything else, the immediate connection to community among the Yiddish actors and their unproblematic self-understanding as Jews sets them apart from the general disposition of Prague Jewry to which Kafka's experiences had heretofore been limited. Giuliano Baioni has aptly noted, "If Kafka loves the Yiddish actors, as he claims several times in his diary, it is because he believes them to be Jews without an identity problem."[47] These Jewish actors, as Kafka repeatedly remarks, exude such a deep sense of belonging that the observer, when watching their performances, does not feel alone but "among them"; Kafka saw the Jews of the East as "bound to each other by their Jewishness in a degree unknown to us" (T 174; D 170). "In short," suggests Enzo Traverso, "the Jews of the East, in his [Kafka's] view, represented the dreamed of *Gemeinschaft* as against those of the West, assimilated, rootless, memoryless, and traditionless."[48] What Kafka had previously observed in the world of the dominant Czech population as the "tremendous advantage of Christians who always have and enjoy such feelings of closeness in general interaction" (T 224; D 222 – trans. rev.) was thus introduced to him in a Jewish vein by the Yiddish actors.[49] Not long after Kafka recorded his initial reflections on the Yiddish actors, his close friend and Prague classmate, Hugo Bergmann, published an essay on Yiddish, "Unsere Stellung zum Jidischen" ("Our Position on Yiddish," 1914), in which he articulated a view complementary to Kafka's: "The Eastern Jew needs only to live, and he lives in a Jewish mode [*er lebt jüdisch*]. This matter-of-factness [*Selbstverständlichkeit*] of being Jewish is due above all to the Yiddish language."[50]

In addition to their strong sense of community and their lack of identity problems, the Yiddish actors most affected Kafka with their attentiveness to language, exhibited in their use of Yiddish in lively dialogues and songs for the stage. In his diary entry from 5 October 1911, Kafka remarks: "Some songs, the expression 'yiddische kinderlach,' some of the acting of this woman [i.e., Frau K.] (who, on the stage, because she is a Jew, draws us listeners to her because we are Jews, without any longing for or curiosity about Christians) made my cheeks tremble" (T 61; D 65 – trans. rev.). The Yiddish actors symbolize for Kafka at once the *Gemeinshaft* that binds them together and the problems that the Western-Jewish writer faces in using German. Kafka sees Yiddish, in stark contrast to German, as a language that is "essentially" Jewish, a language that captures the Jewish spirit with its natural and pure qualities and the vitality of the Eastern Jews. He articulates this linguistic essentialism in a provocative, if also reductionist, passage from his diary of October 1911:

> Yesterday it occurred to me that I did not always love my mother as she deserved and as I could, because the German language prevented it. The Jewish mother is no "Mutter"; to call her "Mutter" makes her a bit strange. . . . We give a Jewish woman the name of a German mother, but forget the contradiction that sinks into the emotions all the more heavily. "Mutter" is especially German for the Jew: it unconsciously contains, together with the Christian splendor, Christian coldness; the Jewish woman who is called "Mutter" therefore becomes not only strange but also foreign. "Mama" would be a better name if only one didn't imagine "Mutter" behind it. I believe that it is only the memories of the ghetto that preserve the Jewish family, for also the word "Vater" is far from meaning the Jewish father. (T 86; D 88 – trans. rev.)

Through his contact with the Eastern Jews of the Yiddish Theater, Kafka came to recognize the linguistic trappings of his identity. Unlike the Yiddish actors, however, Kafka could not rely on his language to preserve the lineage of his Jewishness. In *The Meaning of Yiddish*, Benjamin Harshav indirectly highlights the distinction that Kafka draws between Yiddish and German, between the so-called *mame-loshn* and *Muttersprache*: "The expression *mame-loshn* ('mama-language') is a typical Yiddish compound of Slavic and Hebrew roots, connoting the warmth of the Jewish family, as symbolized by mama and her language, embracing and counteracting the father's awesome, learned Holy Tongue [*loshn-koydesh*]."[51] In a variation of the opposition between Yiddish and Hebrew, Kafka pits the warm, maternal Yiddish against the cold German. The Yiddish actors represent "real Jews" who communicate with each other and who define themselves – their art as well as their lives – in a language that is *truly* Jewish (i.e., a language that, from Kafka's standpoint as a Western "Jew of memory," keeps the traditional past alive in a way that German cannot). Kafka's last love, Dora Diamant, the daughter of an orthodox Eastern Jewish family from Galicia, has suggested that German was "an all-too modern, all-too contemporary language [for Kafka]; Kafka's entire world yearned for an older language. . . . His mind knew finer nuances than those that the modern mind could grasp at all."[52] At the time of his evolving relations to the Yiddish Theater, Kafka appears to have believed, if only fleetingly, that these Jews might "convert" him to their way of life, to their community. As he notes retrospectively in a diary entry from January 1912, "When I saw the first plays it was possible for me to think that I had come upon a Judaism on which the beginnings of my own rested, a Judaism that was developing in my direction and so would enlighten and carry me farther along in my own clumsy Judaism" (T 171; D 167). And yet Kafka is quick to point out that it was not so much Judaism that the Yiddish actors brought to him as it was the feelings of *Gemeinschaft* conveyed in their personalities, their work, and in the particular lifeblood of the *Gemeinschaft*: their language.[53]

### TALKING ON YIDDISH

*Foreign words are the Jews of language.* – Theodor W. Adorno, *Minima Moralia*

*in der heymat home*
*where she does everything to keep*
*yidishkayt alive*
*yidishkayt a way of being*
*Jewish always arguable.* – Irena Klepfisz, *Etlekhe verter oyf mame-loshn / A few words in the mother tongue*

# In Search of Language

*Di gantse velt shtayt oyf der shpits tsung.* *[The whole world stands on the tip of the tongue]* — Yiddish Proverb

On the evening of 18 February 1912, in conjunction with a poetry reading by his new friend, the Yiddish actor Yitzhak Löwy, Kafka delivered an introductory lecture on the Yiddish language before a small audience in the banquet room at Prague's Jewish Town Hall.[54] Considered in terms of its professed aim, this "masterful lecture" (Brod) appears to have been presented as a plea for the understanding of East European Jewish culture, a call for the *Prager Juden* to free themselves from their fear of the *Ostjuden*, and more specifically to free themselves from their fear of the Yiddish language. In his survey of the so-called *Jargon* (a derogatory term, like *Mauscheln*, that Western Jews and Gentiles alike frequently associated with Yiddish, and used here by Kafka in a consciously subversive fashion), Kafka indicates his desire to become closer to a vital Jewish language, its culture, and its community. The lecture thus constitutes a bold defense of the culturally displaced world of the *Ostjuden*. It provides a glimpse into the problems Kafka faced as an assimilated Jew in Prague, writing exclusively in the German language, amidst such diverse political and cultural currents as Zionism, expressionism, neoromanticism, and the bureaucratic forces endemic to modern society.

The task of delivering this introductory lecture on Yiddish came to Kafka with little notice. Originally assigned to Kafka's friend Oskar Baum, it was passed on to Kafka only ten days prior to the scheduled date. According to the notes in his diary, when Kafka was first notified that he was expected to give the lecture, he hastily attempted and even managed to convince Baum to reconsider giving the lecture himself (T 183; D 181).[55] Small wonder that Kafka, once he finally realized that he, and not Baum, would need to deliver the lecture, became intensely nervous: "I was overpowered by uncontrollable twitchings, the pulsing of my arteries sprang along my body like little flames; if I sat down, my knees trembled under the table and I had to press my hands together" (T 181; D 179–80). Similar in intensity to the sensations recorded on 23 September 1912, when Kafka described the unrestrained process of writing "Das Urteil" ("The Judgment"), his reflections on composing his lecture on Yiddish convey the creative act in extemis. To be sure, Kafka's remarks exhibit an abstruse mixture of confidence and insecurity, pride and self-doubt, stimulation and paralysis. With only five days remaining to write the lecture and nothing yet on paper (though days earlier he had asserted that he hoped it would "come straight out of me as though out of a gun barrel" [T 182; D 180]), Kafka explains in his diary the various difficulties that impeded his writing: "The reason is only that incessant excitement has been oppressing me for days and that, somewhat hesitant in the face of the actual beginning of the lecture, I want to write down a few words only for myself; in that way, given a little momentum, I shall be able to stand up before the audience. Cold and heat alternate in me with the successive words of a sentence, I dream melodic rises and falls" (T 182; D 180). During his elaborate preparations, which involved meetings with the *Bar Kochba Verein* and discussions with Hugo and Leo Hermann, Robert Weltsch, and others, the actual writing of the lecture began to take on the character of a personal exploration. As he thinks of the words and the language in which he will give the lecture (the "melodic rises and falls"), he also thinks of himself. Kafka envisions that he will be able to "give a good lecture" but also notes that because of the extreme intensity, he may have no choice but to collapse once it is over (T 181–82; D 180). It is no longer simply a lecture on behalf of the Eastern Jews, nor even on behalf of Yitzhak Löwy. It is, in many ways, an expression of Kafka himself and all of his most intense fears and internal conflicts.

Standing before his audience – anticipating perhaps the fictional (and presumably Jewish) ape figure of Rotpeter in "Bericht für eine Akademie" ("A Report to an Academy," 1919) – Kafka begins his speech with a preliminary supposition: "Before we come to the first poems by our Eastern Jewish poets, I would just like to say, ladies and gentlemen, how much more Yiddish (*Jargon*) you understand than you think" (H 306; RK 263 – trans. rev.). The Western Jews of Prague were asked to dispense with their haughty attitudes vis-à-vis the language of past generations and in turn to realize their affinity with their own language. Through his previous conversations with Löwy, his personal experiences in Prague, and his readings on the history of Yiddish, Kafka realized the need to overcome the stigma attached to Yiddish by assimilated Jews since the Enlightenment.[56] From Moses Mendelssohn's early dismissal of Yiddish as innately regressive to Heinrich Graetz's classification of it as a "halb-tierische Sprache" ("semi-animalistic language"), Yiddish was clearly not welcomed by all of Western Jewry, and in Kafka's time it was still considered a threat to assimilation.

Indeed, as Kafka continues his lecture, he proceeds by responding to the assumed fears of his audience. "I am not really worried about the experience this evening holds in store for you, but I want it to be equally accessible, if it merits it. However, this cannot be the case so long as many of you are so frightened of Yiddish that one can see it on your faces" (H 306; RK 263 – trans. rev.). Fully cognizant of the perceived differences between the Eastern and Western Jews, Kafka constructs an oppositional framework: the unified, foreign *Ostjuden* on the one hand, and the fragmented, assimilated, bourgeois *Prager Juden*, fearful of Yiddish, on the other. As he had done previously for himself when he first viewed the Yiddish actors, he draws a romantically stylized image against which the assimilated Western Jews of Prague might compare themselves. Pointing to the bourgeois pursuit of success and the apparent assimilatory advantages of this pursuit, he provocatively asks his audience why anyone should ever desire to understand Yiddish. "Our Western European conditions, if we glance at them only in a deliberately superficial way, appear well ordered; everything takes its quiet course. We live in positively cheerful concord, understanding each other whenever necessary, getting along without each other whenever it suits us and understanding each other even then. From within such an order of things, who could possibly understand the confused Yiddish – indeed, who would even care to do so?" (H 306; RK 263–64 – trans. rev.). Life among the Western Jews, according to Kafka, was so terribly rational, logical, and well-planned that they would not dare make room for possible disruptions (and, furthermore, saw no need to do so). But Kafka saw a need: greater self-knowledge and a means by which to see through the complacent veneer of assimilation – to see through the ordered, mundane, meaningless lifestyle – into the latent yet ultimately unavoidable problems of the modern German-Jewish consciousness. Yiddish, he contends, represents a vital part of the broader German-Jewish cultural heritage, a language born out of a shared past.

Although he explains that Yiddish is made up of foreign words, Kafka also assures his audience that this merely contributes to the liveliness of the language, by no means reducing its comprehensibility. Moreover, according to Kafka, the audience should need no rational explanations, no grammatical source books, nor interpretational aids, but rather should allow itself to absorb the language, to take a step closer and feel it:

> You begin to come quite close to Yiddish if you bear in mind that apart from what you know, there are active in yourselves forces and associations with forces that enable you to understand Yiddish *intuitively*. It is only here that the interpreter can help, reassuring you, so that you no longer feel excluded and so that you may realize that you are no longer able to complain that you do not understand Yiddish. . . . But if you relax, you suddenly find yourselves *in the midst of Yiddish*. And once Yiddish has taken hold of you and moved you – and Yiddish is everything, the words, the Chasidic melody, and essential character of this East European Jewish actor himself – you will have forgotten your former reserve. Then you will come to feel the true *unity of Yiddish*, and so strongly that it will frighten you, yet it will no longer be fear of Yiddish but of yourselves. (H 308–09; RK 266 – trans. rev.; emphasis added)

Through unmitigated contact with the Yiddish language, Kafka seeks to extend the prevailing notions of Jewishness beyond those commonly held by Western Jewry. "Yiddish is everything," he states: the language, the music, the character of the individual. In his conversations with Gustav Janouch, Kafka is said to have remarked: "I also had difficulties with the language [Yiddish]. Then I discovered that I understood more Yiddish than I had imagined" (J 70). Discussing Yiddish literature, Kafka continues: "Jewry is not merely a question of faith, it is above all a question of the practice of a way of life *in a community* conditioned by faith" (J 109; emphasis added). Kafka's hope that the German-speaking Jews of Prague will feel the meaning of Yiddish, feel the unity of the language, corroborates his implicit idea of a

*Sprachgemeinschaft* – an unadulterated community within the life of the language. The revitalized past of Prague Jews should return to give their present life new meaning as a source of inspiration and renewal. The revivalist implications of Kafka's talk, however, cannot possibly be attributed to him alone. Indeed, many of the ideas he articulates had been presented in contemporary public debates on the Yiddish language, in scholarly books and articles, and in political pamphlets. The single most active figure behind the renaissance of Yiddish as a form of national emancipation was Nathan Birnbaum, born in Vienna in 1864 to Galician parents. Birnbaum had lectured extensively on the significance of Yiddish for the future of Judaism since the turn of the century.[57] Perhaps most famous for coining the term Zionism, Birnbaum organized the first international conference on the Yiddish language in the Austro-Hungarian (today Romanian) city of Czernowitz in 1908, and, in the succeeding years, lectured throughout German-speaking Central Europe. Kafka attended Birnbaum's introductory talk to the Yiddish folksong evening at the Hotel Zentral in Prague on 18 January 1912, just weeks before he gave his own presentation on the Yiddish language at the Jewish Town Hall. Although the original manuscript of Birnbaum's lecture is unavailable, and Kafka's notes only account for Birnbaum's "Eastern Jewish habit" of using such formalities as "my dear ladies and gentlemen" and "my dear," finally referring to such mannerisms as "ridiculous" (T 177; D 173), a lecture from the same year subsequently published in the Zionist journal *Die Freistatt* (*The Sanctuary*), may offer some insight into the revivalist context in which Kafka's lecture might best be situated.[58]

Originally given in 1912 in Yiddish at the *Verein für jüdische Literatur und Kunst* (Association for Jewish Literature and Art) in Königsberg and the *Jüdische Kulturgesellschaft* (Jewish Cultural Society) in Berlin, Birnbaum's lecture, entitled "Sprachadel: Zur jüdischen Sprachenfrage" ("Linguistic Nobility: On the Jewish Language Question"), bears a number of parallels to Kafka's text. Speaking to Western Jewry, Birnbaum cautions his listeners against the false classification of Yiddish as an illegitimate *Jargon*. In explaining the history of Yiddish and its degradation within the German-speaking milieu, Birnbaum offers his own classification of Yiddish as a bona fide *Mischsprache* (mixed language). Like Aramaic and Ladino, Yiddish is a language that has grown out of other languages. However, in Birnbaum's eyes, this makes it no less legitimate. "We truly need not be ashamed of our 'Mischsprachen,'" he asserts. "They are the testimonies to our strength. . . . They point to the false appearance of our assimilation and to the truth of our non-assimilation. They are the most indicative and clear proof of our eternal renewal – the extraordinary loyalty of our people toward itself."[59] As in Kafka's lecture, Birnbaum's remarks direct attention to the great potential he sees for Yiddish, thus undermining the standard prejudices held against the *Ostjuden*. In Birnbaum's counternarrative, the *Ostjuden* are strong, loyal, and unrelentingly anti-assimilationist.

Presumably heard by young, self-conscious Zionists, Birnbaum's lecture speaks directly to the ideological core of the *Freistatt*, fittingly subtitled the *Alljüdische Revue* ("Pan-Jewish Review"). In the editorial statement by Fritz Mordechai Kaufmann and the other *Freistatt* editors, the mission of the journal was "to pave new ways for Western Jewry toward a stronger and totally inclusive *Jüdischkeit* (Jewishness)."[60] The implicit goals were thus to bridge the gap between Eastern and Western Jews by speaking out against the denigration of Yiddish, which according to the editors, "is just as important as the free integration of the strongest and most fertile national values, and thus we will take the first effective step . . . by publishing in each volume high quality, vintage, original Yiddish works" (4). As one of the more poignant *Freistatt* articles on Yiddish, written by an Eastern Jew, proclaimed, "Today Yiddish is not only the strongest cultural medium for the people, but it is also its strongest weapon against assimilation and spiritual servitude [*Geistesknechtschaft*]."[61] Indeed, such ideas as combatting assimilation and forging a more inclusive "Pan Judaism" – and still further, in Kafka's case, attaining a truer sense of "belonging" – underlie the desirability of a *Sprachgemeinschaft* in Yiddish, as it was conceived by Kafka, Birnbaum, Kaufmann, and numerous other German-speaking assimilated Jews.

Kafka's own lecture on Yiddish was generally considered a success by the Prague Zionists in attendance. A review of the event, published in the *Selbstwehr* on 23 February 1912, hailed the "lovely, charming speech given by Dr. Kafka."[62] Even Kafka himself noted a "proud, unearthly consciousness during my lecture . . . strong voice, effortless memory, recognition. . . . In all this are revealed powers to which I would gladly entrust myself if they would remain. (My parents were not there.)" (T 184–85; D 181–82). The strength that Kafka seems to have cultivated in giving the fortuitous lecture comes not only from the subject matter (i.e., from his enthusiasm for the Yiddish language), but also from the fact that he took the stance that he did: against the position of his parents, who were significantly absent from the event. As the *Selbstwehr* review goes on to indicate, Kafka's intended goals of his lecture were on all counts achieved. The review concludes: "The audience, at first a little strangely moved by the unaccustomed language [Yiddish], nonetheless got into the right mood, reached the desired understanding, and received the performance . . . with rich applause. The evening certainly added a great deal to our closer understanding of the Eastern-Jewish spirit" (227). With his speech, Kafka managed to introduce his audience to the language and culture that, during the past months, he had so ardently embraced, while also proving to himself an unknown and often underestimated self-confidence. If only for this one brief moment, Kafka functioned as an effective spokesperson for Jewish self-awareness and the communal "belonging" he experienced at this juncture of his life.

In the obituary published in the *Selbstwehr*, three days after Kafka's death, Felix Weltsch makes a provocative statement about Kafka's sense of language and Jewish identity: "Franz Kafka is one of the most respected masters of the German language. The soul (*Seele*) that wrote in this language, however, is Jewish through and through. Its desperation is Jewish, as are its problematics and its consequences. Still there is the opportunity to uncover the inner connections between this great Western-Jewish writer of the German tongue and his Jewishness."[63] Ironic as it may seem, the "inner connections" of which Weltsch speaks in his obituary may be best illustrated by way of Kafka's observations on the Yiddish language and Eastern Jewry. For it is here, more than anywhere else, that his Jewish identity takes shape. And, of course, it is here that the passionate gestures of belonging reach their most dramatic expression.

Evident in such discussions around 1912–13 as Kafka's and Birnbaum's lectures, as the infamous *Kunstwart* debate (centering on Moritz Goldstein's polemic, "Deutsch-jüdischer Parnaß" ["German-Jewish Parnassus"]), and such articles as Max Brod's "Der jüdische Dichter deutscher Zunge" ("The Jewish Writer of the German Tongue") in *Vom Judentum* and Arnold Zweig's "Zum Problem des jüdischen Dichters in Deutschland" ("On the Problem of the Jewish Writer in Germany") in *Die Freistatt*, German-speaking Jewish authors of Kafka's generation were beginning to reconsider their status in German letters.[64] While very few actually advocated writing in a language other than German (e.g., Yiddish or Hebrew), many looked to these languages for inspiration. Here they found, as Kafka's discussion of Yiddish shows, a sense of Jewishness far different from that experienced in the German-speaking world in which they lived. In some cases, the German-speaking Western Jews identified themselves with the Eastern-Jewish community; in others, they defined themselves against this model. While the German-Jewish discussions of Yiddish seemed to reach a peak in Kafka's time, having first begun at the turn of the century with Birnbaum's early tracts, the search for a *Gemeinschaft* among the Eastern Jews did not end in 1912–13. Indeed, as we shall see in the next chapter, the German tours of the Eastern Front in the First World War brought about another significant encounter with the *Ostjuden*. Here, however, unlike in Kafka's Prague, the Jewish soldiers did not observe the East European Jews on a stage, but rather in their own native setting, the shtetl.

TWO

# The Imagined Community:
# Arnold Zweig and the Shtetl

*In the shtetl, people lived in poverty but were rich in the wisdom of Jewishness.*
– Roman Vishniac

At the close of World War II, before the deaths of millions of Jews had been fully calculated, a volume of photographs depicting the vanished world of East European Jewish life appeared under the generic title *Polish Jews*.[1] The photographer of this volume, Roman Vishniac, had spent the final months before the outbreak of the war capturing images of daily life in the Jewish communities from the Baltic Sea to the Carpathian Mountains. Vishniac's exquisite and often tragic photographs represent "the last pictorial record of the life and character of these people" (PJ 6). The images offer a final glimpse into Jewish life in the towns and cities of Eastern Europe on the eve of catastrophe. As a photo-chronicle, Vishniac's work evokes a distant world of Eastern Jewry that has otherwise all but disappeared. What remains of it is nothing but such images – preserved in the visual arts, literature, and culture – and memories, personal and collective.

For today's viewers, the diverse selection of photos – thirty-one in total – contained in *Polish Jews* documents the complex anatomy of an extinct world. Among the collected photographs are images of young Hasidic boys at the *cheder* (school) in Russo-Poland as well as humble storekeepers and merchants in Cracow, Warsaw, and many smaller, unnamed towns of the region. Portraits of local people – a rabbinical court, an old woman (figure 2), talmudic scholars at study – are juxtaposed with colorful, animated street scenes.

Each photograph seems somehow authentic in and of itself, as well as a true representation of the larger social fabric of the Eastern Jewish

2. Roman Vishniac, *Old Woman*. Roman Vishniac © 1992, International Center of Photography, New York. Courtesy of Mara Vishniac Kohn.

world. It is not only their photographic form that gives them the aura of "real" documentary evidence, of captured historic moments, but also their ability to conjure up a larger, more mythical reality.

In his introductory essay, "The Inner World of the Polish Jew," the Jewish theologian Abraham Joshua Heschel elaborates on what he considers the singularity of the lost world of the Eastern Jews.

## The Imagined Community

In Eastern Europe, the spiritual life of the Jews was lived in solitude. Growing out of its own ancient roots and developed in its indigenous environment, their life remained independent of the trends and conventions of the surrounding world. Unique were their cultural patterns in thinking and writing, unique their communal and individual ways of life. Tenaciously adhering to their own traditions, they were bent upon the cultivation of what was most their own, to the utter disregard of the outside world. Literature for them was writing *by* Jews *for* Jews. They did not apologize to anyone, nor did they compare themselves to anyone else. (PJ 7; emphasis added)

Like other observers before him, Heschel affirms what had traditionally separated the Eastern Jewish world from the outside. The "inner world" of the Eastern Jews was, as Heschel notes, insular, observant, and resolutely communal. Because of this, the *Ostjuden*, as they were commonly referred to in German-speaking Europe, were at once admired and despised, seen as both vibrant and degenerate. For most observers, the urban ghettos of Warsaw, Vilna, and Cracow and the rural shtetls were one and the same; they were seen as *Gemeinschaften* of Eastern Jews who "lived in their own way, without reservation and without disguise, outside their homes no less than within them" (PJ 7).[2]

What is perhaps most fascinating about perceptions of the Eastern Jewish world is the economy of myth that underlies them, an economy that to this day informs standard notions of "shtetl-life" in Eastern Europe, and that, in the early decades of this century, figured prominently in the German-Jewish imagination. Certainly not all Eastern Jews were pious, not all rejected assimilation, not all embraced a communal existence; but this is how they were largely imagined, remembered, and represented in the West. In the German context, from the time that Buber first published his collections of Hasidic tales at the turn of the century, an increasing number of Western Jews had taken an interest in the romantic qualities of the shtetl.[3] They envisioned the shtetl as the home of a purer form of Jewish life, cut off from the modern world, and richly imbued with ancient Jewish tradition. "It was the shtetl," notes Steven Zipperstein, "that came to encapsulate for many the difference between Jewish life in the East and West: between small and big towns, between lives that were static and in flux, between the security of tradition and the uncertainty of the new."[4]

Like Kafka's views on Yiddish, the predominant notions of an affirmative shtetl-life were in great measure antimodern, antibourgeois, and anti-assimilationist. In the wave of Eastern Jewish interest generated by such figures as Buber and Nathan Birnbaum, the shtetl – in its romanticized form – became a favorite icon for the modern promotion of Jewish renewal. There was a burgeoning number of translations of Yiddish tales from the shtetl.[5] Jews also increasingly felt the need to travel east to visit authentic locales firsthand.[6] This desire was greatly stimulated by the German occupation of Poland and parts of Russia during the First World War, when German soldiers, both Jewish and non-Jewish, had the opportunity to witness the Eastern Jews in their local surroundings. There they were able to observe the fundamental traits of Eastern Jewish life, comparing them to the ways of the Western world. Out of these encounters emerged a wealth of literature on the Eastern Jews and their "native" ways, as well as an extensive series of heated debates on the *Ostjudenfrage* (Eastern Jewish Question), as it came to be called.[7]

## MEETINGS IN THE EASTERN WAR ZONE

*Today I am in a very good mood – not to say happy – because I was requested yesterday by the War Press Division Ober-Ost and will travel today to Bialystok. My extraordinarily intense wish to experience the Eastern Jews personally shall be fulfilled.* – Arnold Zweig (1917)

The First World War instilled unprecedented hopes for a greater unity between Germans and Jews in many members of the Jewish communities of German-speaking Europe. Initial support for the German war effort was nearly unanimous among Jewish liberals, conservatives, and Zionists.[8] As the wartime statement of the *Zionistische Vereinigung für Deutschland* (Zionist Organization for Germany) declared, "German Jews! We call upon you, in the spirit of the ancient Jewish law of duty [*Pflichtgebot*], to devote yourself to the service of the *Vaterland* with all your heart, all your soul, and all your ability."[9] Through the putative national and communal bonds of war, a clear majority of Jews hoped to affirm a deeper connection to the German *Volksgemeinshaft*. Not only was it a Jew, Ernst Lissauer, who wrote the beloved German battle song "Haßgesang gegen England" ("Hymn of Hatred Against England"), but it is also well known that a large percentage of German Jews volunteered their services, registering and fighting for the German Vaterland.[10] While some German Jews felt that German victory in the East would help ensure the emancipation of their coreligionists from the yoke of Russian absolutism, others believed that the bonds of war would serve to strengthen the belief in a German-Jewish symbiosis and to establish more firmly Jewish loyalty to Germany. George Mosse has noted that many Jews hoped that the so-called "spirit of 1914" that characterized wartime morale "would lead to a more complete union of Germans and Jews" and would help put an end to the discrimination from which they had long suffered. Mosse suggests that numerous German Jews were still of the belief, first articulated in the early nineteenth century by Gabriel Riesser, that once blood was shed at battle for the fatherland, the "baptism of fire" would further Jewish emancipation.[11] To be sure, there are numerous testimonies of German-Jewish support during the war, and several studies have documented such cases.[12] However, the alleged German-Jewish solidarity was suddenly challenged during the war when scores of soldiers stationed on the Eastern front found themselves in direct contact with Eastern Jews.

German soldiers were generally shocked by the abject conditions in which they found the Eastern Jews: squalor, filth, and horror. Many felt, as an article in one army newspaper put it, as if they had "entered a totally different world, the world of the Orient."[13] The idea of Jews as "Orientals," as symbols of cultural otherness, had long been a part of German and German-Jewish discourse going back to Heinrich von Treitschke's description of German Jewry as "German-speaking Orientals" in 1879 and Karl Emil Franzos's stories in *Aus Halb-Asien* (*From Half-Asia*) of 1876.[14] German experiences on the Eastern front provided the first opportunity to "confirm" preexisting ideas about the Eastern Jews. As Steven Aschheim has argued, "The conditions of war made it easy to fuse myth with reality. Ostjuden had always been stereotyped as dirty, and what the soldiers found as they entered the ghettoes of Poland, Galicia, Lithuania vindicated that idea."[15] Many racial stereotypes, already firmly grounded in the discourse of the previous century, were reintroduced and given credence through contact with Eastern Jews on the front. Confirming the crude and radically contradictory images, Eastern Jews were seen as hagglers, parasites, thieves, and prostitutes on the one hand, and as symbols of purity, faith, and unity on the other. Whether vilified or idealized, these Jews were considered to be "the prototype of Jewishness."[16] These were *real* Jews, in their *real* home, acting in their *real* manner.

While some German soldiers found redeeming qualities in the unique ways of the Eastern Jews, a clear majority considered them degenerate people devoid of cultural worth. This opinion solidified in German soldiers the widespread belief in German cultural superiority. Indeed, there are reports of German battalions performing parodies on stage of the backwards Eastern Jewish life.[17] This sort of German "black-face" was not acted out by gentile soldiers alone. In the eyes of some Jewish soldiers as well, caught as they were in the position of mediator between their long-standing national ties (to the German military) and their new, putative ethnic relations (to the *Ostjuden*), the Easterners seemed a regressive, inferior people. However, a number of Jewish soldiers, though perhaps a comparatively small minority, experienced an ever-deepening bond with the Eastern Jews and an awakened spirit of Jewishness in themselves.

The German occupation of Poland and western Russia lasted for three years, giving the soldiers ample opportunity to observe the Eastern Jews in their native environment. With over two million Jews living in Poland alone, it was impossible to avoid contact with the *Ostjuden*. "Instead of the ghetto coming to Germany," notes Aschheim, "Germany came to the ghetto. Prussian soldiers, impoverished inhabitants of countless shtetls, and middle-class German Jews were flung together – an unprecedented situation."[18] Aschheim aptly calls attention to the central role that the German-Jewish confrontation with the *Ostjuden* had in their still evolving sense of identity, a balancing act between *Deutschtum* and *Judentum* where the Jewish side began to take on more prominence. Not only did the German-Jewish soldiers struggle to comprehend the lifestyle of the *Ostjuden*, but they also observed the relationship between the Eastern Jews on the front and the assimilated Western Jews they knew at home in Germany. An innate affinity between the *Ostjuden* and the German Jews was inevitably construed, posing at once a crisis and a potential renewal for German Jewish identity formation. Needless to say, for German Jewry it was on this level that the most significant transformation brought about by the war took place.[19]

From the Eastern front, reports on the *Ostjuden* were relayed back to Germany in enormous quantity, sparking debates that ranged from questions of cultural and educational reform to citizenship and border rights. Advocates of the Eastern Jews such as Nathan Birnbaum spoke in favor of the independent and flourishing *Kulturgemeinschaft* attributed to the East and the regenerative potential that lay in the proposed East-West solidarity.[20] Conversely, opposition to the *Ostjuden* concentrated on the protection of the German people from the perceived threat of mass migrations of Eastern Jews.[21] Paradoxically, as a result of their own distrust and fear of Russia and Poland, the Eastern Jews became unlikely allies of the German military. Because of this alliance, Germany's *Ostpolitik* developed a vested interest in the Eastern Jews, and they became an even greater concern for German wartime strategists. In sum, the scope of the discussions on the Eastern Jews was vast and the effects equally dramatic. Over time, Germans became more familiar with the issues concerning the Eastern Jews, and the location of the problem was no longer limited to the front but also reached home.

The so-called *Ostjudenfrage* emerged as a familiar and widely discussed issue in wartime Germany, illustrating not only the growing fears of assimilated German Jews vis-à-vis their Eastern counterparts but also the problems surrounding the Jewish Question, in general. In spite of the early Zionist praise of Eastern Jewish culture, many liberal German Jews, who since their political emancipation in the nineteenth century had increasingly adopted the ways of the dominant culture, discovered in the *Ostjuden* a ghost of the past, an unmodernized, unenlightened, *ur*-Jewish relative. Having fashioned their identities around the cultural and political contours of German bourgeois society, German Jews were met with a serious challenge of sustaining undesired associations with the *Ostjuden*, that is, positioning themselves opposite their *Glaubensgenossen* (compatriots of faith). A prominent view held by assimilated German-speaking Jewry is summed up in the reminiscences of Jakob Wassermann in what is arguably one of the sharpest testimonies of the Central European Jewish *Bildungsbürgertum*: "When I saw a Polish or a Galician Jew I would speak to him, try to peer into his soul, to learn how he thought and lived. And I might be moved or amazed, or be filled with pity and sadness; but I could feel no sense of brotherhood or even of kinship. He was totally alien to me, alien in every utterance, in every breath, and when he failed to arouse my sympathy for him as a human being, he even repelled me."[22] Wassermann clearly expresses the views of the assimilated, liberal German Jews who were neither prepared nor willing to accept the easy association of a shared ethnic heritage between themselves and the Eastern Jews. To be sure, the perceived foreignness of the *Ostjude* incited perhaps the greatest fear in the German Jews, who had until now so masterfully integrated themselves into German society. They had entered most professions, participated in politics and culture, and helped shape the modern spirit of the day.

Thus, when in early October of 1916 German-Jewish soldiers were informed by the Prussian War Ministry that they would be officially counted to determine the level of their wartime participation, an event that came to be known as the *Judenzählung* (census of Jewish soldiers, or more literally, "Jew count"), belief in a cultural and spiritual union with Germany was immediately put in check. The measure, which claimed to be a result of "complaints from the population that large numbers of men of the Israeltic [sic] faith who are fit for military service are either exempt from military duties or are evading their obligation to serve under every conceivable pretext," explicitly demonstrated the German presumption that Jewish participation in the war was less than adequate.[23] Given this suspicion, many Jewish soldiers felt as if their Germanness were in question. What had seemed like a prime opportunity to prove the depth of the "German-Jewish symbiosis" was now fiercely challenged by the *Judenzählung*. As Michael Brenner has observed, "German Jews had entered the war with high hopes of gaining recognition as integral parts of the German *Volksgemeinschaft*. Even the toll of twelve thousand Jewish lives in the battlefield, however, was not sufficient to create the 'community of the trenches.'"[24] Hence, those Jews who had originally expressed their unequivocal support for the German wartime effort were now more apt to reconsider their position. An exemplary case, revealing this change, may be observed in the wartime career of the German-Jewish writer Arnold Zweig.

Stationed on the Western front at the time that the census of Jewish soldiers was administered, on 15 February 1917 Zweig wrote an emotionally charged letter to Martin Buber, describing the personal insult and betrayal he felt. "The 'Judenzählung,'" he confessed, "was a reflection [*Reflexbewegung*] of unheard sadness for Germany's sin and our agony. . . . If there was no antisemitism in the army, the unbearable call to duty would be almost easy. However, to be subjected to such despicable and wretched creatures! I now regard myself personally as a captured civilian and a stateless foreigner."[25] The onetime vigorous support and loyalty of German Jews to the German war effort could no longer, as Zweig claims, sustain the blows of rejection that the *Judenzählung* and other forms of wartime antisemitism posed to them.

Like many German-Jewish soldiers, Zweig had initially supported the German war effort. Already in August 1914, he wrote to his friend Helene Weyl, telling her of his enthusiasm for what he regarded as the "deeply binding power of the *Kulturgemeinschaft*" that had been intensified by the war. "Greater Germany [*das große Deutschland*] is here again," he wrote, adding that as a Jew "I will take a passionate interest in Germany's destiny. . . . Indeed, in my inherently Jewish way I will make Germany's concern into my own concern."[26] Curious as it may seem, Zweig had expressed a similar will to make Germany's literary concern into his own in his "Zum Problem des jüdischen Dichters in Deutschland" ("On the Problem of the Jewish Writer in Germany") of the previous year.[27] His early enthusiasm for staking out a space in the German literary and cultural realm carried over into the war years in a new manifestation. Although he volunteered as early as 1914, due to his bad eyesight he was excluded from service until April 1915. Following the initial months of training in Germany, Zweig served in Belgium, Hungary, and Serbia until April 1916, when he was finally stationed in France for over a year.

During his first year of duty in the army, Zweig remained a loyal *Vaterlandsverteidiger* (defender of the Fatherland), even to the point of insisting on being married in uniform in July 1916. However, after the devastating experience of the *Judenzählung*, Zweig not only began to revise his otherwise positive views of the war, he also began to realize that it pitted Jews against Jews.[28] Based on his experiences, Zweig wrote and published the semifictional short story "Judenzählung vor Verdun" ("The Jewish Census at Verdun") in the *Jüdische Rundschau* of November 1916. In it, Zweig tells an ominous tale of how dead German-Jewish soldiers are summoned from their graves to be counted. They line up, announcing their respective identities as Jews: "Mosaischer Konfession," "Israelit," "Deutscher jüdischen Glaubens," "Jude, ja."[29] Indeed, the haunting, traumatic content of the story recalls the actual experiences of the wartime census in a macabre, surreal setting. The story ends starkly: "And I awakened from this abrupt, harsh, heart-wrenching horror."[30] Zweig's own "awakening," brought about by the *Judenzählung* and the final acknowledgment that Jews were fighting against Jews, was confirmed when, in June 1917, he was transferred to the Eastern region of Ober-Ost (in Lithuanian Kovno) to serve in the special wartime press division. There, as he traveled to the various shtetls in Lithuania, Zweig witnessed for the first time the problems that the Eastern Jews faced during the war – animosity and ill-treatment from both sides of the battle – and, more importantly, the unique community they maintained in the face of such conditions.

While on the Eastern front, Zweig also first came into contact with Hermann Struck (likewise stationed at Ober-Ost), an artist, printmaker, and graphic designer.[31] Zweig was extremely impressed by Struck's work, as it captured for him the unique spirit of the Eastern Jews that he too had so sympathetically observed.[32] When in spring 1918 Zweig was presented with the opportunity to collaborate with Struck on the project that produced *Das ostjüdische Antlitz* (*The Face of Eastern Jewry*, 1920), he showed immediate interest. In a letter of May 1918, Zweig wrote to Martin Buber of the project as he envisaged it:

> In an already firmly established project, I am going to write a full account of the Jews of the East, as I have come to know them

among the Lithuanian Jews. In a text written in conjunction with some fifty new lithographs by [Hermann] Struck, I am going to establish the claim that I now simply write down here: the Jewish human being is indestructible, non-distortable, non-distractible, is oriented towards purity, sincerity, and candor. Even in the most confusing and tempting conditions, he remains more pure than, as far as I could see, his cohabitants – indeed, how much more brilliantly and more honestly he will rise, where he is able to create according to the laws of his spirit. [33]

For Zweig, the Eastern Jews were the model for the future of Jewry: they embodied everything needed to revitalize the Jewish spirit, the answer – as fashioned in such elevated terms – to the crisis that was plaguing Western, in particular German, Jewry. This kind of unconditional praise and support for the Eastern Jews among Zweig and other German-Jewish soldiers came to serve as an antidote to the traumatic experiences of the war, especially the *Judenzählung*, and a growing sense of rejection on both national and communal levels.[34]

Zweig's letter to Buber makes clear that the ideological message of his project with Struck was already intact in 1918. Though it might seem that at that time Zweig was placating Buber, who, in his earlier work on Hasidism had illustrated – in a similarly romantic fashion – the benefits of community, Zweig's desire to demonstrate his views in his account of the Eastern Jews gradually became his own.[35] In its own right, Zweig's project represents a candid attempt to offer a corrective to the misconceptions of East European Jewry, to portray the Eastern Jews as vibrant, healthy, and inspirational souls.[36] To be sure, Zweig's desire to redeem the *Gemeinschaft* of Eastern Jews was motivated not only by the wish to benefit from the *Ostjuden*, but also to encourage a conscious Jewish renewal on the part of Western Jews.[37] Indeed, the creation of a positive image of the Eastern Jew played an integral role in the creation of a positive image of the Western Jew.

### THE FACE OF THE *OSTJUDE*

*I certainly understand how the average German Jew no longer feels a kinship [Verwandtschaft] to the Eastern Jews; indeed, he has really lost it for the*

*most part, as he has become more philistine, more bourgeois. But I, and peo-*
*ple like myself, must feel this kinship in an unmitigated way.* – Franz Rosenzweig (1918)

Arnold Zweig's preoccupations with Eastern Jewry, Zionism, and the
potentials for Jewish renewal did not begin on the Eastern front. Born
in 1887 in the Lower Silesian town of Glogau to assimilated parents,
Zweig, like many of his contemporaries, grew up in a modern German-
Jewish household. He attended numerous German schools and uni-
versities, finally pursuing a degree in philosophy, literature, and philol-
ogy (though he never went on to complete his doctorate). Like many
of the more self-conscious German Jews of his generation, Zweig discovered an interest in Jewish matters beginning to blossom around
1911–12, when he published his short works *Aufzeichnungen über eine
Familie Klopfer* (*Notes on the Klopfer Family*, 1911) and *Novellen um Claudia* (*Novellas about Claudia*, 1912), both of which deal with questions of
assimilation and Jewish identity.[38] Zweig's engagement with the German Zionist project can be traced to these early years, when he became
acquainted with the writings of Buber and began to contribute to such
journals as *Die Freistatt* and the *Mitteilungen des Verbandes der jüdischen
Jugendvereine Deutschlands*, as well as to the *Bar Kochba* anthology *Vom
Judentum*.[39] Until the outbreak of the war, Zweig's literary career followed a path of Jewish issues and concerns, perhaps most poignantly
expressed in his *Ritualmord in Ungarn* (*Ritual Murder in Hungary*,
1914), a tragic play based on a Jewish blood libel case from the late nineteenth century. However, as Jost Hermand has pointed out, the period
in which *Das ostjüdische Antlitz* was published marked a high point in
Zweig's contributions to the Jewish press and, together with his war
experiences, was the time when Zweig was most concerned with his
Jewish identity.[40]

By the summer of 1919, Zweig had completed his project with Struck,
and first began to publish parts of it in Buber's *Der Jude* before the
book itself appeared in 1920.[41] Given the continuous debate on the *Ostjudenfrage*, which essentially reached its peak in the same year as the
publication of *Das ostjüdische Antlitz*, as well as the rising tide of Eastern European anti-Jewish pogroms, the time was right for an insight-

ful contribution that would respond to these currents of discourse. "This book," announces the introduction to the first edition, "speaks about the Eastern Jews as written by somebody who attempted to observe them."[42] The implicit didacticism of the project lay in the plan to show a Western audience the Eastern Jews "as they are," to demonstrate deep ties to the Eastern "brothers and sisters."[43] As was immediately noted by one contemporary critic, the work represented the culmination of Zweig's "lively cohabitation [with Eastern Jews] during the war" on the Eastern front and the well-informed – indeed, well-aimed – observations he made while he was stationed there.[44] Of course, *Das ostjüdische Antlitz* says as much about Zweig as it does about its subject matter. Zweig himself admits to becoming an apologist for the Eastern Jews, the result of which is not only a defense of Eastern Jewry but also a document of the "human transformation [*Verwandlung*] of the author" (DoA 7). Thus, self-legitimation is a product of the legitimation of the *Ostjuden*.[45]

What had been initiated by Zweig as an "extraordinarily intense wish to experience the Eastern Jews personally" develops into a more intensive experience of himself. Like Kafka's treatment of the Yiddish language and culture, Zweig's work serves to accentuate, while aiming to overcome, the gulf separating Eastern and Western Judaism. The "testimony" that Zweig's project seeks to convey must be seen just as much as a testimony of German-Jewish crisis in the face of Eastern Jewish communal vitality. In the tradition of Heinrich Heine, who in 1822 had already traveled through Poland observing the Jewish inhabitants of the shtetls, Zweig embarks on a type of *Bildungsreise*, in which the lifestyle of a distant culture provides a catalyst for broadening the notions of the self.[46] In each of these cases, the travels to the East, "to the Jews," are symptomatic of the author's disenchantment with life in the West and the pressing challenges to German-Jewish assimilation.

Zweig's text is divided into five parts, each of which presents a specific component of the Eastern shtetl-community. In near-genealogical fashion, he begins with the figure of the old, wise man, the patriarchal embodiment of tradition, and concludes with the figure of the young Jewish boy instilling hope in the future of Judaism. In the main body of

Zweig's text there are expositions on the Eastern Jewish institutions, the synagogue, the schools, as well as a chapter on the Eastern Jewish family and the role of women in the community. There is also a chapter dedicated to the ideological nature of Eastern Jewish life, the youth movement, Zionism, and revolutionary Socialism. Each section is illustrated with lithographs by Struck, some more explicitly addressed in the text than others. As any student of East European Jewish history would recognize, Zweig is less concerned with providing a disinterested, factual account of the *Ostjuden* than with rendering a portrait of an admirable community that might serve as a model for the future of Judaism. He himself openly admits to the highly subjective character of his study, remarking: "If anywhere, it should be said here that this book is not supported by literature and not by reports, but rather by the present condition of life and of the spiritual gift of observing. It is as right or wrong as the configuration itself which life presents to the observer. Hence the gaps, hence the exaggerations: it is a testimony" (104).

Yet, as much as Zweig is aware of the problematic method of his work, he proceeds unabashedly with his mythical, highly politicized narrative of Eastern Jewish life. As we know from his correspondence with Buber, Zweig already had his agenda in mind when he undertook his project. Moreover, the nature of the accompanying illustrations by Hermann Struck clearly inspired and strengthened the tone of Zweig's discourse. Around the same time that he began work on *Das ostjüdische Antlitz*, Zweig noted in his review of Struck's art that the "politicization of art" is what made his work so effective. "The language of the artist is the language of his work," wrote Zweig in 1918; "the politics of the artist is the sentiment of his form, and is the intensity of the creation and its language."[47] The same claim could be applied to Zweig's text. Iconographically, Struck's work operates from within a specific Zionist vernacular, conveying precisely the political "intensity" that Zweig highlights in his review. By the time Zweig began to collaborate with Struck, the graphic artist had already established his name among German Zionists. As early as 1913, in conjunction with the Eleventh Zionist Congress, Struck had created the widely celebrated etching of Theodor Herzl, rendered in a distinguished, profile pose.[48] Much like his later lithographs of the Eastern Jews, Struck's Herzl – considered by many Zionists the "countenance of the movement" – represents a vital mixture of pride, grandeur, and tasteful Jewishness, effectively aimed at inverting the negative stereotypes of Jews projected by anti-semites.[49] In capturing both formal clarity and mythical elegance in his work, Struck achieves the effect of a visually politicized message of Jewish national strength and beauty.

At the beginning of *Das ostjüdische Antlitz*, we observe a similar effect. An old Jewish sage, the wise man, stares into the past and into the future. Rendered proudly in his skullcap, beard, and side-locks, he symbolizes at once Jewish history and lore, devout spirituality tempered by tenacity (figure 3).

For Zweig, the politics of Struck's art gives weight not only to the individual lithographs but also to his own accompanying text. Struck, too, consistently employs sentiment with formal description to elevate the political content of his argument. Of the opening figure of *Das ost-jüdische Antlitz*, the old Eastern Jew, Zweig writes: "He turns his eye away from me and into the distance, which is nothing more than time. His profile leads us like a falling drop of water on his beard, that dissolves into foam and clouds. The nobility of his posture and his nose, the spirituality of his pensive and swollen forehead, play off against the hard, defiant ear and come together in his gaze, which neither demands nor relinquishes, neither yearns for nor bemoans what it is. And the gaze absorbs a distance about which we know that it is nothing but time" (13). Zweig's lyrical use of language – his poignant inflections of a heightened pathos – guides the reader to a more spiritual plane where myth, politics, and imagination intersect.

The Eastern Jewish elder is, according to Zweig and Struck, not merely a human being who dwells in the Lithuanian shtetl; he is also a symbol of "purity, serenity, and wisdom" (42). At times, it is as though Zweig were examining biblical figures rather than ordinary people, a treatment that is perhaps best articulated in his concluding discussion of the young Jewish boy as Abel (figure 4). Such mythologizing is clearly intended to help readers sublimate the realities of everyday life in the shtetl and any negative preconceptions of the *Ostjuden*. Like Roman Vishniac's photographs in *Polish Jews*, Struck's old man is not to be

3. Hermann Struck, *Old Eastern Jew*. Courtesy of the Leo Baeck Institute, New York.

4. Hermann Struck, *Young Eastern Jewish Boy*. Courtesy of the Leo Baeck Institute, New York.

taken simply as an individual; he represents a prototype in the mythical landscape of shtetl-life (figure 5).

Both Struck's and Vishniac's works share a starkness of portraiture that evokes a distinct rawness and the sense that each image hangs suspended in time.

5. Roman Vishniac, *Old Man*. Roman Vishniac © 1992, International Center of Photography, New York. Courtesy of Mara Vishniac Kohn.

### ROMANCING THE SHTETL

*In the ghetto, the life of the Jewish* Gemeinschaft *was self-contained and encompassed everything – not only religion, but custom, law, language, and family life, all in one.* – Adolf Böhm (1913)

In conjunction with a 1993–94 Judah Magnes Museum exhibition on the shtetl, curator Florence Helzel delineated two major traditions through which artists – among them Hermann Struck – represent the shtetl. They do so, she writes, "either by mirroring a realistic slice of life or by idealizing it. The majority of the art does not concentrate on the prevalent abject poverty, drudgery, and terror-filled pogroms. Instead, the shtetl is remembered for the warmth of familial relationships, the joy of celebrations, and the fervent study of the Torah."[50] This tendency toward idealization is certainly true of both Struck and Zweig, whose representations rarely make mention of the negative aspects of shtetl-life, while prominently featuring noble and inspirational virtues. As in modern Yiddish literature, which abounds with folkloric types (e.g., "Fishke the Lame," "Bontshe the Silent," and "Tevye the Milkman"), the figures in Zweig's texts and Struck's lithographs symbolize the folkloric inhabitants of the shtetl.[51] They are members of the community as imagined and romanticized by its interpreters. This is a tradition, as Helzel points out, that extends from prewar Europe to post-Shoah America. Anthropologists Elizabeth Herzog and Mark Zborowski's renowned cultural history of the shtetl, *Life is With People*, shows how the perpetuation of the shtetl-myth continues to be reinvented:

> For its inhabitants, the shtetl is less the physical town than the people who live in it. "My shtetl" means my community, and community means the Jewish community. Traditionally, the human rather than the physical environment has always been given primary importance. Emphasis on the Jewish portion of the community was inevitable, for historical developments had excluded it from membership in the larger community. Socially and legally it was an entity in itself, subject to special laws and responsible – within strict limits – for regulating and conducting itself.[52]

The isolation of the shtetl has become for many the paramount feature of its existence and the main reason for its uniqueness. In the romanticized discourse, this isolation is also one of its most prized ideals. Historian Steven Zipperstein has argued that the images of the shtetl derived from the fictional literature and art of the last century "are the images that have come to represent in contemporary Jewish memory the texture of East European Jewish life – often culled from the literary world of Mendele Mocher Seforim, Sholom Aleichem, and [I. L.] Peretz. It is these that have proven immeasurably more influential than historical literature."[53] Even in modern Yiddish literature itself, as Irving Howe has suggested, "an impulse arose among Yiddish writers – most notably in the later stories of Peretz – to romanticize the very world [i.e., the world of the shtetl] that Mendele had so bitterly attacked."[54] Of course, after the Shoah, the romantic impulse became even more tempting.

Yet, more than three decades before Herzog and Zborowski published their anthropological examination, well before anybody could ever have imagined what would transpire in Auschwitz, Arnold Zweig focused on similarly romantic aspects of the *Ostjuden* as he noted the fundamental structures of the Eastern Jewish community: "The Jews of the East want to live according to their own Jewish ways, in their own cultural sphere, with their own beliefs, and with their own languages" (DoA 10). Hence, the self-contained "purity" of the shtetl – and it is the ideal of purity to which Zweig repeatedly refers – stood out as antithetical to the assimilated, fragmented, and diffuse communities of the West. Unlike the enlightened Jews of Germany, who observed the main principle of Haskalah Jewry, namely, "Be a Jew at home and a human being outside," the Eastern Jews remain Jews both in their public and private personas.[55] This overt adherence to tradition, as Zweig makes clear, is what has maintained the ways of the Eastern Jews over time. "And this nationality [*Volkstum*], obstinately preserved, in language, costume, rituals, and spirituality adopted from, and changed only slightly since the fourteenth and fifteenth century, appears to be unchangeable and tenacious like an old man who is not threatened by illness" (DoA 21). The old man, whose symbolic weight had already captured the attention of Zweig and Struck, embodies the radical preservation of tradition among Eastern Jews as conceived in stark contrast to that among their Western counterparts. In his *Reise in Polen* (*Journey to Poland*, 1926), the German-Jewish novelist Alfred Döblin, offers a strikingly similar observation of the Eastern Jews: "They are a nation," he writes. "People who know only Western Europe fail to realize this. The Jews have their own costumes, their own language, religion, manners and mores, their ancient national feeling and conciousness."[56]

Quite similar to Alfred Döblin, Joseph Roth, and others who, following Zweig, "journeyed to the Jews" in the 1920s, Zweig presents observations on the Eastern Jews consistently made within the comparative framework of an East-West, traditional-modern, *Gemein-schaft-Gesellschaft* dichotomy.[57] The Eastern Jews, as Zweig emphasizes time and again, are for German Jewry the symbols of organic wholeness, vital spirituality, and promise for the future. By contrast, according to Zweig, Western Jewry stands in an acute crisis: "Condemned to atomization, to the loss in each and every Jew, as indeed among the Jews of the West every Jew has suffered from loss of Jewishness? Condemned to assimilation, to 'modernity,' to 'contemporaneity' [*Jetztzeit*], to Europe, to *Mischmasch*?" (DoA 42). Echoing the Zionist rhetoric on Jewish decline, Zweig calls attention to the perceived dangers of Jewish life in the West. Like Felix Theilhaber, whose *Untergang der deutschen Juden* (*The Decline of German Jewry*, 1911) warned of the deleterious effects that an assimilated, urban capitalist society might have on Judaism, Zweig's text outlines the legacy of post-Enlightenment German Jewry.

> We know that our forefathers were relatives of the men we find today in the shtetls of Lithuania, Poland, and Galicia; no, we know that they lived in the Frankish hill regions and the German plains like us. Today we speak different languages, think different thoughts, live a different Judaism, eat different dishes, measure by different standards, and we have exchanged a part of our soul with Europe, giving up a part of our Jewish one. It has formed not quite five generations of us, this European destiny and its freedom, its new air, its wonderful and artistic values, its integrating and expropriating breath. And then it took the most explicit crisis to bring us to our senses: crisis of the heart, crisis of memory, crisis of the countenance. . . . The old Jew of the East, however, preserved his face. It looks at us from the tales of Mendele [i.e., Mendele Moykher Sforim], this face: sincere and dreamy and of a *purity* which can be purchased only at the cost of abandoning the broader activities and the happiness of broader activity. (DoA 13–14; emphasis added)

Zweig constructs a narrative that traverses the history of assimilation and, finally, leads to the perceived "crisis" of Western Jewry. He taunts assimilated Western Jews, hoping in turn to lead them to a more conscious awareness of their Jewishness.

Despite the differences that separate the two cultures, Zweig suggests that a return to a more traditional and "pure" lifestyle (here embodied in the Yiddish tradition of Mendele Moykher Sforim that he cites) might bring the Jews together. Zweig is not asking that the Western Jews make countermigrations en masse to the Eastern shtetls, nor does he explicitly wish for all of assimilated Jewry to make *aliyah* (immigration) to Palestine (however implicit this may be in his argument). How, then, should the Jews of the West, now living in the thick of modern civilization, become more like their brothers in the East? Does this transformation simply amount to the abandonment of Western lifestyle in favor of the traditions of the *Ostjuden*?[58] While Zweig entertains these questions, he does not offer conclusive answers. Instead, he presents the redeeming qualities of Eastern Jewish life for consumption by his readers as a self-conscious critique of modernity. For Zweig, the *Gemeinschaft* of Jews represented in the shtetl is to be held up to the Jews of the German *Gesellschaft* as a means of raising Jewish national and spiritual awareness (i.e., as an ideal by which Jewish identity may be newly defined).

Zweig also discusses one further distinction between the life of the shtetl and modern Jewish life of the West in regard to spirituality and religious practice. He notes the firm convictions held by the Eastern Jews who follow the laws of the Talmud, the "mind of the Jew" (DoA 56), as he calls it, and thereby maintain a strong connection between religious belief and ritual. For Zweig, the *Ostjude* at prayer, with his shoulders covered by his prayer shawl, his eyes fixed upon the ancient text, links himself to the Jewish chain of being. Zweig regards prayer among the Eastern Jews as the "bearer of the Jewish soul" (44), the spiritual core of Jewish life. Most unique in the Eastern act of prayer is the loud, communal, responsive procession of the congregation, a clear contrast to the German-speaking West, where the push towards universalization often included German translations of Hebrew liturgical texts, organ music, and German sermons. For its "naturalness," its perceived purity, its unmitigated spirituality, Eastern Jewish prayer became a popular point of discussion in the German-Jewish literature on the *Ostjuden*. Like Kafka, who, following evening Yom Kippur services at Prague's Altneu Synagogue in 1911, noted in his diaries the unique method of prayer he witnessed in three praying Eastern Jews, Zweig focuses on the distinctiveness of Eastern Jewish spirituality.[59]

In the second part of his text, devoted entirely to prayer and Eastern

Jewish ritual, Zweig himself examines "typical" Eastern Jewish scenes of prayer, paying close attention to the Western Jewish variant: "Yes, prayer is still loud in the East. In each hour of praying, the passion of the charge towards the height of God is progressively kindled. And for superficial, Western eyes and ears, this is an embarrassing and tasteless experience: these relentless voices, these jolting figures, these foreignly articulated, wailing, groaning melodies storm together in a wild, screaming chorus that, even outside the walls of the synagogue, resonates like the rush of a distant surge, like the shouting of a wild mass" (46). The community of Eastern Jews at prayer provides for Zweig yet another vivid reminder of the conflict between Eastern and Western life. Unlike the West, where the division between religion and state ostensibly keeps politics from entering the religious domain, among the Eastern Jews the synagogue, or *Schul*, as Zweig refers to it, is both a *Volkshaus* (house of the people) and a *Gotteshaus* (house of God). The continuity between the Jewish people and God, between *Gemeinschaftsformen* and ritual, makes the act of prayer an ideal representation of the continuity of Eastern Jewish life as a whole (figure 6).

The political message conveyed through Struck's image of prayer and Zweig's text is national renewal. "Renewal: that is the division between us and the others. . . . 'Back to the torah'" (157), as Zweig states in his treatment of the youth movement, calling for a more "full" and "pure" sense of nationality. "The spirit of *Gemeinschaft*," he continues, is revealed in the "name of God" (157–58). To be sure, the forces of national renewal extend beyond the religious and spiritual realm.[60] Maintaining a position already anticipated in his letter of 1918 to Buber, Zweig believed that national renewal would come about through a fundamental transformation of community. From the Eastern front, he expressed to Buber his belief that the national unity of the Jewish people could not be forced. "It is something natural," he remarks, "like everything organic, it emerges; like everything godlike, it adapts itself. In the meantime, if we Jews, together with other Jews, organize a *Gemeinschaft* in which the human being can express most purely the best powers of his human nature . . . we will produce something that will become national."[61]

For Zweig, a significant component in the expression of Jewish

6. Hermann Struck, *Praying Jew*. Courtesy of Leo Baeck Institute, New York.

nationality is "Arbeit und Land" ("work and land"), along with the preservation of traditions, myths, and heroes. The ideology of Jewish renewal, as envisaged by Zweig, is a blend of revolutionary Socialism (Landauer, Luxemburg) and utopian Zionism (Buber). In his discussion of work and land, it becomes clear that his image of a Jewish homeland resembles more an idealized large-scale kibbutz than a national state.[62] In Zweig's view, portraying the Eastern Jews as a people of farmers and craftsmen counteracts the notion of Jews as born merchants and bankers (162). Further, to enhance this perceived Jewish Socialist legacy, Zweig invokes the deaths of Rosa Luxemburg and Gustav Landauer as martyrs of the movement, indeed martyrs of the Eastern Jews. In his eulogy to Rosa Luxemburg, Zweig goes on to call her "the Jewish revolutionary of the East."[63]

In Zweig's "imagined community," a utopian form of Zionism and socialism merge in the shtetl, and the shtetl in turn becomes the reinvented model for the future. Zweig turns to the Eastern Jews, as they represent for him "the last segment of the Jewish people that has produced and kept alive their own new songs and dances, customs and myths, languages and *Gemeinschaftsformen*" (42). They are the prime source for a revived Jewish identity. As is so often the case with national discourses, Zweig's "imagined community" is conceived in its most romantic form, virtually devoid of shortcomings, and charged with a mythical, indeed messianic essence.[64] And so "the countenance of the Eastern Jew" finally becomes, in the last sentences of Zweig's treatise, "the countenance of the Messiah," a theological inversion where the young Eastern Jewish boy resembles Abel and the old Eastern Jewish man resembles the prophets.

It was through the publication of *Das ostjüdische Antlitz* that Zweig made his mark as a defender of the *Shtetl-Gemeinschaft*. As Moritz Goldstein noted in his review of 1922, Zweig's text makes possible the recognition and legitimation of "Jewish commonality" and, in so doing, helps see to it that "Eastern Jewry will always be able to be protected against haughtiness and ignorance."[65] Not all critics greeted Zweig's program with such enthusiasm. In Martin Buber's journal, *Der Jude*, Paul Zucker took Zweig to task for what he called "self-glorification" [*Selbstverherrlichung*].[66] Under the provocative title "Mythos der Gegenwart" ("Myth of the Present"), Zucker's review accused Zweig and Struck of oversentimentalization and misuse of stereotype. Above all, Zucker was highly suspicious of the cleverness with which Zweig and Struck lead the reader to respond affirmatively to the alleged "primal instincts" (*Urinstinkte*) of the Eastern Jews.[67] And yet it is precisely the sentimentalization and uncritical defense of the Eastern Jews that made Zweig and Struck's joint project so appealing to German Jews. To lead the reader to a more affirmative response, as Zucker astutely notes, was certainly their goal.[68]

In the afterword to his 1929 reprint of *Das ostjüdische Antlitz*, Zweig asks a question that anticipates the ultimate demise of the Eastern Jewish community and the vanishing of these "faces": "Perhaps we, the generation of the war, were the last ones who were able to see the old Eastern Jewish countenance."[69] Here, as in many parts of Zweig's text, there is a nostalgia for an ostensibly more humane epoch, a pure community. However, Zweig was not the last to witness the face of the old Jew. Indeed, the "imagined community" that Zweig envisions in his work continued to thrive – in the popular press, in the cinema, in the arts – throughout the 1920s. The Eastern Jew tended either to continue bearing the romantic aura that Zweig and Struck depicted or to have the sense of *Shtetl-Gemeinschaft* converted into the embodiment of a new *Gesellschaft* – the Jew as city dweller, modernist, and urban threat. What made the latter possible was, as we shall now see, the conflation of Eastern Jewish and German-Jewish identities with the notion of the Jew as modern German city dweller.

# THREE

# Weimar Cinema, the City, and the Jew: Paul Wegener's *Der Golem: Wie er in die Welt kam*

*Perhaps, instead of thinking of identity as an already accomplished historical fact, which the new cinematic discourses then represent, we should think of identity as a "production," which is never complete, always in process, and always constituted within, not outside representation.* – Stuart Hall

Deep in the bowels of the city, underground among the prostitutes, the pimps, the gamblers, the criminals and their victims, shady inhabitants live in filth, struggling to survive in uninhabitable conditions. On a street corner, a lone hooker speaks in visionary words: "From day to day the city's getting bigger, while the people in it are getting smaller and smaller."[1] Violence, shock, horror, and the commodification of human desire constitute the chief forces of the big city.[2] Urban modernity's ever-expanding process of industrial growth takes its toll on human beings, and under these conditions – in Rainer Werner Fassbinder's provocative play, *Der Müll, die Stadt und der Tod* (*Garbage, the City and Death*, 1975) – a sense of fear and foreboding pervades the city street.

Enter the "Rich Jew," the quintessential representation of the thriving industrialist, the modern capitalist who buys up abandoned space in the city only to sell it at a higher price. He is the slumlord who manipulates the powerlessness of his fellow citizens, who dominates physical, financial, and political exchange and, above all, for whom "the city redeems itself in its forgiving gestures" (GCD 183). Much like late-nineteenth- and early-twentieth-century reactionary discourse on Jewish identity, Jewishness is codified here in the terms and metaphors of the city: in short, as the embodiment of capitalism, urban exploitation, and power. Such representation suggests a symbiotic relationship where the city needs the Jew as much as the Jew needs the city. For as the "Rich Jew" asserts, "The city protects me, it has to, as I am a Jew. . . . The city needs the unscrupulous businessman who allows it to transform itself. It must protect him" (170–71; trans. rev.). As a key force in the transformation of the city, the "Rich Jew" functions as modernist, the fuse igniting urban explosion. As "the city gobbles up its children," it becomes clear that not only the city but also the Jew bears responsibility. And while the other inhabitants of the city suffer from severe distress, the "Rich Jew" masters the urban economy: "I go through this city as if it weren't chaotic, uninhabitable like the moon, as though it were open, honest, straight up and down. And I laugh all the while, grinning 'til my teeth grind to stubs" (177).

Although it certainly could be, the setting partially reconstructed here is not taken directly from the late nineteenth or early twentieth century, not from the theorists of the Jewish origins of capitalism, nor from the theorists of race, nor from the numerous literary and cultural texts treating this topic in the 1920s.[3] Rather, it comes from a German drama written just over two decades ago, a text unmistakably indebted to a modernist legacy of Jewish identity formation that draws on the codes and metaphors of the big city, namely, Fassbinder's *Garbage, the City and Death*. With his provocative two-part play, the German filmmaker, playwright, and enfant terrible abruptly ended his final season as the artistic director of Frankfurt's prestigious Theater am Turm, 1974–75, in an enormous outburst of controversy. Critics repeatedly attacked Fassbinder's work for its insensitivity to the problem of representing a Jewish figure (the "Rich Jew"), often pointing to the crass distortion of the Jew and the lack of complexity Fassbinder's characterization offers. Germany's most prominent conservative daily newspaper, the *Frankfurter Allgemeine*, pronounced Fassbinder's play a work of "left-wing fascism," while a spokesman from B'nai Brith called it "political pornography" and "a disgusting anti-Semitic tirade."[4] By linking the "Rich Jew" to corrupt practices in commerce, as Marx had done – albeit under far different pretenses – over a century before in his *Zur Judenfrage* (*On the Jewish Question*, 1844), Fassbinder joined the debate on how to define Jewish identity in modern German mass society.[5]

All distortion aside, *Garbage, the City and Death* opens discussion of some of the most difficult problems that modern German society has faced: industrialization, urbanism, national and cultural identity crises.[6] By casting a spotlight on the "Rich Jew," Fassbinder's text explores the position that the Jew occupies within this complex network of social tensions, thereby grappling with problems of Jewish representation. His portrayal of the Jew invokes modern fears of exploitation and urban domination in a manner that is remarkably similar to the images of the Jew in classical Weimar cinema, emphasizing the continuation of an acutely modern problem: the vexed situation of the Jew in German urban life. As the contemporary playwright Heiner Müller notes, "Fassbinder's *Garbage, the City and Death* uses a victim's [the "Rich Jew's"] revenge to describe the devastation of a city in huge, harsh images."[7] Like his cinematic works, Fassbinder's play presents its characters – most notably, the "Rich Jew" – in precisely the amplified terms that Müller observes. The editor and translator of the English rendition of Fassbinder's play, Denis Calandra, has offered the following assessment of the controversy surrounding its production: "Probably the strongest argument against *Garbage* is that it may unwittingly subscribe to the syllogism Jew = Finance = Exploitation: Jew as someone who will put his people's status as victim to work for him in the marketplace" (GCD 14). Fassbinder's work, and the debate that would later come to be known as the "Fassbinder affair," is of course deeply embedded in the postwar, post-Shoah climate of the Federal Republic of Germany.[8] And yet, in spite of the fact that it emerges from the historically specific moment of Frankfurt in the 1970s, Fassbinder's rendering of the Jew addresses a broad series of questions to which Weimar cinema responds: What is the role and status of the Jew in the modern German city? How does defining the identity of the Jew hinge upon the negative image projected against an opposing affirmative image (i.e., upon the crude juxtaposition of Jewishness with Germanness)? And if defined in the terms and metaphors of the big city, what relationship does the Jew have to the conditions of modernity?

Taking into consideration the stakes of the Fassbinder debate, it is instructive to apply this set of concerns back to the problems of modern German-Jewish representation in general and, more specifically, to the problems of Jewish identity formation in Weimar cinema. For it is precisely on this representational level that Fassbinder's *Garbage, the City and Death* might provide us with a theatrical prism through which to refract the complexities of Jewish identity formation. Although conspicuously absent from Fassbinder's play, modern German political and cultural history necessarily informs many of the questions that his work implicitly raises. In the following discussion, I wish to account as much for the historical as for the aesthetic and, in particular, for the area in which these two realms intersect. I thus hope to demonstrate how the historically specific, while fully obscured in both Fassbinder and in the select examples of Weimar cinema that I examine, significantly underlies the images that these works project.[9]

### THE RETURN OF MYTH IN THE NAME OF HISTORY
*Always they treat it as a legend, till something happens and turns it into actuality again.* – Gustav Meyrink (1915)

During the initial years of the Weimar Republic, the urban masses were deeply affected by the volatile political situation, the economic decline, and the heterodox cultural climate, which together produced a potentially explosive atmosphere. "In the streets of Berlin," writes Siegfried Kracauer in one of his early articles on film, "one is not seldom struck by the momentary insight that one day all this will suddenly burst apart. The entertainment to which the general public throngs ought to produce the same effect."[10] As the so-called "theater for the little people" (Döblin) or "the psychoanalytic couch for the poor" (Guattari), the cinema has often been seen as a medium that bespeaks the collective desires, wishes, dreams, anxieties, and nightmares of the audience.[11] Early Weimar cinema, with its predilection for haunted, mysterious, faraway settings, often operated in this fashion, concealing the tensions of the contemporary and real within the fictional, removed cinematic space. An especially threatening horror film of 1920 builds both on the social and psychological constellation surrounding the moment in which it was produced, as well as on the cultural constructs it projects.

One of the pioneers of German cinema, Paul Wegener was originally a theater actor trained under Max Reinhardt. He had declared his commitment to film innovation with the haunting classic *Der Student von Prag* (*The Student of Prague*, 1913), which he wrote in collaboration with Hanns Heinz Ewers. Prefiguring his later golem films, *Der Student von Prague* began by taking samples from modern and ancient legends and transforming them into a visual tale of horror and deception. Here Wegener revealed the intense fascination and engagement with which identity questions were being treated in Germany's visual arts during these years. With its staged shots of Prague's Jewish cemetery and its focus on the dark underbelly of the human spirit, Wegener's early film juxtaposed the Jewish elements with the German, the Eastern with the Western, the ancient with the modern. Throughout much of his film career, Wegener exhibited a sustained preoccupation with the "strange visions" and "demoniac forces" that appealed most to the fantasies and fears of his modern viewers.[12]

When the Berlin premiere of Paul Wegener's third and final golem film, *Der Golem: Wie er in die Welt kam* (*The Golem: How He Came into the World*, 1920), opened at the Ufa Palast am Zoo on 29 October 1920, the German audience likely had at least some familiarity with the golem legend (a stock parable of human creation), having been exposed over the previous decades to numerous renditions.[13] Aside from Wegener's first two golem films, *Der Golem* (*The Golem*, 1915) and *Der Golem und die Tänzerin* (*The Golem and the Dancer*, 1917), there had been a great number of literary treatments of the golem myth: from Arthur Holitscher's *Der Golem: Ghettolegende in drei Aufzügen* (*The Golem: A Ghetto Legend in Three Acts*, 1908) and Gustav Meyrink's *Der Golem* (*The Golem*, 1915) through Chayim Bloch's *Der Prager Golem; Von seiner "Geburt" bis zu seinem "Tod"* (*The Golem of Prague: From his "Birth" to his "Death"*, 1919), German culture of the 1920s had already encountered its share of adaptations of the ancient Jewish legend. And yet what was most significant was not the familiarity with the past adaptations of the theme, but rather how the legend now fit into what Stephen Greenblatt has termed "the circulation of social energy" – the broader understanding and widely shared perceptions of Jews at the time in which the film was produced.[14]

Opening with the banishment of the Jews from the German Empire set in the film, the first scenes of the *Golem* speak immediately to the lingering Jewish Question. As the film's fictionalized documentary insert – the *Dekret wider die Juden* (*Decree Against the Jews*) – reads: "We can no longer neglect the many grave complaints against the Jews, who crucified our Lord: they despise the holy Christian ceremonies; they endanger the lives and property of their fellow-men as well as non-Jews; they practice black magic. We decree that all Jews must abandon the city [ghetto] before the new moon."[15] Indeed, the guise of sixteenth-century kabbalistic legend assumed in the film merely serves as an allegory of the feared threat of urban domination.[16] For in this light, Rabbi Loew's mystical talents poignantly underscore his ability to transform the city, while his construction of a mechanical robot strikes a highly resonant chord in the then contemporary discourse on industrial production. "The creation of the Golem," remarks Kabbalah scholar Gershom Scholem, "is then in some way an affirmation of the productive and creative power of Man."[17] As the rabbi works in his study creating his mystical and technological wonder – a scene that Fritz Lang's characterization of Rotwang in *Metropolis* (1927) undoubtedly cites – the consummate modernist asserts his productive powers. He operates on his own terms, creating the mechanical object of horror, the ultimate symbol of modernity (figure 7).[18]

Not unlike the rabbi himself, the automated golem additionally serves as an embodiment of the urban metropolis (figure 8). He is the commodity and instrument of exchange produced by the Jewish engineer and, as such, appears as the cause of both fear and desire. It is in the figure of the golem that the rabbi transforms the biblical Adam – himself referred to in talmudic legend as a "golem" – into the modern Jewish robot. The blurred boundaries separating the ancient legend from the contemporary realm of political and cultural life around 1920 elicit a variety of questions on the Jewish position as an agent of exchange, technician, industrialist, "strange magician," and mad scientist. How, for example, does the *Wunderrabbi* and technological mastermind Loew cultivate and wield his authority?[19] Why, in a climate of great instability, do the Jews of the city pose a threat both to the German Empire within the film and to its contemporary counter-

7. Rabbi Loew creating the golem. Photo courtesy of The Museum of Modern Art Film Stills Archive.

part, the Weimar Republic at large? And how does a Judeo-Christian myth of creation resonate with the myth-based construction of Jewish identity?

Though Wegener's film is set in the sixteenth-century Prague ghetto, Rabbi Loew masters the economy of the city far more like a Weimar statesman (à la Walther Rathenau) – or, alternatively, more like Fassbinder's figure of the "Rich Jew" – than a premodern alchemist. Considered in the wake of the Versailles Treaty, as well as Hitler's formal announcement of his twenty-five point party program for the Deutsche Arbeiter-Partei (German Workers' Party, the precursor to the Nazi Party), Loew's negotiating power over the Jews in the German Empire might be seen to comment on the territorial struggles of the Republic. Indeed, as arbitrator between the German Empire and the ghetto world, Loew functions as foreign minister of the ghetto Jews.[20] In these images of the Jew, conveyed respectively through political, theat-

8. The golem at the ghetto's gate. Photo courtesy of The Museum of Modern Art Film Stills Archive.

rical, and cinematic representation, the past and present "flash into a constellation," as Walter Benjamin attests, forming "a dialectic in a standstill."[21] To be sure, the glimpse of the past in *The Golem*, evoked in the sixteenth-century ghetto setting, casts light onto the present, circumscribing the Jew's presence in the modern German city.[22]

In a brief essay from 1915, "Schauspielerei und Film" ("Acting and Film"), Wegener himself claimed that he had hoped to achieve precisely this effect in his *Golem* project. "Here everything is tailored to the image," he declares, "to the merging [*Ineinanderfließen*] of a fantasy-world of past centuries with everyday life."[23] Anticipating Benjamin's observations on the dialectical relationship between past and present, the images in Wegener's film produce an analogous type of antilinear, polyphonic constellation. In terms of the relation that such celluloid images have to the common notions of Jewish identity, the liminal realm separating reality from fantasy provides an indeterminate space for communicating myth in the name of history.

Traces of the physical world blend with the fantasies of the cinematic world, revealing one of the cinema's greatest affective potentials. In an article from the *Frankfurter Zeitung*, Siegfried Kracauer summed up this unique characteristic: "The capacity to stir up the elements of nature is one of the possibilities of film. This possibility is realized whenever film combines parts and segments to create strange constructs. If the disarray of the illustrated newspapers is simply confusion, the game that film plays with the pieces of disjointed nature is reminiscent of the *dream* in which the fragments of daily life become jumbled."[24] One of *The Golem's* central scenes, in which the rabbi visits the emperor's Rose Festival, illustrates the visual conflation of twentieth-century industrialism and ancient fantasy. Known to the court as the "strange magician," Rabbi Loew premieres his golem creation before the audience of the emperor's palace, boldly displaying his aesthetic power.[25] Inside the lavishly decorated court, the wizard-like rabbi appears at once submissive, as he kisses the emperor's ring, and almighty, as he orchestrates the "show." While the camera focuses on Loew's position among the audience at the emperor's court, the dimly lit "strange magician" takes on increasingly amplified dimensions (figure 9).

Not unlike Robert Wiene's *Das Cabinett des Dr. Caligari* (*The Cabinet of Dr. Caligari*, 1920) – which premiered only months before Wegener's *Golem*, and in which the mad scientist and sideshow performer Caligari exhibits his somnambulist Cesare before an eager crowd of spectators – Loew stands prominently framed alongside his golem "show" as the guests of the court curiously observe. Just as Cal-

9. Rabbi Loew as the strange magician. Photo courtesy of The Museum of Modern Art Film Stills Archive.

igari maintains control over his monster, Loew manipulates the movements of his robot-figure, withholding the secrets of his act. In fact, the rabbi himself asserts, "He is *my servant* and *my creation*, called Golem, more I may not tell you" (46; emphasis added).

In Rabbi Loew, Wegener characterizes the Jew as master of the power over the spectacle – over the aesthetic medium – a power that is repeatedly emphasized throughout the film.[26] Indeed, the subsequent series of scenes at the Rose Festival further affirms this trait. In a remarkable metacinematic gesture, the rabbi conjures a film-within-a-film sequence of the biblical Exodus story through which his individual technological mastery as well as the status of the Jews forced to flee their homeland are duly invoked. Masses of Jews walk across the screen, mirroring ancient doubles of Loew's fellow ghetto inhabitants. Amidst the Jewish procession a lone figure reaches the center of the screen, abruptly turning toward the court spectators. Although one might at first glance recognize this figure as Moses, in his expository script Wegener addresses him not as Moses but as "Ahasverus, the eternal Jew" (50).[27]

In the role of "eternal Jew," the bearded mythical figure feigns a portrait of the exiled condition of the Jews in the emperor's city, who likewise face expulsion from their non-Jewish domain. By invoking the figure of Ahasverus, not only does the Jewish Question return to the foreground, but the mythical foundation of the film expands: the golem legend, the Exodus passage, and the invocation of the "Wandering Jew" make the film's narrative both culturally and historically familiar yet fantastically remote. Already exposed to the stock motifs and metaphors of *The Golem*, as well as to the Faustian and biblical inflections, the audience can identify the cinematic rendition in terms of its rootedness in German culture, while nonetheless distancing themselves from the bizarre (read: Jewish) miracles on the screen.[28]

Analogous to the interaction of the golem narrative with the present, the skewed Exodus citation embodied in "Ahasverus" resonates with the story that Wegener's film tells. Both the figures in Loew's "show" and the figures in Wegener's narrative must flee from the places they have made their home – the Exodus Jews in Egyptian exile and the ghetto Jews in the German city. Both face persecution in their respective host countries and therefore must seek freedom. The blurred configuration of genres, time periods, and images conveys a jumbled composite of history, fiction, aesthetics, and myth.[29] By introducing the biblical passage in the film, the past reemerges in the form of narrativized myth, imbricated with the historical immediacy of the modern Jewish Question. As witnessed in Hans Karl Breslauer's film of 1924, *Die Stadt ohne Juden* (*The City Without Jews*), and less overtly in F. W. Murnau's *Nosferatu, eine Symphonie des Grauens* (*Nosferatu, a*

*Symphony of Terror*, 1922), the question of expelling the unwanted inhabitants of the city provoked a wide range of responses in the years surrounding Wegener's production.[30]

The aesthetic production of the biblical scene and the creation of the golem raise the theological problem of profanely imitating the Divine, that is, the iconoclastic disavowal of the paramount Jewish biblical commandment against the creation of images resembling God or anything in the heavens or on earth (Ex. 20:4; Deut. 5:8).[31] As the Jew, the artist, and the producer, Rabbi Loew invokes replicas of sacred figures, thereby defying the biblical proscription of images (*Bilderverbot*). In the intertitle announcing the rabbi's intentions, Loew instructively states, "Allow me to show you, dear ruler, the fathers of my people" (47). Loew's "show" offers precisely the mimetic photo-quality representation of the Jews against which he is proscribed. As Theodor W. Adorno remarks, "The Old Testament prohibition of graven images can be said to have an aesthetic aspect besides the overt theological one. The interdiction against forming an image – of something – in effect implies the proposition that such an image is impossible to form."[32] Adorno's statement critically underscores the destructive nature of the film aesthetic. Unlike Benjamin, whose notion of cinema envisions a potentially redemptive aesthetic, Adorno insists on film's lack of autonomy and fetish character. When considered in light of Wegener's *Golem*, Adorno's thoughts point to a double fetishization, as the Jew on the screen creates a further projection of the biblical passage. In his earliest reflections on antisemitism, "Elemente des Anti-Semitismus" ("Elements of Anti-Semitism," 1944), written in collaboration with Max Horkheimer and Leo Löwenthal, Adorno implicitly commented on the fetishization and desecration of Jewishness: "The morbid aspect of anti-Semitism is not projective behavior as such, but the absence from it of reflection. When the subject is no longer able to return to the object what he has received from it, he becomes poorer rather than richer. He loses reflection in both directions: since he no longer reflects the object, he ceases to reflect upon himself, and loses the ability to differentiate."[33] The masses of Jews projected onto the screen in *The Golem* cannot possibly reflect the individuality of the living Jew. Rather, as Adorno would argue, they merely represent one-dimensional replicas of the absent object that can never be fully reproduced.

Interestingly, in a 1920 lecture on the future of film delivered at the *Filmliga* in Berlin, Paul Wegener spoke of an innate danger in film that he calls the "Lebenslüge," the misrepresentation of life and nature. He observes how filmic images, in their unmediated affective capacity, "schematize," "stereotype," and graft characteristics onto an individual or a people (*Volk*).[34] As contradictory as his statement may appear against the backdrop of his *Golem* film, Wegener himself reveals an awareness of the problems of misrepresentation. For as seen in the film's portrayal of the Festival of the Roses and the film-within-a-film projection, the nature of the filmic enterprise is called into question. Although Rabbi Loew explicitly tells the viewers of the court to show respect for his creation ("No one may speak or laugh; otherwise, terrible disaster will occur" [48]), they do not know how to behave at the movies — a scene reminiscent of the confusion in Edwin Porter's classic, *Uncle Josh and the Moving Picture Show* (1902) — mocking the fictional images before them as if they were real.[35] The court audience, led by the jester, ridicules the Jews on the screen, affirming their odd appearance and the stark difference between Rabbi Loew's wandering Jews and the gentile viewers. This scene speaks directly to Adorno's critique of a certain kind of mimesis in his discussion of the *Bilderverbot*. According to Adorno, what is most dangerous in this mode of representation is the mimicry of the Jew. As the Nazi's myth-machine would later propagate, the Jews here become mere caricatures, types devoid of any human individuality.

To understand the implications of Wegener's version of the golem legend for the identity formation of Jews both on and off the screen, it is necessary to note the film's predilection for myth-based, caricatured constructions of Jewishness. Shown variously at work, at prayer, in the streets, and in acts of intrigue and conspiracy, the Jews of the ghetto city exude a sinister air. Among Wegener's repertoire of Jewish figures, the viewer encounters a succession of threatening characters: Rabbi Jehuda, the elder of the community who must be consulted in the decision to act with power against the emperor's banishment; Famulus, the rabbi's scheming, vengeful assistant, who turns the golem loose only to run amok after the rabbi has already thwarted the emperor's plan for Jewish expulsion; and the rabbi's unruly daughter, Miriam, whose oversexed gaze lures the gentile court messenger Florian into the ghetto, resulting in his death and the near destruction of the city. As in the caricatured portraits of Jews widely appropriated for German and Austrian political campaigns in the years surrounding the film's production, and as in the 1920 publication of the German edition of the *Protocols of the Elders of Zion*, the film's depiction of Jewishness reveals a strong bent toward a feared invasion.[36]

Just as the film's fictionalized documentary insert, the *Dekret wider die Juden*, declares that Jews "work black magic" and "endanger the lives" of Christians, *The Golem*'s portrayal of the main Jewish characters confirms these claims. Rabbi Loew mysteriously produces the robot-like golem out of clay – a scene stylized with thick clouds of smoke, wizard's garb, and pseudokabbalistic sorcery – while his manipulative "show" before the gentile court persuades the emperor fearfully to retract his decree (in the face of catastrophe, following the court's profane mockery of Loew's "show," the emperor begs, "save us, and I will pardon your people" [52]). Such ominous attributes of the Jew foster a clear division between the dark mysterious ghetto and the enlightened empire, between Jewish sorcery and German culture, between the perceived threat of Jewish power and the vulnerable German state. In this sense, Wegener's film presents an iconography of Jewishness that far exceeds the mythical foundation of the golem story, and thus highlights the many disparate contemporary issues surrounding Jews in Weimar Germany.

## THE GERMAN CITY AND THE JEWISH QUESTION

At the same time that such early German films as Stellan Rye's *The Student of Prague* (1913) and Paul Wegener's *The Golem* (1915) were projecting uncanny images of Jewish presence, Jews themselves were fiercely struggling with self-definition.[37] In the main German metropolitan centers, Jews sought to account for their position in the big city. Numerous public discussions and debates on the question of Jewish identity and its evolving forms appeared both in the German and German-Jewish public press. Writing in the pages of *Die Freistatt*, Arnold

Zweig presented his personal reflections on the problem of the Jewish writer in prewar Germany, which for him was above all an urban problem: "The Jew is a city-dweller, not from birth, but historically forced [*erzwungen*]; indeed, beyond that stirringly deep yearning to somehow share a vast community [*Gemeinschaft*] together with many of his own kind, he is the man of the big city. For him, the big city becomes the surrogate for the lost community of people [*Gemeinschaft des Volkes*] in his own state."[38] In this particular instance, Zweig attempted to legitimize the city as a form of ersatz community, which for him, in the face of modernity, had replaced the original Jewish homeland. He notes the prescient desires among Jews for a unified *Gemeinschaft* – a topic that he would later explore in *Das ostjüdische Antlitz* (1920) – while also recognizing the countervailing urban development of a "Surrogat für die verlorene Gemeinschaft" ("surrogate for the lost community").[39] As an *Ersatz-Gemeinschaft*, and not as a true unified community, the German city becomes a place where Jews tend to define themselves in terms of their Germanness more than their Jewishness.

Already in 1916 a series of heated debates on the Jewish Question, indeed "a veritable pamphlet war" prefiguring the Weimar treatment, took place in the major German cities.[40] Of paramount importance in these discussions were three main points: the status of the *Ostjuden* in modern civilized German society (i.e., in the German city); the impact they might have on the identity of German Jewry; and the risks, limits, and possibilities of cultural assimilation. In Berlin, responding to widespread attacks on Eastern Jewish cultural and political legitimacy, the prominent Zionist Adolf Friedemann offered an impassioned plea for support for the *Ostjuden*, noting the recent discovery of preserved Jewish life in the East and the mutual heritage shared by German Jews and their Eastern brothers and sisters. "The terrible war that we live through," he observes, "has suddenly created the necessity for the German Jews to address a problem from which the majority of German Jews in the past frightfully ran away – namely, the resolution of our relationship to the *Ostjuden*."[41] Friedemann goes on to emphasize the vital importance of seeing to it that the flourishing Jewish life of the East does not experience the backlash of emancipation: the massive trend in baptisms, the destruction of Jewish family life, and, most significantly, the disruptive forces of the cities. The Jewish concentration in the big cities, according to Friedemann and other Zionist leaders and scholars, only further contributed to the cultural and spiritual disenfranchisement from which Jews in the modern world suffered, whereas the Eastern way of life maintained a deeper sense of *Volksgemeinschaft* removed from this world.[42]

Friedemann's critique of the city was echoed in a lecture of the same year by Rabbi Felix Goldmann. Similar to such Zionist social scientists as Arthur Ruppin, Ignaz Zollschan, and Felix Theilhaber, Goldmann called attention to the "industrial growth" and the "big-city induced damages" to Judaism. Goldmann's lecture underscores the modern affinity that the Jew in general, and the German Jew in particular, had with the city: he is, as Goldmann argues, representative of the "typical city dwellers with genuinely urban professions." Goldmann's assessment of the modern German Jew as urban prototype and cause of Jewish decline follows a discursive line to which many reactionary modernists, Jew and gentile alike, ascribed.[43] This brand of Jew, which Goldmann and others link to the German big city, was widely seen as the prime symbol of cosmopolitan mass society (*Massengesellschaft*). By contrast, according to Goldmann, the Eastern Jew "carries with him the future of our *Gemeinschaft*. . . . The future of Judaism lies, in fact, only in the East and that is for us the point of the *Ostjudenfrage*."[44] Clearly celebrating the role of the *Ostjude* as the last authentic Jew, a sentiment that has been fittingly characterized as the "cult of Eastern Jews," Goldmann's remarks accentuate a position supported only by the more extreme advocates of Eastern Jewish culture and staunch opponents of German-Jewish assimilation.[45]

During the years surrounding the First World War the definition of Jewishness was no longer merely derived from one's declared religion (which, in the past, had been possible to circumvent through conversion to Christianity), but rather from one's ethnically defined lineage, from one's race.[46] While German Zionists focused on the rapid decline of Judaism due to modernization and urban growth, German nationalists exploited such data to support their claims of the impending *Verjudung* (Jewification) of *Deutschtum* (Germanness), the Jewish contamination of the German city.[47] Equally important, however, was the fact that the *Ostjudenfrage*, having entered into the discourse of racial and ethnic identity, reemerged within the broader parameters of the *Judenfrage*. While previously regarded, at least by liberal Germans, as "German Citizens of Jewish Faith," the Jews of Germany were now identified not as German Jews but simply as Jews, racially defined and iconographically marked by the traits of the *Ostjuden*.

By this point, the modes of identity formation had notably changed, whereby the shift in the trappings of identity among the German and Eastern Jews produced widespread confusion and personal strife among Jews and non-Jews alike. In his account of the social psychology of German Jewry, Gershom Scholem postulates, "To question the German identity of German Jews – and this was exactly what my generation was doing between 1910 and 1920 – was not regarded as purely theoretical dialectics but as a personal provocation and a destructive attack against something held taboo."[48] As Scholem suggests, lively debates on the Jew's position in the modern big city continued to capture the attention of the Germans and Jews throughout the 1920s. Articles on the *Judenfrage* filled German newspapers and journals, political campaigns decorated their platforms with caricatures of the (Eastern) Jewish threat, and, most dramatically, Weimar cinema discovered a popular social, cultural, and political question through which to pursue the perceived problems of the big city.[49]

Just as the Eastern Jewish Question had been conflated with the general Jewish Question, the *Ostjude* became a master icon of identification for the Jews at large. In the cinema, then, signs of Jewishness had to rely on cultural references to overt differences such as stereotypical Eastern Jewish physiognomy, religious and ritualistic symbols, and ghetto markings, while also relying on the latent anxieties of ostensibly specific Jewish trades and professions (e.g., urban industrialists, free-market capitalists, revolutionary intellectuals, and scientists). One of the great fears about assimilated German Jews was precisely their lack of overt characteristics, indeed their mastery of blending in with the gentile majority. Hence, a great enigma for Weimar cinema was how to represent the Jew if not by invoking the stereotypical physiognomic traits of the Eastern Jews. Although the films of the Weimar era dealing with Jewish subjects did not necessarily aim at propagating antisemitism, nor at inciting violence against Jews, the cinematic construction of Jewishness widely partook of various historical, socio-political, and cultural discourses inflected with notable anti-Jewish strains. What is most remarkable, however, is not so much that the filmic discourses of Weimar Germany incorporated anti-Jewish currents as how these currents were employed to convey the perceived notions of Jewishness.

While these currents are most explicit in Wegener's *Der Golem: Wie er in die Welt kam* (*The Golem: How He Came into the World*, 1920), similar inflections of Jewishness and urbanism existed in numerous other films from the period: F. W. Murnau's *Nosferatu, eine Symphonie des Grauens* (*Nosferatu, a Symphony of Horror*, 1922), Fritz Lang's *Dr. Mabuse, der Spieler* (*Dr. Mabuse, the Gambler*, 1922) and *Metropolis* (1927), Hans Karl Breslauer's *Die Stadt ohne Juden* (*The City Without Jews*, 1924), and G. W. Pabst's *Die Büchse der Pandora* (*Pandora's Box*, 1928). And yet, because of its exemplary status – as both a classic Weimar horror film and an especially rich treatment of the Jewish Question – and its broad-based appeal, Wegener's *Golem* best demonstrates the distinct ways in which film addresses the question of Jewish identity. Wegener's film represents the Jew on three distinguishable levels: first, the mythical, in the act of creation of the golem and the fantastic display of Jewish production; second, the physiognomic, both in the Jewish figures of the film and the spaces they occupy; and third, the political, in the subtle and not so subtle allusions to the Jewish Question and the fears of Jewish revolutionary power. These levels of representation illuminate the problems of constructing Jewish identity in German mass society of the 1920s, how the Jew stands in relation to this society, and finally how identity formation occurs within the aesthetic medium of the cinema.

## THE ARCHITECTURE OF THE JEW

*The gray soul of medieval Prague has been molded into these eccentric and errant crypts. They suggest a kind of Jewish Gothic – a blending of the flame-like letters of the Jewish alphabet with the leaf-like flame of Gothic tracery.* – Herman G. Scheffauer (1920)

As was certainly well known at the time, after the German defeat in World War I, waves of migration of East European Jews increased in unprecedented numbers, heightening the already acute awareness of the Jewish presence. The approximately 90,000 Eastern Jews who lived within German borders prior to the war nearly doubled, as another 70,000 immigrants joined their countrymen in the West during and after the war.[50] If, as Georg Lukács claimed in 1913, the cinema is to present a visual documentation of "everyday activities in the streets and markets," then *The Golem*'s focus on the crowds that occupy the ghetto city would seem to foreground the awareness of the Eastern Jewish masses.[51] A 1920 review of Wegener's film appearing in the Weimar film journal *Der Kinematograph* notes this imperceptible line separating the cinematic from the real world: "The crooked buildings, the twisty alleys of the ghetto, indeed even the people who appear in inexhaustible fullness, are without any distortion of a non-reality [*Unwirklichkeit*] that is removed from everyday life."[52] The Jewish setting, the *Kinematograph* critic suggests, along with the Jews portrayed on the screen, correspond to the common images of Jews in Weimar society. Symbolizing both the modern assimilated German Jews and the immigrant *Ostjuden*, these celluloid Jews, or what Alain Finkielkraut would later call "imaginary Jews," evoke at once capitalistic dominance, political prowess, and scientific insight on the one hand and stifling swarthiness, exotic practices, and ghetto sensibilities on the other.[53]

Signifying a meeting ground for the Jewish city dwellers, the streets in Wegener's film fuse with the masses, becoming a unified symbolic expression of the stylized setting. The amorphous crowds of Jews in the streets, swarming through the various passageways, resemble the arteries of an urban body (figure 10).[54]

In an article from the *Neue Berliner Zeitung*, published just days before the debut of Wegener's film, Joseph Roth noted the overwhelming presence of *Ostjuden* in Berlin: "On the whole, 50,000 human beings [Jews] have come to Germany after the war. It appears, of course, as if it were millions."[55] It is precisely this sense that is so dramatically evoked in *The Golem*. Like so much of the late nineteenth- and early-twentieth-century reactionary discourse on Jewish identity, the ghetto

10. The urban masses of the ghetto. Photo courtesy of The Museum of Modern Art Film Stills Archive.

Jews in *The Golem* are perceived as the quintessential urban *Volk*.[56] By combining Jewish and urban iconography, Wegener obscures the differentiation of the Jewish masses immersed in the animated quality of the city. "It is not Prague," explains Wegener in a *Film-Kurier* interview introducing the film, "that my friend, the architect [Hans] Poelzig, has erected. Rather it is a poem of a city [*Stadt-Dichtung*], a dream, an architectural paraphrase of the golem theme. These alleys and squares should not call to mind anything real; they should create the atmosphere in which the golem breathes."[57] Given the remarkable visibility of the *Ostjuden* within the postwar German city (most prominently in the Scheunenviertel of Berlin) and the Eastern Jewish swarms occupying Poelzig's fantasy city, the critique of the *real* contemporary problem, whether willful or inadvertent, cannot be overlooked.[58] Poelzig himself expressed the desire to make the ghetto buildings speak Yiddish – according to his biographer Theodor Heuss, he once claimed that "at least the buildings should jabber" ("wenigstens sollten die Häuser mauscheln") – which only affirms the artfully constructed bond of Jew and city, a bond that discursively runs from the nineteenth century through the postwar period.[59]

Because in silent cinema nothing can speak in audible terms, everything speaks in visual terms. In the same 1920 *Film-Kurier* interview with Wegener, the director proclaimed, "Film is not narrative; film is also not drama; film is, above all, moving image."[60] Just as Hans Poelzig had hoped, the buildings that were to communicate in Yiddish thus do in fact conjure an air of *Yiddishkeit* (figure 11).

The distorted shapes, dark cavities, and hunchback structures all serve to characterize the figures who occupy its expressive space. "The endlessly twisting staircases," writes Lester Friedman, "narrow crowded streets, dimly illuminated rooms, and sinister bellow-lit figures encourage us to believe the Emperor is correct: these people do practice black magic and are a threat."[61] In her aesthetic and cultural history of Weimar cinema, *The Haunted Screen*, Lotte Eisner observes the fantastic atmosphere of the Jewish ghetto city in Wegener's *Golem* and the integral relationship that the setting has to its inhabitants: "[T]he houses in the Prague ghetto, which have sprouted like weeds, seem to have an insidious life of their own 'when the autumn evening

11. The architecture of the ghetto. Photo courtesy of The Museum of Modern Art Film Stills Archive.

mists stagnate in the streets and veil their imperceptible grimace.' In some mysterious way these streets contrive to abjure their life and feelings during the daytime, and lend them instead to their inhabitants, those enigmatic creatures who wander aimlessly around feebly animated by invisible magnetic current."[62] The ghetto city, as Eisner argues, draws a portrait of the Jewish body defined in graphically urban terms. Poelzig's buildings convey the Jewishness of the ghetto as the site from which a specific "physiognomy" emerges.

In view of the lively responses elicited by the expressive architectural mystique of Poelzig's ghetto city – that is, by the enigmatic space of the Jew – it is worth considering some of the critiques by the film's earliest commentators both in Germany and abroad, as they almost invariably focus on this aspect of Wegener's film. Paul Westheim's review in the *Kunstblatt* recalled the atmospheric tension projected between the ghetto walls and the synagogue, conveying what he pronounced a "strongly expressive unity of scenery"; Hermann Scheffauer's American critique observed an "eerie and grotesque suggestiveness" of the houses and streets in the Golem's city. "The will of this master architect," Scheffauer continues, "animating façades into faces, insists that these houses are to speak in jargon – and gesticulate."[63] The physiognomy of the Jew – a subject that at the time of the film's debut was widely explored in literary, popular, and *völkisch* writings – emerges in Wegener's film in the architectural construction of Jewishness. As attested by the creators of the film and their critics alike, the contemporary face of the Jew emanates from the historical surface of the ghetto buildings.[64]

A choice passage from Gustav Meyrink's bestselling *Golem* novel of 1915 serves to illustrate the background of the aesthetic innovation incorporated in the so-called "Jewish Gothic" (Scheffauer) of Poelzig's film sets: "How uncanny and depraved they [the buildings] all seemed. Erected without plan, from the look of them, as fortuitously as so many weeds rising from the ground. Two of them were huddled up together against an old yellow stone wall, the last remaining vestige of an earlier building of considerable size. There they had stood for two centuries now, or it might be three, detached from the buildings around them; one of them slanting obliquely, with a roof like a retreating forehead; the one next to it jutting out like an eye-tooth."[65] As in Wegener's fantasy film of some five years later, Meyrink's fantastic novel features the eery world of the Prague Jewish ghetto. Similar, too, is the contemporary resonance that both texts achieve in their respective treatments of the mysterious Jewish legend: playing, in effect, on the innate curiosity and exoticism attributed to the story.

12. Hans Poelzig, film poster, 1920. © Bildarchiv Preussischer Kulturbesitz.

13. Hans Poelzig, lithograph. The Museum of Modern Art, New York. Photograph © 1998 The Museum of Modern Art.

The unusual quality of this ethnically encoded architecture, or cinematic production of *Jewish* space, found prominent expression in the publicity materials printed for Wegener's film (figures 12 and 13).

In the 1920 posters for *The Golem*, reportedly designed by Poelzig, the profiles of the dark Jewish figures – the inhabitants of the ghetto as well as the golem himself – reflect the oblique shapes of the city buildings towering above. As in the film's representation, the Jews in the advertisement vividly mark the city's physiognomy. Huddled beneath the monstrous ghetto buildings, the figures in Poelzig's poster maintain the same posture as the ghetto architecture itself. Like the *Ostjuden* portrayed in political caricatures of the 1920s, these Jews connote dark, scheming, and intrusive elements that threaten to invade the German body politic. As Anthony Vidler has recently noted, "'light space' is invaded by the figure of 'dark space,' on the level of the body in the form of epidemic and uncontrollable disease, and on the level of the city in the person of the homeless."[66] In Wegener's *Golem*, the homeless

Jews similarly radiate the darkness of a spreading epidemic, a problem which on the narrative level of the film takes a distinct turn in the sexual relationship between Rabbi Loew's daughter, Miriam, and the emperor's knight, Florian.

In this melodramatic subplot, the affair between the rabbi's daughter and the gentile messenger, the symbolic interaction is hardly as insignificant as critics like Eisner and Kracauer have suggested. Indeed, to dismiss the subplot as merely a secondary parallel storyline is to overlook the highly charged issue of interracial relations and the threat of the Jewess. It is, after all, Miriam's enticing gaze that lures Florian into her web, while her sexual transgression ultimately leads to violent disaster. (In a plot for revenge, the golem is unleashed by the jealous rabbi's servant – himself having shamefully discovered the gentile "stranger" in Miriam's bedroom – only to murder Florian and, in his rage, to set the ghetto city aflame.) Next to Rabbi Loew, Miriam appears to be the most dangerous of the Jews occupying the ghetto. Moreover, as a modern Sulamith figure, her body imagery exudes a dark, haunting eroticism, representing not only a threat within the context of the film, but also within the context of writings on Jewish sexuality and interracial relations around the year 1920.

Well before Wegener's production, the threat of sexual and racial relations between Germans and Jews had long been a topic of popular literature, politics, and the visual arts. In the new wave of antisemitic writings following a brief boom at the end of the nineteenth century, Artur Dinter's best-selling novel *Die Sünde wider das Blut* (*The Sin Against Blood*, 1918) warned the German *Volk* against the effects of racial mixing. Pitting the German and Jew against each other, Dinter asserted that German-Jewish procreation causes an evil revenge manifest in the so-called sin against blood: the German race, so the argument goes, is irreparably polluted by even the slightest infusion of Jewish blood.[67] In the cinema, this topic would be picked up again only two years after Wegner's *Golem* in F. W. Murnau's *Nosferatu*, a film that, when viewed against the historical backdrop of Eastern Jewish migration and the discourses of parasitism, insanity, and sexuality, clearly reveals an acute fear of Jewish contamination (*Verjudung*). Not entirely unlike Fassbinder's "Rich Jew" in *Garbage, the City and Death*, the plague-bearing Eastern capitalist in Murnau's *Nosferatu*, played by the Jewish actor Max Schreck, buys up property in the gentile city, causing the near annihilation of the dominant population. He destroys all who enter into his path, conspires with the (Jewish) pathological real estate dealer (played by the Yiddish Theater actor Alexander Granach), and engages in sexual intercourse with members of the Western gentile *Volk*.[68] Near the end of Fassbinder's *Garbage*, in one of its most chilling scenes, the German figure Hans von Glück utters the following words, emphatically stating his fears of Jewish domination: "He's sucking us dry, the Jew. Drinking our blood and blaming everything on us because he's a Jew and we're guilty. . . . He has the banks and city hall on his side. . . . The Jew knows his business well, fear's a stranger to him, he's not frightened by death"(180–81). On a discursive level, the ostensibly Jewish figures in *Garbage*, *Nosferatu*, and *Golem* are all portrayed as unsavory, swarthy, threatening creatures who inhabit dark, haunted, and urban spaces.

Such depictions of Jews were certainly not limited to "artistic" productions of the time. On 24 February 1920, only eight months prior to the Berlin premiere of *The Golem*, Adolf Hitler introduced his twenty-five point party program for the German Workers' Party. In this document, he set the tone for a newly defined, rejuvenated, and unified German *Volk*. In addition to demanding the abrogation of the Versailles Treaty and the re-Germanization of the postwar nation, Hitler announced the crucial stipulation to his vision of the German Reich: "No one who is not a member of the nation can be a citizen. No one whose blood is not German blood, regardless of creed, can be a member of the nation. Thus no Jew can be a member of the nation."[69] Drawing his definitions in pseudoscientific racial terms, Hitler believed that the Jew could never become a German, for he could never change his biological identity. Moreover, like the message signaled in Artur Dinter's novel, Hitler's perception of the Jew emphasized the revolutionary threat to *Germanentum*, that is, Jew as "parasite, vampire, bloodsucker, contaminating the Aryan race."[70] In a speech given in August of the same year, he forcefully stated his agenda vis-à-vis the Jews: "The impact of Jewry will never pass away, the poisoning of the people will not end, as long as the causal agent, the Jew, is not removed from our midst."[71] The German state, according to Hitler, had to cleanse itself of the damaging forces inflicted by its Jewish inhabitants. As in *The Golem's* fictionalized *Dekret wider die Juden*, the Jews had to be expelled from German soil.

Wegener's *Golem*, which he himself declared a "powerful film, perhaps my most powerful," responds to the Jewish Question by presenting the threat of the Jew.[72] Though the mystification of this question in the ancient Jewish legend might otherwise prevent the audience from focusing on the actual issue, the profusion of indicators referring to the various problematic conceptions of Jewishness around 1920 serves to position this question among the central and most salient features of the film. In the equation of Jewish identity with urban identity – and thus the fear of Jewish urbanization – the Jewish Question remains, at least implicitly, within the narrative, iconographic, and historical emplotment of the film. Wegener not only exploits the mythical content of the golem story in a way that radically accentuates common perceptions of Jewishness, but he also constructs a veritable "architecture of Jewishness," framing these images in the urban setting. The fecundity of such images lies in the multilayered meanings they offer to the observer and the perspectives rendered through the interaction between viewer and image.

Although we cannot possibly estimate the impact that these images had on the audience of 1920, the potential seems extraordinary.[73] While such images doubtless spoke to the problems of Jewish identity, they equally underscored the crisis of German identity. For Jewish identity during the years of the Weimar Republic could not be defined without reference to the German – in its opposition, and in its connection. To explore the ways in which Jews are portrayed in film during the 1920s is not simply to suggest that these images travel a course which leads directly to Nazism, the destruction of the Jews, and mass barbarism. Similarly, Weimar cinema does not, as Kracauer claims in *From Caligari to Hitler*, provide a key to uncovering the alleged psychological disposition of a nation.[74] Rather, the power and poignancy of this medium lies in its role in defining an identity, one that was constructed – and continues to be constructed – through memory and fantasy, history and myth.

# FOUR

# Culture in Ruins:
# Walter Benjamin's Memories

*In a century in which memory has been more than ever before under threat, Benjamin offers us a body of work in which the demands of modernity are investigated alongside the ethical demands of memory. To speak, write and think in memory of Walter Benjamin, to commemorate his centenary, is to be in memory of a writer for whom the requirements of memory were pressing and ineluctable – it is to be in memory of the fragile value of memory itself.* – Laura Marcus/Lynda Nead

Perhaps this century's most celebrated German literary critic, cultural historian, and man of letters, Walter Benjamin has been examined from a remarkably wide range of angles, appropriated within a host of disparate and often contradictory programs, and considered anew in light of evolving critical methodologies. Regarded at once as a utopian Marxist, Jewish messianist, and historical materialist, Benjamin has elicited responses from commentators in such disciplines as art history, sociology, and political science and from such diverse theoretical enterprises as feminism, new historicism, Marxism, and post-structuralism. As Axel Honneth has recently noted, "Scarcely any other author of this century has been able to trigger so many waves of reception in so short a time: hardly any other seems to possess the same stimulating potential for generating new efforts at interpretation as Benjamin."[1] In recent years Benjamin's writings have experienced a veritable renaissance, a rediscovery of their profound cultural, political, and social "actuality."[2]

Rather than focusing on the wide range of interpretive entries into Benjamin's work, a daunting task that numerous Benjamin critics have endeavored to undertake in recent years, the scope of the following chapter will be limited to the critical tension in Benjamin between Jewish memory and identity construction on the one hand, and the forces of modernity on the other.[3] Central to this discussion is Benjamin's conception of memory and Jewish identity, as developed from his earliest diary entries, letters, and short essays, through his major works, and finally up to the last notes before his suicide in September 1940. From this standpoint, we will explore the ways in which Benjamin articulates his sense of Jewishness and the bearing that such articulations have on his theoretical and cultural projects. In fact, Benjamin's sense of Jewish memory might be finally seen as a critique of modernity and of the concomitant developments within German-Jewish culture.

Anson Rabinbach has remarked that Benjamin's late correspondence with Gershom Scholem from 1932 to 1940 should be viewed as "an extended discussion of the fate of the Jewish and German intellectual traditions on the eve of catastrophe."[4] In the case of Benjamin – perhaps more than any other of his contemporaries – we find a figure who stands on the threshold of this "catastrophe," whose life and work both embrace and resist the problems of salvaging history and tradition while confronting modern technological progress. Benjamin's work takes us through the crisis of community and the confrontation with mass society, through the redemptive gestures of memory and collection, and finally into the catastrophic realm of destruction and defeat.

Modernity, for Benjamin, was the historical epoch that ushered in great socio-political, aesthetic, and ontological transformations as well as the new possibilities, attractions, and perceived dangers of technological advancement. Benjamin's home was the modern German metropolis of Berlin, where he lived on and off from his birth on 15 July 1892 until the spring of 1933, and finally the French capital of Paris, where he lived as an exile from Nazi Germany until his suicide in September 1940.[5] During his lifetime, Benjamin witnessed firsthand the late nineteenth-century turn toward industrialization. As he observed in what might be considered his most exacting critique of modernity, "Das Kunstwerk im Zeitalter seiner technischen Reproduzierbarkeit" ("The Work of Art in the Age of Its Mechanical Reproduction," 1936), around 1900 – also the temporal marker of his childhood memories –

modern technological progress began to change Western culture irreversibly: the arts, politics, and society. Here Benjamin notes the potentially "heightened presence of mind" brought about by the shock effects of the cinema, mass media, and big-city life, while also recognizing the adverse implications of technological reproduction for classical and traditional arts. Only three years later, in his essay on Baudelaire, "Über einige Motive bei Baudelaire" ("On Some Motifs in Baudelaire," 1939), Benjamin would argue that already in mid nineteenth-century Paris, Baudelaire "had indicated the price for which the sensation of the modern age may be had: the disintegration of the aura and the experience of shock" (GS I-2, 653; I 194). Modernity, then, represents an epoch in which tradition has "fallen ill" (Kafka), in which the aura of a work of art and the authenticity of real experience can no longer go unchallenged, and the big-city sensibilities portend new ways of seeing.

Benjamin's view of modernity accentuated the fragmentary, disjointed, inauthentic qualities of twentieth-century life, and his sense of Jewish identity was certainly affected by his modernist sensibility. Jewish identity, then, was largely conceived of as displaced and ephemeral, shaped by the contours of modern German cultural and spiritual life and the competing developments of Zionism, romanticism, Socialism, and the German Youth Movement. Like his critique of modernity, Benjamin's conception of Jewish identity incorporates strains of nostalgia for a past order, for authenticity and original wholeness; yet there is also a strong will to read the future in the past. Here the major point of intersection between Benjamin's conception of modernity and Jewish identity emerges within the sphere of memory. "The anticipation of what is new in the future," writes Jürgen Habermas in his excursus on Benjamin's philosophy of history, "is realized only through remembering [*Eingedenken*] a past that has been suppressed."[6] Indeed, Benjamin's conception of modernity and the problem of Jewish identity is in many ways oriented towards "remembering" a past in ruins, recollecting the fragments, and extracting their redemptive and utopian potentials. His model for understanding this constellation is neither normative nor teleological, but rather antinomian and apocalyptic. It aims at rendering memory operative – and, to a great extent, constitutive – in the process of critical illumination.

*When I was born the thought came to my parents that I might perhaps become a writer. Then it would be good if not everybody noticed that I was a Jew.* – Walter Benjamin (1933)

Walter Benjamin came of age during a time when Jewish cultural life in German-speaking Europe was entering a new phase. In the wake of the nineteenth-century emancipation movements and the continued assimilation of Jews into the mainstream of German culture and society, the generations before Benjamin had largely managed to achieve financial success, even if it was at the expense of abandoning their Jewishness. This was certainly the case of the generation to which Benjamin's father, Emil Benjamin, a wealthy Berlin art dealer, belonged. Like many of the assimilated German-Jewish fathers of the fin de siècle, Emil Benjamin was a prime example of bourgeois German Jewry – a Jewry that celebrated Christmas as a national German holiday, that privileged the ideals of *Bildung* and *Deutschtum* over the vanishing traditions of *Judentum*, and that often fully neglected or repressed its tenuous status within German culture and society.[7] Benjamin's generation, however, challenged the complacency of the German-Jewish bourgeoisie, cultivating instead a "new Jewish sensibility" that no longer oriented itself around the principles of emancipation and the ideals of *Bildung*.[8] Generally more leftist in political orientation, this generation's diverse currents of thought incorporated a curious blend of Socialism, youthful neoromanticism, and utopian messianism. Although the young Jews of Benjamin's generation were weaned on the staples of German Enlightenment culture, well-versed in Kant, Lessing, Goethe, and Schiller, they had also personally experienced the rise of political and racial antisemitism, the dramatic impact of East European Jewish migration during the First World War, and the dissemination of cultural and political Zionism. Brought up in this rapidly changing era, they were more apt than previous generations to confront what they saw as the many shortcomings of assimilation.

In the spheres of literature, philosophy, politics, and the arts, the status of Jewishness had increasingly come under attack by Jews and non-Jews alike. The construction of Jewish identity, to be sure, took on new meaning. Under the spiritual guidance of Ahad Ha'am, Martin Buber, and Theodor Herzl, more young German Jews began to identify with various branches of Zionism. Some, of course, continued to hold fast to the tenets of German liberalism and the ideals of the Enlightenment; still others rejected the values of Jewish national and cultural renewal altogether. It should come as no surprise that Benjamin's own sense of Jewishness was imbued with the various conflicting strands of this cultural and political climate.

Although Benjamin's position on Judaism, his attitude towards his own Jewishness and his opinion of the evolving Jewish currents around him, remained in flux until his death, what stayed consistent was his ongoing effort to articulate the ambivalence he felt. From the time that Benjamin first became involved in the German Youth Movement in 1911 until he wrote his theses on the philosophy of history in 1940, he considered issues of Jewish concern alternately on the periphery and at the core of his thought. Like his later stance on Marxism, Benjamin's commitment to Judaism was one that yielded many idiosyncratic and contradictory strains. And as was the case with Marxism, Benjamin's position on Judaism made it possible for him to theorize about *Judentum* and its socio-cultural, political, and moral potential (e.g., in his discussions of Zionism) without bringing it to the practical sphere of everyday life. To be sure, as he would finally admit to Gershom Scholem in 1926, both "religious [Judaism] and political [Marxism] observance" meet in the realm of ethical decision, in the realm of the concrete – an area where Benjamin showed continued apprehension.[9] Benjamin's most critical reflections on *Judentum* reveal a vacillation between the developments of modern German-Jewish identity formation and German modernity.

Benjamin's sense of Jewish identity, though continually shifting, underwent a series of recognizable phases that are no less real for their ambiguity. In his early debates around 1912–13 on Zionism and the German Youth Movement with Ludwig Strauß, Kurt Tuchler, and other young German Zionists, Benjamin engaged in the revived search for a "new Jewish community." This phase nearly coincides with a second one – or, rather, a series of phases – in which Benjamin continued to challenge his sense of Jewish identity through a growing relationship with Gershom Scholem, which he maintained during the most productive and most frustrating stages of his life and career. Later, while he was exploring the possibilities for Jewish tradition and culture under the tutelage of Scholem, he entered a period in which Judaism is for the most part dealt with on an implicit, esoteric level, that is, a period in which he pursued more explicitly universalistic projects such as his treatises on language philosophy, German romanticism, and the origin of German tragic drama. Finally, in the last phase of his career, Benjamin's work enters a period that extends from his studies on Proust and Baudelaire of the late 1920s to his *Passagen-Werk* (*Arcades Project*, 1928/29–1940), where he deals with Judaism and the competing currents of Marxism and dialectical materialism. Benjamin's unique conception of Judaism takes shape around these four phases, particularly around the incomplete shift from his sense of a potential for a Jewish intellectual *Gemeinschaft* to the crass confrontation with the modern *Gesellschaft*.[10]

On Passover, the eight-day Jewish celebration commemorating the deliverance from Egypt, Benjamin writes in his diary entry of 12 April 1911: "Today is *Yontev*. I just read in the Haggadah. – At dinner, Mr. Charitz always says: 'So, what is one supposed to do on *Yontev*?' (i.e., cook) One does not say *guten Tag*, but rather *gut Yontev*" (GS VI, 232). Here the fragmentary portrait of the Passover holiday preserves the memory of Benjamin's early encounters with Jewish ritual and lore, an encounter that reappears episodically in his later memoirs. In Benjamin's brief discussion of the Jewish holiday and its rituals, we discern subtle traces of his autobiographical project (e.g., memory, hope, redemption) transmitted through reading from the Haggadah. According to Jewish historian Yosef Hayim Yerushalmi, Passover is "preeminently the great historical festival of the Jewish people, and the Haggadah is its book of *remembrance* and *redemption*. Here the memory of the nation is annually renewed and replenished, and the collective hope sustained."[11] Though for Benjamin the cultural memory inscribed in the Haggadah might not best be seen as the "memory of the nation," the questions of remembrance and redemption, as we shall see, are recurring questions that occupy a central position in his public and private writings. In the notes from his Passover diary entry, Benjamin goes on to mention the three-armed candelabra, the matzohs eaten for breakfast, and finally declares summarily that "we live according to the rituals of the Passover-week" (*wir leben in der Pessahwoche*) (GS VI, 233).

Although Benjamin announces his engagement with the Jewish holiday, a degree of uncertainty and skeptical reservation about the Passover traditions remains present. In the same diary entry, he goes on to reveal his split position on the role of Jewish ritual, thereby highlighting what for German Jewry had increasingly become a secularized act: "Thank God we didn't have a Seder. It certainly would have been very interesting and might have even moved me. But it would have struck me as *profane theater* [*unheiliges Theater*]. – Nonetheless, tonight I traveled back five hundred years in world history" (GS VI, 233; emphasis added).[12] As an eighteen-year-old student, Benjamin is clearly self-conscious about his participation in the Jewish festival of remembrance in the Haggadah and thus critically observes the rituals. On the one hand, Benjamin's negation of the Seder as "profane theater" calls the Passover ritual into question, while on the other, his statement acknowledges the historical and mnemonic power of the journey into the past made possible through reading from the Haggadah. While Benjamin appears to convey a genuine interest in the Jewish holiday and its rituals, he also maintains a critical position on the ritualistic Seder *performed* by assimilated German Jewry. Given the repeated encounters with this two-sidedness in Benjamin's response to Judaism, it seems possible to view his earliest debates as the foundation for those in the many years to come. This ambivalence in Benjamin will later become an interest in his renewed explorations of the historiographic potential of memory for the project of modernity.

During the years 1912 and 1913 – a transitional moment in which Scholem locates both the "crisis of German-speaking Jews" and the subsequent "Jewish awakening" – Benjamin engaged in numerous heated discussions about the German Youth Movement, Zionism, and the possibilities of building "a new Jewish community."[13] Key testimony to these debates can be found in Benjamin's correspondence with the German Zionist (and future son-in-law of Martin Buber), Ludwig Strauß. Situated in the wake of the controversy surrounding the 1912 publication of Moritz Goldstein's "German-Jewish Parnassus" in the *Kunstwart*, Benjamin's letters express his views on German Zionism, its political and cultural variants, and the tasks for the future. Just as Goldstein's polemic had brashly outlined the problems of the German-Jewish intellectual – the lack of legitimacy and the one-sided love affair – Strauß's response and Benjamin's subsequent interpretation both address the absence of a young Jewish intellectual *Gemeinschaft* and the need for a better understanding of Jewish identity in the Diaspora. German-Jewish writers and intellectuals, according to Goldstein, could no longer feel at home in the German cultural milieu and so had to redefine Jewish self-understanding. This self-understanding was to come about through the "organization of Jewish intellectual life" either in Germany (in the case of Benjamin) or in Palestine (in the case of Strauß).[14] Upon careful examination of the letters, it becomes apparent that this period was a time in which Benjamin's most intense early thoughts on his sense of *Judentum* – of Judaism and Jewishness – first crystallized.

While Benjamin initially expresses a willingness to recognize and support the ideas of Zionism, he also makes clear to Strauß that Zionism alone has not shaped his own identity.[15] He explains that although he considers his Jewishness something "essential" (*Kernhaftes*), he also feels a great indebtedness to his years of active involvement in Gustav Wyneken's branch of the German Youth Movement. In a letter of 10 October 1912, Benjamin discusses the mixed currents that informed his early intellectual growth: "As I hardly need to tell you, I was raised in a liberal fashion. I had my most decisive spiritual experience [*Erlebnis*], before Judaism ever became *important* [*wichtig*] or *problematic* [*problematisch*]. All that I really knew about it [Judaism] was antisemitism and an ambiguous piety. As a religion it was foreign to me, as a nationalist enterprise it was unknown" (GS II-3, 836; emphasis added).[16] The "decisive spiritual experience" to which Benjamin refers is in fact the time he spent under the aegis of Wyneken. Until the summer of 1912, Judaism had simply not been a vital concern for Benjamin. In fact, the previous years with the *Freie Schulgemeinde* (Free School Community) of Wickersdorf in the Thuringian forest had left a lasting allegiance to the ideals of the Youth Movement and set the foundation of his thought. Franz Kafka is said to have once remarked in conversation with Gustav Janouch that "Gustav Wyneken and his friends wish[ed] to escape from the grip of our machine world. They turn[ed] to nature and to man's most ancient intellectual heritage."[17] Similar to their Zionist counterparts such as *Jung-Juda* and *Blau-Weiß*, Wyneken's Youth Movement sought to discover a community outside of the hustle and bustle of the modern city; with their shared discourses of *Volk*, *Gemeinschaft*, and *Erneuerung*, both the Zionist and German Youth Movement looked to nature for the revitalization of organic harmony.[18] However, in his debate with Strauß, Benjamin also reveals a great indebtedness to the universalist ideals of the Enlightenment rather than to the Zionist conception of Jewish culture. For Benjamin, individual religions do not have particularized origins, but rather function as parts of universal humanist values.[19] He takes note of the fact that the members of the Wickersdorf community were largely Jews, but adds that they are Jews with a "dualistic conception of life" (GS II-3, 837), indeed a conception where the German was on par with the Jewish.

In light of such a critique of Judaism, it is worth noting the parallels between the remarks in his diary entry of 1911 and those made in the letter to Strauß: What Benjamin had first dubbed "profane theater" in his diary of 1911 seems to resonate with his later reference to "an ambiguous piety." Both statements challenge the value of normative Judaism and Jewish ritual, and point to Benjamin's skeptical view of the legacy of bourgeois German-Jewish assimilation. This general pattern in Benjamin's stance on Judaism – a vexed position between *wichtig* (important) and *problematisch* (problematic) – extends over the years without significant modification.

At once wary of and fascinated by Buber's notion of a "Jewish experience" (*jüdisches Erlebnis*), Benjamin shows signs of a complex struggle to define his position in his discussion with Strauß, as he reveals reservations about Zionism alongside a firm embrace of Jewish culture and Jewish identity.[20] He concludes his letter to Strauß with an impassioned statement that highlights his idiosyncratic position: "Over the last months everything has become clear to me. From the point of view of Wickersdorf [i.e., Wyneken], not purely speculative nor totally emotional, but rather from the outer and inner experience, I have found my Jewishness. I have discovered that which I regard highest in ideas and people to be Jewish. To articulate all of what I have recognized as a formula: I am a Jew and if I am to live as a conscious human being, then I must live as a conscious Jew" (GS II-3, 837). Though it remains unclear whether he fully acknowledges the move toward a more pure form of *Deutschtum* within the Youth Movement, along with the antisemitic and chauvinist strains that accompanied this shift, Benjamin's experiences in Wickersdorf manage to remind him of his Jewishness.[21] Referring to the Jews as "peoples of memory," Pierre Nora has argued that in Jewish tradition, "which has no other history than its own memory, to be Jewish is to remember one is such."[22] Similarly, by accounting for his position within the lineage of Jewish culture and tradition – albeit from an unusually affirmative standpoint – Benjamin's exchange with Strauß enforces his self-conception as a Jew. In fact, at this point, Benjamin goes so far as to declare his loyalty to a form of "cultural Zionism" (Ahad Ha'am), "which recognizes and works for the Jewish values in all areas" (GS II-3, 838).[23]

Nevertheless, the subtle skepticism toward Judaism that one finds in his Passover diary entry from the preceding year has not completely vanished. Rather, it reappears in a different form, namely, as a critique of German "political Zionism" à la Herzl, which for Benjamin separates itself from "cultural Zionism" in its half-heartedness (*Halbheit*). So as to highlight the "imperfection" he sees in political Zionism, Benjamin invokes the inner transformation of cultural Zionism and the "essence" (*Wesen*) of Judaism expressed by Buber in his *Drei Reden über das Judentum* (*Three Lectures on Judaism*, 1911), asking himself whether Jewish work for Palestine or Jewish work for Europe is more urgent. "I am connected here [i.e., Europe]," he responds to Strauß. "And it would be terrible for Europe if it lost the cultural energies of the Jews" (GS II-3, 838). Similar to his liaison to Wyneken and the German Youth Movement, Benjamin's position on Zionism construes a moral allegiance to the cultural life of Europe as opposed to the political Zionists' allegiance to Palestine. For Benjamin, politics has no place in the spiritual and cultural realms of Judaism. Accordingly, he asserts that in the eyes of the political Zionists, "Zionism [was always] a matter of political organization. At the inner core, their personality was by no means shaped by Jewishness: they propagate Palestine and drink [*saufen*] like Germans" (GS II-3, 838). In spite of his high opinion of cultural Zionism, particularly Ahad Ha'am's notion of the spiritual center of Judaism, accompanied by his own self-conception as "a conscious Jew," the ambivalent undercurrent remains present throughout his writings on Judaism.

Some contemporary Benjamin scholars have challenged the pivotal role that Gershom Scholem played in Benjamin's intellectual career. Yet when considering Benjamin's notion of Judaism, Scholem's influence is incontestable. In his sustained contact and ongoing correspondence with Scholem from 1915 to 1940, Benjamin privately explored numerous Jewish concerns, many of which never quite reached expression in his published work. In the same sense that Kafka's relationships to Yitzhak Löwy and, to a greater extent, Max Brod helped build his awareness of Jewish culture, Benjamin's ties to Scholem were definitive in shaping his sense of Jewish identity. As Benjamin would ultimately confess to Scholem in the spring of 1930: "Living Judaism I have certainly encountered in no other form than in you. The question of my relationship to Judaism is always the question of how I stand – I do not want to say in relation to you . . . but rather in relation to the forces that you have aroused in me" (*Briefe* II, 513; *Correspondence*, 364 – trans. rev.).

From the outset of their relationship, Benjamin and Scholem both rejected the assimilated German-Jewish bourgeoisie and the liberal Jewish establishment. Their first meeting in autumn of 1913, at a gathering under the auspices of the *Jung Juda* Zionist youth organization and the faction of Wyneken's group involved in the *Sprechsaal der Jugend* (Youth Forum), marked a search for an alternative *Gemeinschaft* among young German Jews. In an illuminating passage from his memoir of their friendship, Scholem tells how early on in their relationship Benjamin had declared, "If I ever have a philosophy of my own . . . it somehow will be a philosophy of Judaism" (*Friendship*, 32; cf. *Benja-*

*miniana*, 62).[24] Although one might attempt, as have Gillian Rose and Irving Wohlfarth, to expound a *Jewish* reading of Benjamin's work, that is, a reading that examines specifically Jewish motifs and sources in Benjamin, I would suggest instead that his thought is marked by various attempts of his own – many of them failed – to include aspects of Judaism, or rather "Jewishness," in his writings.[25] Scholem's role in these attempts cannot be underestimated. Whether he was acting to secure Benjamin a stipend from Judah Magnes (then president of the newly founded Hebrew University in Jerusalem) to learn Hebrew in 1928, or providing his input on the halakhah and aggadah for Benjamin's Kafka essay of 1934, Scholem's extensive knowledge of Jewish tradition and culture was omnipresent in Benjamin's "Jewish" life.

In the early 1920s, in the midst of their developing relationship, when Benjamin first announced his attempts to learn Hebrew at the University of Berlin and after his recent acquisition of various Judaica titles from Jewish secondhand booksellers, Benjamin suddenly announced plans to publish a journal with an unapologetic Jewish character. Named after Paul Klee's painting *Angelus Novus*, Benjamin's journal, as he envisioned it, would provide a forum for Scholem's translations of S. J. Agnon's "Synagogue" and for "Rise and Fall" by Benjamin's childhood friends, the brothers Fritz and Wolf Heinle; it would also include a critique of Prague Zionism by Scholem, and other literary and nonliterary works from the German and German-Jewish cultural milieu (*Briefe* I, 280–81; *Correspondence*, 193; cf. *Friendship*, 104–105). Due to rising inflation, the journal was never launched. However, it is possible to speculate on the path it might have taken. As Benjamin makes clear to Scholem, his desire to participate in the widespread debates on Jewish culture and the Jewish Question would have found a proper forum with the establishment of the journal. Toward the final stages of plans for the journal in 1922, in one of Benjamin's letters to Scholem, written on Rosh Hashanah, the Jewish New Year, he refers to *Angelus* as an individual being who wishes to show that he is in fact a "a good Jew," and thus he sends New Year's greetings to Scholem (*Briefe* I, 289; *Correspondence*, 199).

Benjamin's discussion of Jewish and German-Jewish matters continued in his correspondence with the former priest and German Shakespeare critic Florens Christian Rang, exhibiting further that the Jewish Question remained important to him during the early 1920s. In a letter of November 1923, Benjamin discusses with Rang "the current situation of Germanness" and the "genuine Germanness" that Rang represents vis-à-vis Benjamin's "Jewish self" (*Briefe* I, 310; *Correspondence*, 214–15). Alluding to the recent assassinations of Walther Rathenau and Gustav Landauer, Benjamin reflects on the potential dangers of Jewish public participation in German political and cultural life. It is in this letter to Rang that Benjamin arrives at a truly provocative summation of the Jewish Question:

> Here, if anywhere, we are at the core of the current Jewish Question: the Jew today endangers even the best German cause for which he stands up *publicly*, because his public German expression is necessarily venal (in the deeper sense). It cannot produce a certificate of authenticity. Secret relationships between Germans and Jews can be maintained with an entirely different kind of legitimacy. As for the rest, I believe that my principle is true and apt: nowadays everything having to do with German-Jewish relationships that has a *visible impact* does so to their detriment; furthermore, nowadays a salutary complicity obligates those individuals of noble character among both peoples to keep silent about their ties. (*Briefe* I, 310; *Correspondence*, 215 – trans. rev.; emphasis in original)

As if to revisit the unsettled dispute surrounding Moritz Goldstein's *Kunstwart* debate, Benjamin questions the appropriateness of outwardly Jewish contributions to German cultural and political causes. With his eyes fixed upon the public discourse of the Jewish Question, he reads the increasingly tenuous ties between Germans and Jews as a practical sign of the need for secrecy, for silence about his Jewishness, especially in his public writings.

During the 1920s, while continuing to explore Jewish culture (he had an orthodox Passover Seder with Scholem at the home of Moses Marx in Berlin in 1922), Benjamin also began to immerse himself in Marxist thought. In 1924, while visiting the island of Capri, he initiated an intense relationship with the Latvian Marxist Asja Lacis, who for Benjamin symbolized an extreme counterpart to Scholem (i.e., a turn against Jewish tradition). As Ernst Bloch puts it, "she [first] acquainted him with Marxist trains of thought" and encouraged him to explore the critical potential of this new domain.[26] In conjunction with his intense discussions with Lacis on the possibilities of radical Communism, Benjamin, who at approximately the same time first read Lukács's *Geschichte und Klassenbewußtsein* (*History and Class Consciousness*, 1923), increasingly turned his attention toward class and ideological critique. He then faced a shift in his theoretical focus that would close the gap between materialistic theory and practice. During this same period, however, Scholem continued to emphasize the need in Benjamin for further study of Jewish culture and tradition. At a meeting in Paris with Benjamin's old Berlin friend Franz Hessel in 1927, Scholem and Benjamin addressed their own rendition of the Jewish Question: "Was Judaism still alive as a heritage or an experience, even as something constantly evolving, or did it exist only as an object of cognition?" (*Friendship*, 136). While Scholem claimed to see Benjamin's renewed interest in Judaica during their Paris reunion, the commitment on Benjamin's part was undoubtedly faint. Though he had actually agreed to come to Palestine in August of 1928 and dutifully accepted a stipend to learn Hebrew, Benjamin ultimately acknowledged his acute indecision regarding his travel plans: "I am encountering a pathological vacillation which, I am sorry to say, I have already noticed in myself from time to time" (*Briefe* II, 493; *Correspondence*, 350 – rev. trans.). In this letter of June 1929, Benjamin makes clear that his journey to Palestine can never be realized, given the political implications that such a visit entails (e.g., more serious considerations of making *aliyah* [immigration to Palestine] and a deepening commitment to Judaism and political Zionism). It was perhaps what Benjamin, in reference to his canceled plans to visit Palestine, described as "pathological vacillation" that also determined his still ambiguous relationship to Judaism, a relationship that for many years he had maintained only in private – in the spirit, and in the mind.

From 1916, when Benjamin first began to work on his theory of language, "Über Sprache überhaupt und über die Sprache des Menschen"

("On Language as Such and the Language of Man"), until the publication in 1928 of his failed *Habilitationsschrift*, *Der Ursprung des deutschen Trauerspiels* (*The Origin of German Tragic Drama*), his published writings deal with Judaism in a largely covert fashion. Though he continued to discuss Judaism with Scholem and to read Buber, Rosenzweig, and other modern German-Jewish writers, he did not fully participate in Jewish circles. In fact, when invited in 1916 to contribute to Martin Buber's journal *Der Jude*, Benjamin declined, insisting that his "inability to say something clear on the question of Judaism" reflects the "inchoate stage" of the journal and, more implicitly, the "inchoate stage" of his own sense of Jewishness (*Briefe* I, 127; *Correspondence*, 81). Aside from his philosophical musings on the origin of language and the Talmudic mode of interpretation, he rarely deals explicitly with Jewish concerns. Some Benjamin scholars have suggested that during this period a sublimated Judaism is to varying degrees dispersed throughout Benjamin's work. Irving Wohlfarth, for example, notes that "in his work [Judaism is] so deeply inscribed that it only seldom appears as such and – as Scholem determines – is to be comprehended 'almost only in distant tones.' Even more, in Benjamin Judaism appears to come into effect most intensively where it disguises itself behind an incognito."[27] Critics such as Wohlfarth have viewed the period between the First World War and Benjamin's 1929 fiasco as fertile ground for the intellectual development of Benjamin's sense of Jewish identity. However, it is not until after 1929, when Benjamin suffered from his failed academic career, failed marriage, and severe monetary instability, that he began to consider the question of Jewishness in an explicit fashion.[28] To a large extent, Benjamin's early reflections on Judaism resurfaced precisely at the same time that he began to reflect on his childhood memories.

It is not easy to find direct references to Jewish culture in Benjamin's published writings before his famous Kafka essay of 1934, which appeared in the German Zionist *Jüdische Rundschau*. However, a rarely noted encyclopedia article entitled "Juden in der deutschen Kultur" ("Jews in German Culture") of 1929 and published in the German edition of the *Encyclopedia Judaica* (GS II-2, 807–13) reveals at least a tentative commitment to Jewish culture several years earlier. In this often neglected work, Benjamin provides a modest outline of the history of Jewish participation in German literature, philosophy, sociology, and politics. In the first part, "In den Geisteswissenschaften" ("In the Humanities"), Benjamin presents brief, schematic entries on Moses Mendelssohn, Salmon Maimon, Leopold Zunz, and the *Wissenschaft des Judentums*. He discusses the socialist politics of Marx and Lassalle and the pioneering Zionism of Moses Hess; finally, he provides a survey of the neo-Kantian philosophy of Hermann Cohen and the phenomenology of Edmund Husserl. After a short tour through the sociology of Georg Simmel, with a cursory look at Sigmund Freud's psychoanalysis, Benjamin arrives at the second part, "In der Dichtung" ("In Literature"). Here he discusses the works of Rahel Varnhagen, Berthold Auerbach, Heinrich Heine, and Ludwig Börne, along with the Jewish participation in subsequent modernist movements from naturalism through expressionism. While touching only superficially on the actual biographical and literary texts, the main point of the essay seems to be to observe the great number of Jewish writers, poets, and playwrights who contributed to the shaping of German modernism.

Despite the brevity of this undertaking, Benjamin's observations on Jews in modern German culture demand further consideration. In the marginal comments of his galley proofs, Benjamin noted that the printed version of his article was "heavily shortened and purged of its essence" (GS II-2, 807). Scholem explains, however, that Benjamin's disapproval of the article stemmed above all from the apologetic character that it acquired during editorial revision – precisely the point Benjamin himself makes regarding his Kafka article in the *Jüdische Rundschau* five years later. Yet the fact that Benjamin was commissioned to write an article for the *Encyclopedia Judaica*, and that he assumed the unexpected role of "expert" on Jewish culture, indicates a much deeper dedication to Jewish learning than his public persona otherwise reveals. For, as is quite clear in various sections of the encyclopedia article, Benjamin offers insights, however cursory, that only a serious student of Judaism could offer. As Scholem aptly points out, the encyclopedia article represents "the first one [i.e., published essay] in which he expressed himself in concentrated form on a Jewish subject" (*Friendship*, 160). Whether or not he had been coached by Scholem during his undertaking remains unclear. Yet his engagement with Jewish culture and Jewish lore – albeit from a more critical perspective than the article officially presents – is indisputable. Indeed, following his brief stint with learning Hebrew in the late 1920s, Benjamin sustained at least a peripheral engagement with Jewish matters – cultural, theological, and political.

Benjamin's conception of Judaism remains caught in a dialectic between *wichtig* and *problematisch*. The more affirmative his views become, the larger the need to recoil, to infuse his Jewishness with a more radical negation. If we view this negative dialectic between Judaism and modernity as emblematic rather than as a conflict to be resolved, its two sides appear mutually illuminating rather than exclusive. Furthermore, a corollary to this dichotomy in Benjamin's position on Judaism can be traced in his theory of memory, a theory that, to a greater extent, also represents an attempt to come to terms with his identity in the face of modernity.

## MEMORY AND COLLECTION
*Forgetting lengthens the period of exile. In remembrance lies the secret of redemption.* – Baal Shem Tov[29]

In the Jewish tradition of the Torah, the ubiquitous command *Zakhor* (Remember!) instructs the Jewish people to take account of their history and culture through the ever-recurrent acts of remembrance. From the ritual celebrations (e.g., Passover, Rosh Hashanah, Yom Kippur) to the scriptural warnings ("thou shalt not forget!" Deut. 25:17), memory plays a paramount role in Jewish identity formation.[30] Walter Benjamin seemed to have this in mind when in his "Über den Begriff der Geschichte" ("Theses on the Philosophy of History," 1940) – a *confessio in extremis* (Scholem) from the very last lines of his œuvre – he wrote: "We know that the Jews were prohibited from investigating the future. The Torah and prayers instruct them in remembrance, however."[31] For the exiled German-Jewish intellectual his (re)collections hold together the ruins of his past – lost youth, lost *Heimat*, lost security of the nineteenth century – reassembled under the ominous historical conditions of the impending fascist storm. Indeed, memory offers Benjamin the ultimate hope of messianic redemption: "For every second of time was the strait gate through which the Messiah might enter" (GS I-2, 704; I 264).[32]

Since Benjamin was writing as a German-Jewish refugee in Paris, under some of the most adverse conditions in his life, it is instructive to read his work in reverse, that is, to move from his historical theses and his incomplete notes from the *Passagen-Werk* through his hallmark essays of the 1930s on such key figures as Proust, Baudelaire, and Kafka, and finally to examine how his discussion of memory might be located on the threshold of his opus. Particularly unique in Benjamin are the special relationships between memory and modernity, and between memory and Jewish identity. Most importantly, reading Benjamin in this fashion will allow us to examine more carefully how his thought developed during the time he worked on his memoir-project.

The idea of reading Benjamin in reverse comes not from his astute commentators, but from the trajectory of his own thought. In his now famous interpretation of Kafka's "Das nächste Dorf" ("The Next Village," 1914–17), Benjamin establishes its primacy. "For my part," he writes, "I give the following interpretation: the true measure of life is memory [*Erinnerung*]. Retrospectively, it traverses life with the speed of lightening. As quickly as one turns back a few pages, it has gone back from the next village to the point where the rider decided to set off. He whose life has turned into writing, like old people's, likes to read this writing only backward. Only so does he meet himself, and only so – in flight from the present – can his life be understood" (GS VI, 529–30; R 210 – trans. rev.). Like Kafka – who once remarked that he considered himself "nothing but literature" (*nichts als Literatur*) – Benjamin's interpretation reveals the immediate relationship he has to writing and the historical and biographical need to account for his life as it is mediated through writing. "Walter Benjamin the person," explains Theodor W. Adorno in his introductory essay to Benjamin's two-volume collection of letters, "was from the very beginning so completely the medium of his work – his felicity was so much one of the mind – that anything one might call 'immediacy of life' was refracted."[33] This is the same Benjamin who, rather than migrate to Palestine upon the invitation of Scholem, set out to become "Germany's foremost literary critic" (*Briefe* II, 505; *Correspondence*, 359). In a peculiar sense, Benjamin's passion for literature, and his ambition to pursue it until his death, testifies to his sustained passion for exploring memory. For Benjamin, literature constituted a repository for memory, both personal and cultural. As a literary critic and as a Jew, Benjamin invoked his memories in order to mediate the two realms that his life so tenuously straddled. While Benjamin was acutely aware of the various manifestations of danger in the present – the rise of fascism, the atrophy of experience, and the violent state of mass society – he sought refuge not in the present, but rather in the possibilities of redemption in the past.

Once more, there is a dialectic – between tradition and modernity, between redemption and doom, between hope and despair – to which Benjamin's mature writings respond. Quite strikingly, this same dialectic can be found in Benjamin's observations on Kafka in his letter to Scholem of 12 June 1938: "Kafka's work is an ellipse with foci that lie far apart and are determined on the one hand by mystical experience (which is above all the experience of tradition) and on the other by the experience of the modern city-dweller" (*Briefe* II, 760; *Correspondence*, 563).[34] Like Kafka, Benjamin positions himself along the boundary between two realms: the first of tradition, especially a "tradition falling ill"; and the second, the conditions of *Gesellschaft*, of the big city and the modern sensibilities it inspires. In his mature writings, Benjamin frequently explores both the evolution of the modern *Gesellschaft* and his countervailing predilection for storytelling, for the memory-oriented position of narration and self.

It is this need to turn back to history and storytelling, to remember the past, and then to direct it towards the future, that Benjamin's 1938 interpretation of Kafka so brilliantly expresses. "Principally," remarks George Steiner, "Benjamin is a remembrancer. No modern sensibility has ached more vividly towards the scandal of the unjustly forgotten. . . . None has striven harder to recuperate the stricken past in order to embody it in the justifying motions of the future."[35] As we know from his historical theses and his notes from the *Passagen-Werk*, Benjamin's notion of culture and history is inextricably bound up with the idea of remembrance. For it is remembrance that first actualizes the past in its renewed form; it is remembrance that enables Benjamin to seize hold of his past experiences while in exile; and, perhaps most significantly, it is remembrance that connects the strands of his identity as a critic and as a Jew.

In Benjamin's historiographic writing, the will to recuperate and to repair (*tikkun*) emerges from an intense interest in the "past in ruins." It is a relationship to history markedly determined by a destroyed past and thus, in Benjamin's case, viewed through the lens of a destroyed present.[36] In his sixth thesis on the philosophy of history, he writes, "Only the historian will have the gift of fanning the spark of hope in the past who is firmly convinced that *even the dead* will not be safe from the enemy if he wins. And this enemy has not ceased to be victorious" (GS I-2, 695; I 255). What remained for Benjamin in the last years of his life, the 1930s onward, was what he himself termed "hope in the past," a redemptive and highly messianic impulse that seeks to transcend the destroyed past by actualizing its potential in the present. Expounding on this idea, Adorno has observed that for Benjamin, "history had long been written from the standpoint of the conqueror and therefore had to be (re-)written from that of the defeated."[37] Indeed, Benjamin's own history, both on the personal and collective level, is the story of the defeated. It is a history of failure – the same type of "failure" (*Scheitern*) that Benjamin finds so characteristic of Kafka (*Briefe* II, 764; *Correspondence*, 566) – destruction and defeat.

Continually addressed in Benjamin's œuvre, the concepts of memory (*Eingedenken*, *Erinnerung*, and *Gedächtnis*) and collection (*Sammeln*) form a vital current in his work.[38] In his cultural and literary essays, in his writings on language and translation, his urban portraits and his arcades project, the idea of memory stands out as the most salient of all motifs. Seen in reverse, from his theses on the philosophy of history back to his hallmark essays, the power of memory and collection lie at the core of Benjamin's attempt to recapture the past.[39] Benjamin's life itself is reversed in the recovered fragments of his past – without full completion and yet without losing the hope of redemption. Richard Wolin has recently observed that Benjamin, with his relentless vision of redemption, maintains a certain "methodological primacy of remembrance" through which he pursues his historical, cultural, and personal collections.[40] Similarly, it is this impulse that serves as the guiding light in Benjamin's discussions of the eminence of storytelling, the modern decay of experience, and the crisis of community.

Benjamin developed his theory of memory over many years and in a wide variety of textual settings. Central to his theory are the relation of the past to the present and the dialectical tension outlined in his theses on the philosophy of history. If Benjamin's notion of memory incorporates the Jewish commandment to remember (*zakhor*), then, as Stéphane Moses remarks, "the temporal perception of the Jewish tradition, of these so-called archaic cultures, stands much closer to him than that which underlies modern philosophy of history [*Geschichtsphilosophie*] since the Enlightenment. Hence, the way that the Jewish practice of remembrance [*Eingedenken*] responds to the past is comparable to the way that the ancient technique of soothsaying relates to the future: in both cases, it has to do with the actualization of distant times in the experience of the present."[41] In memory, the historian decodes traces of the past left behind in the present. His sense of time is thus both retrospective and prospective, while maintaining a pivotal footing in the present moment.

Like the patriarchal storyteller in Kafka's "Das nächste Dorf," Benjamin reflects on the past, relying on memory in order to pass on his experiences to future generations. For Benjamin, then, there seems to be a narrative obligation invoked in his notion of storytelling. He recognizes within it a fundamental relationship to community and identity. In his study of national and communal identity, Benedict Anderson points to this problem and its relation to identity construction: "Awareness of being imbedded in secular, serial time, with all its implications of continuity, yet of 'forgetting' the experience of this continuity . . . engenders the need for a narrative of 'identity.'"[42] Benjamin's lament on the decline of the storyteller similarly foregrounds this impulse, as does his position on Kafka articulated in his diary account of conversations with Bertolt Brecht in 1934. While in Denmark, visiting Brecht at his Svedenborg summerhouse, Benjamin engages in a heated debate with Brecht on Kafka's text "Das nächte Dorf." By interpreting

Kafka's parable as an apotheosis of memory, storytelling, and tradition, Benjamin elicits a strong reaction from Brecht, who calls his comrade's reading "Jewish fascism," mystical obscurantism devoid of the desired Marxist apparatus.[43]

As a further corollary to memory, the idea of experience in Benjamin's writings has a specific communal function. "Experience," he writes in his essay "Der Erzähler" ("The Storyteller") of 1936, "which is passed on from mouth to mouth is the source from which all storytellers have drawn" (GS II-2, 440; I 84). Just as Kafka's "Das nächste Dorf" shows memory passing from one individual in a community to the next (in this case from the grandfather to the grandson), Benjamin's essay on storytelling focuses on both the discursive and the "local." In this regard, Benjamin's treatment of memory corresponds to Ferdinand Tönnies' conception of *Gemeinschaft* as a communal and primal force unifying a cultural group.[44] "*Memory*," Benjamin continues in his critique of the storyteller, "creates the chain of tradition which passes from generation to generation" (GS II-2, 453; I 98). Martin Jay rightly points out that for Benjamin the "historically grounded notion" of *Erfahrung* extends beyond the position of the individual to the "community, which could transmit the tales of the tribe through oral traditions such as story-telling. Thus, it was the Haggadic quality of truth, its ability to be handed down from generation to generation, like the Passover story, through collective memory rather than official historical records, that marked genuine experience."[45] Indeed, there is a certain *Gemeinschaft* of storytelling – and, of course, a *Gemeinschaft* of experience – that localizes within it such fundamental structures of identity as language, culture, religion, and family. Small wonder that Benjamin so firmly embraces these concepts at precisely the same moment in which the world around him experiences the pains of an ever-decaying *Gesellschaft*.[46] In a concrete sense, Benjamin's predilection for collecting reminders of his bourgeois childhood – books, postcards, children's memorabilia – represents a further attempt at salvaging pieces of his shattered world.[47]

Although Benjamin points out in his essay on the storyteller that the advent of the modern novel has replaced the traditional model of storytelling with a less communal, less epic form, he also notes exceptions to this in the writings of Leskov and in his favorite novelist, Marcel Proust. Benjamin sees in Proust an acute sensitivity towards memory – "the epic faculty *par excellence*," as he calls it – that imparts to *À la Recherche du temps perdu* the traits of the storyteller. Indeed, Benjamin insists that Proust's thirteen-volume work undertook "to restore the figure of the storyteller to the present generation" (GS I-2, 611; I 159). In his essay entitled "Zum Bilde Prousts" ("The Image of Proust," 1929), Benjamin notes that Proust's memory-project consists of a web of memories and "the ornaments of forgetting," a true *textum* in the Latin sense. It is not the individual experience of the novelist, but rather the communal experience of the storyteller that Proust's tightly woven story conveys. Proust's concept of *mémoire involontaire*, Benjamin adds, represents "the rejuvenating force which is a match for the inexorable process of aging. When the past is reflected in the dewy fresh 'instant,' a painful shock of rejuvenation pulls it together." (GS II-1, 320; I 211). As is readily discernible in Benjamin's historical theses and his *Passagen-Werk*, Proust's lessons for remembering the past convey to Benjamin the forces of history that distill such buried moments out of the past and, in renewed form, reconceive them as flashes of the present. In his later work, discussing "a Messianic cessation of happening," Benjamin also speaks of the potential for "blasting a specific life out of the [past] era or a specific work out of the lifework" (GS I-2, 703; I 263). Although here Benjamin's examination of shock clearly anticipates the destructive side of remembrance (indeed, the very "blasting" that it entails), behind his notion lies the hope, if only fleeting, for ultimate redemption.

Another of the great inspirations for Benjamin's intellectual labors on memory and collection is Charles Baudelaire. In his readings of Baudelaire, we encounter Benjamin's most radical confrontation with the shocks of modern life and the impact on human memory. As a principal translator of Baudelaire's poetry into German and the author of a series of studies from "Über die Aufgabe des Übersetzers" ("On the Task of the Translator," 1923) to "Über einige Motive bei Baudelaire" ("On Some Motifs in Baudelaire," 1939), Benjamin had a particularly intimate relationship to Baudelaire's writings. To Benjamin, Baudelaire's poetry offers insight into the depths of urban life – especially as it comments on the raw experience (*Erlebnis*) of modernity, decay, and the new modes of perception. Just as Benjamin's later writings on technology, cinema, and violence all respond to the jolts of modernity, Baudelaire's work records a similar experience decades earlier. In his "lyrical stirrings of the soul," the French poet recognizes the shocks of consciousness, prefiguring some of the most important problems Benjamin treats in his own writings on the conditions of modernity and the city dweller. In particular, Baudelaire's prose poems and critical writings provide a model for Benjamin's miniatures on Berlin. As one might note in Baudelaire's text entitled "The Crowds" (1861), the inspiration for Benjamin's penchant for urban exploration looms large: "Not everyone has the gift of taking a plunge into the multitude: there is an art to enjoying the crowd."[48] As we see in his later memory fragments from *Berliner Kindheit*, Benjamin is clearly indebted to Baudelaire for introducing him to the joys of the street, the lessons of urban strolling (*flâneuren*), and the minutiae of modern life. If, for Benjamin, Proust made the nineteenth century *memoirenfähig* (fit for memoirs), then Baudelaire seems to have made the modern age fit for critique, for illuminating elements of the past through a heightened mode of perception. Benjamin finally notes that Baudelaire "indicated the price for which the sensation of the modern age may be had: the disintegration of the aura in the experience of shock" (GS I-2, 653; I 194).

As Benjamin came closer to embarking upon his memory project, the piquancy of memory intensified. In fact, Scholem tells how in 1932 Benjamin wrote to him that his childhood memoirs should represent "individual expeditions into the *depths* of memory."[49] It is surely no coincidence that during the same time that Benjamin reflected on his *Berliner Kindheit*, he also produced a series of reflections on the functions of memory. One such fragment, "Ausgraben und Erinnern" ("Excavating and Remembering," 1932), defines the complexity of gathering one's past: "Language shows clearly that memory [*Gedächtnis*] is not an instrument for exploring the past but rather its medium. It is the medium of past experience, as the ground is the medium in which old cities lie in ruins. He who seeks to approach his own buried past must conduct himself like someone who digs" (GS IV-I, 400–401; R 25–26 – trans. rev.).[50] In his own memory-project, Benjamin approaches his buried past as a type of cultural archeologist; at his excavation site, he burrows beneath the ruins of his past, salvaging the retrievable scraps. Benjamin collects his findings (*Fundobjekte*) in their fragmented form, as "images, severed from all earlier associations, that stand – like precious fragments or torsos in a collector's gallery – in the prosaic rooms of our later understanding" (GS IV-I, 400; R 26). According to his theory of memory – in this case, of *Gedächtnis* – the human memory does not function as an instrument able to produce willfully *mémoire volontaire*, but rather serves as the "medium of experience," as the method by which the past is actualized. And, in the *textum* of his memories, the strains of Benjamin's Jewishness reemerge. Benjamin does not recreate the past mimetically "the way it really was" à la Ranke, but rather reorganizes these collections of miniatures – the fragmented ruins – in an "epic" and "rhapsodic" manner, cutting through the layers, unraveling the various psychological strands of memory. "Collecting," suggests Hannah Arendt, "is the redemption of things which is to complement the redemption of man."[51]

Shortly before Benjamin began to record his childhood memories, he published his essay on book collecting, "Ich packe meine Bibliothek aus" ("Unpacking My Library," 1931) in Willy Haas's prominent literary journal *Die literarische Welt*.[52] We know from accounts by his contemporaries and from the catalogue of Benjamin's books included in the seventh volume of his *Gesammelte Schriften* (*Collected Writings*, 1972–89) that Benjamin was a devoted book-collector with highly eclectic taste (GS VII-I, 437–76). Not only did he have an extensive collection of children's books, but also of French literature, German philosophy, and Jewish history. In a letter to Scholem from December 1931, Benjamin claims to own between 1,200 and 2,000 volumes (*Briefe*, 544; *Correspondence*, 387).[53] For Benjamin, books constituted a foundation for his pursuits and, as an extension of his historical identity as a collector, his raison d'être.[54] "To renew the old world," he writes in his essay on book collecting, "that is the collector's deepest desire when he is driven to acquire new things, and that is why a collector of older books is closer to the wellsprings of collecting than the acquirer of luxury additions" (GS IV-1, 390; I 61). Like his reflections on the archeological nature of digging up one's past, Benjamin's discussion of the collector attributes memories to the objects he uncovers, indeed to the "chaos of memories" itself. The collector's project thus aims at remembering the histories attached to these objects: "not thoughts but images, memories. Memories of the cities in which I found so many things . . . are piled up around me" (GS IV-1, 396; I 67).

By holding fast to the lost time contained in his materialized memories, the collector acts as custodian of the past as well as surveyor of the future. He is, as Benjamin calls him, the *Lumpensammler*, the "ragpicker," who sifts through the trash of history, cataloging his inventory and serving as curator of his collections (GS V, 574–75).[55] "Collection is a form of practical memory" (*eine Form des praktischen Erinnerns*), he writes in the section entitled "Der Sammler" ("The Collector") from his *Passagen-Werk* (GS V, 271). As in his essay on book-collecting, Benjamin is concerned here not just with the process but with the world that his collections preserve. He further defines the project of the collector as a "battle against distraction" (*Kampf gegen die Zerstreuung*), dialectically strapped between chaos and the order of historical narrative and historical construction. As he remarks at the conclusion of his notes on collecting, this type of "productive disorder is the canon of *mémoire involontaire* as well as of the collector [himself]" (GS V, 280). In other words, through collection the *Lumpensammler* tentatively orders his memories as the lexicon of his own identity. Moreover, through the material possession of memory, as Benjamin points out in a fragment from his *Berliner Chronik* (*Berlin Chronicle*, 1932/38), pleasure is ascribed to the collector's passion: "With the joy that I remember [*erinnere*], another is fused: that of possession in memory [*Erinnerung*]. Today I can no longer distinguish them: it is as if it were only a part of the gift of the moment I am now relating, that it, too, received the gift of never again being wholly lost to me – even decades have passed between the seconds in which I think of it" (GS VI, 515–16; R 57 – trans. rev.). Similar to the theory of constellation outlined in his arcades project as well as the theory of historiography expressed in his philosophical theses, Benjamin's theory of collecting bears a sharp contemporaneity: while he remembers the past, he does so from the standpoint of the present. At once collector and "memory artist," Benjamin surveys his miniatures in their kaleidoscopic form, examining the "blinded [*Verblendetes*], the nature-bound [*Naturhaftes*], the diffuse [*Diffuses*] under a microscope."[56] Indeed, Benjamin observes his collections of ruins from the past through the lens of the now, the *Jetztzeit* (a condition notably operative in the writing of his own fragmented childhood memoirs). In this regard, Benjamin's notion of memory and collection appears to run parallel to what Jürgen Habermas has called *rettende Kritik* ("rescuing," or "redemptive critique"), that is, "rescuing [the] past charged with the *Jetztzeit*." "It ascertains," Habermas adds, "the moments in which the artistic sensibility puts a stop to fate draped as progress and enciphers the utopian experience in a dialectical image – the new within the always-the-same."[57]

We encounter this phenomenon most poignantly in Benjamin's fragmentary memory episodes in *Berliner Kindheit*. In these episodes the collector as "memory artist" opens up the world of the past, attempting to reenliven "lost time." Benjamin becomes an "interpreter of fate" who yearns to distill the prophetic out of the secret world embodied in his "collections." Through his concept of collection, Benjamin establishes the prophetic mode that memory has for him, the vision of the future embodied in the frozen memories of "extinct ages." In a brief section of his essay on book collecting, deleted before publication, Benjamin appears to reveal the hidden agenda of his project: "The collector freezes his fate" (GS IV-2, 998).[58] As collector, Benjamin aims not only to reorganize images and objects, holding fast to lost time, but he also attempts to anticipate his fate from these ruins: akin to the "rückwärts gekehrter Prophet" (F. Schlegel), or the "angel of history" in his historical theses, the collector has his "face . . . turned toward the past" (GS I-2, 697; I 257). As Peter Szondi has argued, like the collector's impulse, memory "seeks tokens of the future in the past."[59] In an uncanny passage from his collection of modern literary, philosophical, and cultural miscellany, *Einbahnstraße* (*One-Way Street*, 1928), Benjamin anticipates the method of his autobiographical project: "Like ultraviolet rays memory shows to each of us in the book of life a script that invisibly glosses the text as prophecy" (GS IV-1, 142; R 89 – trans. rev.).

## Culture in Ruins

*We understand the ruins not before the point that we ourselves are ruins.* –
Heinrich Heine

In September of 1932 Benjamin writes to Scholem that he had "begun a
series of vignettes, half of which are now finished, called *Berliner Kindheit um 1900* – a portrayal of my earliest memories" (*Friendship*, 189); it
is the first time that he makes mention of his memoir-project. These
short reflections, which, as Benjamin further announces, are meant to
"portray individual expeditions into the depths of memory," continued to occupy his work schedule for the next six years. Without ever
managing to publish them in their entirety, Benjamin worked inter-
mittently on his memory episodes – in Ibiza, Palermo, Berlin, and finally in Paris – until late 1938, a period in which he also undertook to
reread Proust, to reconsider the conditions of modernity, and to dedi-
cate himself to his chef d'œuvre, the *Passagen-Werk*.[60] Written in the
style of his fragmentary *Denkbilder*, indeed remarkably similar to Ernst
Bloch's *Spuren* (*Traces*, 1930), Benjamin's memoirs are comprised of
observations on the cultural topography of the city as well as inner reflections of the subject. They are thus "not only the mysterious work of
memory [*das geheimnisvolle Werk der Erinnerung*] – which is really the
capacity for endless interpolations into what has been – but also, at the
same time, the precaution of the subject represented by the 'I'"(GS VI,
476; R 16 – trans. rev.).

Opening his reflections on childhood by referring to the "art" of getting lost in the city, Benjamin claims that his undertaking "fulfills the
dream, of which the first traces are left as labyrinths on the blotter
pages of my notebooks" (GS IV-1, 234). Like the travel memories, the
philosophical aphorisms from *Einbahnstraße*, and the incomplete
notes in his *Passagen-Werk*, his childhood memoirs have a certain fragmented quality, illuminating the minute pieces of historical and cultural ruin. Interspersed among the numerous discontinuous episodes
that constitute *Berliner Kindheit*, we discover what Adorno later called
"an attempt to recover one's childhood."[61] With a messianic bent similar to his historical theses, Benjamin's autobiographical project "means
to seize hold of memory as it flashes up at a moment of danger"

(GS I-2, 695; I 255). He fervently rejects the method of writing a traditional linear autobiography that, in his own words, "has to do with
time, with sequence and what makes up the continuous flow of life.
Here [i.e., in *Berliner Kindheit*] I am talking of a space, of moments and
discontinuities" (GS VI, 488; R 28).

Although those memory episodes from *Berliner Kindheit* that overtly thematize the problem of Benjamin's Jewish identity are not in the
majority, the foundation of his project is notably imbued with the most
Jewish aspects of his writing. As Scholem has observed, "Among the
Jewish categories which he [Benjamin] introduced as such and upheld
to the last is the messianic idea . . . and above all the notion of remembrance [*Idee des Eingedenkens*]."[62] When read within the nexus of
his early reflections on his Jewishness and his later discourse on memory, Benjamin's *Berliner Kindheit* reveals a current that runs through
the bulk of his work: the trajectory of origin, messianism, collection,
and destruction. Similar to his earliest reflections on Jewish identity as
a young student, in particular his diary entries from 1911 and his correspondence with Ludwig Strauß in 1912, as well as in his later debates
with Scholem, Benjamin's position vis-à-vis Judaism itself consistently
vacillates between skepticism and affirmation. To be sure, the contradictory nature and acute ambivalence of Benjamin's early stance – characteristic of Jewish intellectuals in German modernism in general – was
only exacerbated by the extreme conditions of exile during his later
years.

At the core of *Berliner Kindheit*, the clearest example of Benjamin's
reconfrontation with his Jewish upbringing appears under the heading
"Erwachen des Sexus" ("Sexual Awakening"). Benjamin tells a story
that highlights his position caught between his responsibilities toward
the Jewish traditions of his family and the erotic forces of the streets of
Berlin. On Rosh Hashanah, he fails in his attempt to escort a distant
relative to the synagogue, encountering instead "a sexual awakening
under the oddest circumstances." The stage for Benjamin's recollection
is the interior of Berlin at the fin de siècle, the same streets in which he
"later roamed about at night, during *migrations that never came to an
end*" (GS IV-1, 251; emphasis added). Much like a dream sequence, it is

not the exact details, but rather the cultural milieu and the psychological complexity of the memory that find expression:

> It was in one of the streets that I later roamed about at night, during migrations that never came to an end, that I was surprised, when the time came, by an awakening of sexual desire under the oddest circumstances. It was on the Jewish New Year, and my parents had made arrangements to have me admitted to some religious ceremony. Probably it was a service at the reform synagogue, which my mother, on grounds of a family tradition, held in some sympathy, whereas my father's upbringing inclined him more to the orthodox rite. However, he had to give way. I had been entrusted for the holiday to the care of a distant relative, whom I was to fetch on my way. But whether because I had forgotten his address, or because I was unfamiliar in his neighborhood, it became later and later, and my wandering became increasingly hopeless.

In the fashion of the Parisian *flâneur* – or the Parisian émigré – the first-person narrator of "Erwachen des Sexus" wanders through the labyrinth of the city, traversing its passages, searching for refuge in the urban space. Both the memory episode and the wandering that takes place therein bear a certain disorienting, endless quality; indeed, the ambiguous time barrier and the fragmented sense of reality evoke a blurred reproduction of memory. As the subtext of Benjamin's memory in "Erwachen des Sexus," Benjamin's parents' conflicting practices of Judaism and his own skepticism of this heritage color the narrative. His struggle to express his commitment to Jewish culture and ritual finds an even greater subversion in his memories of the Berlin streets from the 1930s than had been experienced in the countryside at Wickersdorf in the early 1910s. Further, if we consider the time during which he wrote these lines, we might also recall the struggles with Scholem, whose repeated invitations for Benjamin to visit Palestine were met only with Benjamin's indecisive responses.[63]

Indeed, Benjamin incorporates these feelings of wavering allegiances and indecision into the remainder of his memory episode. Like others of his generation, Benjamin finds his commitment to Judaism challenged by the lure of modernity:

There could be no question of my going to the synagogue on my own, since my guardian had the entrance tickets. Of this misfortune, the blame was carried by my reluctance towards this nearly unknown relative, to whom I had been entrusted, and my suspicion of the religious ceremonies that merely resulted in public embarrassment. In my state of total disarray, a sudden burning wave of anxiety came over me – "too late, the synagogue is over" – and before it had subsided, at exactly the same moment, another came, this time one of perfect indifference – "whatever happens, it doesn't concern me." And both waves merged together in my first feeling of pleasure [*Lustgefühl*]: the violation of the holiday united with the procuring street, which made me anticipate for the first time the forces with which it would serve my awakened desires. (GS IV-1, 251; R 52–53 – trans. rev.)

The proclaimed "sexual awakening," as it were, occurs for Benjamin via the erotic forces of the street, here starkly contrasted with his failed religious observance. Judaism and sexuality come into conflict in the modern joy of urban strolling; the "violation" of Jewish ritual by Benjamin is affected by his focus on the pleasures of the street. It is no wonder that Scholem, who first read parts of the manuscript of *Berliner Kindheit* as early as 1932, encouraged Benjamin to cut "Erwachen des Sexus" from the manuscript. "I urgently advised him to delete this section," he writes in a brief explanatory note, "because it was the only one in the whole book in which Jewish matters were explicitly mentioned, thus creating the worst possible associations. There would have been no point in leaving out this section if his Jewish experiences had been voiced in other sections as well, but it would have been wrong to have kept it in this isolated position" (*Correspondence*, 401). Scholem's fears call attention to the unresolved status of Benjamin's Jewishness, realizing perhaps that his memory episode might offer a striking glimpse into his still acute ambivalence. In a variation of his earlier observation of the Passover Seder in 1911, Benjamin's memories in "Erwachen des Sexus" level an additional critique of his family's traditions: Benjamin's "suspicion" (*Abneigung*) of the Rosh Hashanah service and the "embarrassment" (*Verlegenheit*) echo the remarks made twenty years earlier: the "profane theater" (*unheiliges Theater*) of the Seder in the first instance, and the "ambiguous piety" (*unbestimmte Pietät*) he considers characteristic of Judaism in the second.

Benjamin's autobiographical text recalls, reorganizes, and finally reanalyzes the frozen images of his memories from the perspective of his present state of exile. As he writes in the introduction to the final edition of *Berliner Kindheit*, the *Fassung letzter Hand*:

> I consider it possible that such images are reserved for one's own fate. Still, they do not hope for established forms, as is the case with those images – for centuries in natural preservation – at the command of memories of a childhood spent in the countryside. By contrast, the images of my big-city childhood – in their inner shape – are perhaps capable of prefiguring later historical experience. At least in these images, I hope one is able to note how much he – of whom we are speaking – later lost the security that filled his childhood. (GS VII-1, 385)

Benjamin's memories convey both his personal experiences and the experiences of an historical epoch. They offer specific images of his own fate, while shedding light onto images of the larger surrounding cultural milieu. A certain chain of continuity is forged through the act of remembrance, fusing the world of the past with the world of the present, and even prefiguring, as Benjamin tells us, historical experience.[64] In his memories we encounter a series of experiences that seem to repeat themselves throughout his later life.

The Jewish family conflict, for example, with its underlying stream of assimilation, reappears at numerous points. One episode, "Bettler und Huren" ("Beggars and Whores") evokes the mediated perspective of the childhood environment: "In my childhood I was a prisoner of the old and the new West. In those days my clan inhabited these two districts with an attitude of stubbornness [*Verbissenheit*] mingled with self-pride [*Selbstgefühl*], turning them into a ghetto which it regarded as its fief" (GS IV-1, 287; I 28 – trans. rev.). Here Benjamin directs his critique at the most salient traits of his family, stubbornness and self-confidence. In her analysis of this passage, Hannah Arendt aptly links the two traits addressed by Benjamin to his family's sense of Jewish identity. "The stubbornness" suggests Arendt, "was toward their Jewishness; it was only stubbornness that made them cling to it. The self-confidence was inspired by their position in the non-Jewish environment in which they had, after all, achieved quite a bit."[65] By participating in the metropolitan subculture – here he senses a certain "union with the streets" – Benjamin strays from the family milieu in which he feels so "hopelessly stifled" into the distracting world of urban chaos. Rather than remaining within the walls of the bourgeois "ghetto," maintaining the practices of his class, Benjamin forges an alliance with the streets. He turns away from his assimilated Jewish upbringing in search of his own locus of identification. For the generation of German-speaking Jews to which Benjamin belongs, the city becomes the breeding ground for rebellion against the bourgeois culture of the parents. It is the place where modernity intersects with the revival of spiritual currents.[66]

Most striking perhaps in Benjamin's account is the remarkable tension that brings together urban modernity (the shocks, erotic allure, and sheer force of the street) and German-Jewish culture (as represented at once in rejection of family tradition and the qualified embrace of new forms of *Judentum*). When understood as an ongoing dialogue between Judaism and modernity, Benjamin's memory episodes appear to extract these tensions from the continuum of history and hold them up in the light of the present – a veritable displacement of the story and its teller. And although the passages of *Berliner Kindheit* should not be read as a traditional autobiography, they do in some ways construct, as Benjamin himself once noted, "the most precise portrait I shall ever be able to give of myself" (*Briefe* II, 589; *Correspondence*, 424). The "portrait" that Benjamin's memoirs evoke is finally one of multidimensionality, a pastiche of past projects and debates, reworked in the present, and relentlessly directed toward the faint hope of a messianic future.

For Benjamin, momentary flashes of the past help to cast light onto the path toward redemption. In the second of his theses on the philosophy of history, he writes: "The past carries with it a temporal index by which it is referred to redemption" (GS I-2, 693; I 254). Similarly, in *Berliner Kindheit*, he claims that there are experiences, images, actual sites in his memories that bear redemptive "signs of the coming" (256). Berlin's zoological garden affords Benjamin this type of projected vision: "It was a prophetic corner. Just as there are plants which one regards as having the power to peer into the future, so too are there sites which possess the same power" (GS IV-1, 256).[67] That Benjamin returns as an uprooted "homeless refugee" in the episode "Abreise und Rückkehr" ("Departure and Return") would seem to allude to the lingering uncertainty of his adverse conditions in Parisian exile, while the sounds of the military band in the episode "Zwei Blechkapellen" ("Two Brass Bands"), conveying something uniquely dehumanizing in their tones of fascism, appears to anticipate the mass wave of National Socialism. In this regard, Benjamin's childhood memories express a mournful tone, an awareness of a final departure and imminent destruction.[68]

Although Benjamin's mnemonic search for his lost *Heimat* also functions as a search for a future *Heimat*, he points out that it is a future "in which they forgot us" (GS IV-1, 252). If the past draws the blueprints for the future, then, by the same token, the future must also transport certain elements of the past. On 15 July 1932 Benjamin writes a short prose piece, "In der Sonne" ("In the Sun"), that reinscribes this mode of thought in terms of Jewish messianism: "From the Hasidim there is an expression of the coming world, which purports, 'everything will be arranged as it is with us.' Just as our room is now, so it will be in the coming world. . . . Everything will be as it is now, just a little different" (GS IV-1, 419). In the messianic world, as envisioned by Benjamin, there will be a return of "community."[69] By refiguring the past in the discourse of Jewish redemption, Benjamin's autobiographical project attempts to infuse the ruins of the past with the hope of a messianic future; his understanding of redemption seems to function in the original sense of "return" and restoration.[70] In this regard, the cyclical "return of the same" that Benjamin cites from Nietzsche underscores the thrust of his enterprise. Unlike the Hasidic proverb, however, the security and sense of community in Benjamin's childhood can never be fully restored. For him, the destruction of the past does not culminate in the transcendence to a messianic kingdom.

In *Berliner Kindheit*, the subtle traces of German Jewry and the overt conditions of German modernity together determine the production of Benjamin's memories. The clash of his family practices, accompanied by the erotic discovery of the big city and the projections of homelessness, technological progress, and mnemo-technical decay, emerge from within the space of Benjamin's memory. Just as Benjamin's larger plans indicated the hope of chronicling a "tradition of the oppressed," his own personal story seems to fit into such a tradition in which the end result can appear as failure and defeat.[71]

With their apocalyptic edge, Benjamin's childhood memories present a history that can end in nothing but catastrophe. The crisis and eventual collapse of the German *Gesellschaft*, though perhaps implicitly desired in the more destructive side of Benjamin's notion of memory, results in final destruction when placed within Benjamin's personal story. What is left in the future are merely traces from memories of the past. Benjamin's "quest for time gone by, for lost time," according to Peter Szondi, "is, in sum, a quest for the lost future," or, as Benjamin himself calls it, "a future in which they forget us" (GS IV-1, 252).[72] A tragic life doomed to destruction "under the oddest circumstances," Benjamin's own history offers just that. For in the end, even the deepest hopes for future redemption were, in his words, "all in vain" (GS IV-1, 248).

MONUMENTS TO THE VANISHED

*Die verwandelte Zeit sieht uns grausam an;*
*Sie will nicht mehr zurück.*
*Die Vision der Erlösung in Qualen zerrann.*
*Was bleibt, ist verworfenes Glück* – Gerhard Scholem (1943)

*We human beings now have the power to exterminate ourselves; this seems to be the entire sum of our achievement.* – James Baldwin

In a letter of May 1938 to the publisher Karl Thieme, Benjamin announces the message of his *Berliner Kindheit*: "It has something to say to thousands of persecuted Germans" (GS IV-2, 968). For Benjamin, his memories represent not merely "an allegory of his own destruction," as Adorno has suggested, but the fall of an entire epoch – the decline of German modernism, the end of the Weimar Republic, and finally the destruction of Jewish intellectuals in German cultural life and that of European Jewry at large. Benjamin further accentuates the extremity of his situation when, in the same letter to Thieme, he asserts: "Due to its subject matter, it [*Berliner Kindheit*] will have trouble finding a publisher." It was by no means an accident that Benjamin's memories of a bourgeois Jewish childhood in fin-de-siècle Berlin – "Bilder der Endzeit" ("images of the final era"), as Bernd Witte has called them – first appeared in complete form five years after the war, after the Shoah.[73] And even then, when the 1950 edition showed little sign of success, the publisher Peter Suhrkamp noted, "These pieces will likely remain undigested for a long time."[74] Like the memories of other Jews who perished under the Nazi regime, Benjamin's childhood memoirs still remain largely "undigested." Only recently have they become a greater source of interest among scholars and critics.

Benjamin's life came to an end on 25 September 1940, when he committed suicide outside the Spanish bordertown of Portbou, but his memories have persisted. They continue to inform contemporary thought, scholarship, and reflection. And now, more than ever, Benjamin's memories have come to be regarded as the memories of many. This is perhaps most evident in a recent monument dedicated to Walter Benjamin. Intended to commemorate the fiftieth anniversary of his death in 1990 and the one-hundredth anniversary of his birth in 1992, a memorial was built at Portbou by the Israeli sculptor Dani Karavan and was finally inaugurated in May 1994 (figures 14 and 15).

Inscribed on a sheet of glass, located at the end of the steel construction, are the words from one of Benjamin's own *passages*: "It is more difficult to honor the memory of the nameless than that of the famous. Historical construction is devoted to the memory of the nameless" (GS I-3, 1241). This glass sheet and the words written upon it separate the crashing waters of the Mediterranean Sea from the cliffs above the Bay of Portbou. It is a transparent yet final wall blocking the elongated steel shaft that leads – by way of some eighty-five steps – from land to the

14. Dani Karavan, *Passages* (view from afar). Portbou, Spain. Photograph: David Schorr.

15. Dani Karavan, *Passages* (view from within). Portbou, Spain. Photograph: David Schorr.

water. Under the Benjaminian title, *Passages*, Karavan's monument to Walter Benjamin attempts to incorporate his concept of memory into a work of art, a work that is to honor the memory not only of the author (who has arguably achieved his share of posthumous fame) but also that of the nameless, the countless who similarly perished in their respective attempts to flee the fascist storm that engulfed Europe under Hitler. And it is certainly not insignificant that Benjamin's words – which at least one critic has called "monuments" in their own right – set the tone of the monument.[75] Karavan's main objective, as he explained in an interview, was to offer "a memory of Walter Benjamin's story" and to create "a place of meditation and of commemoration of all the people whose fate Benjamin symbolizes."[76]

This truly site-specific monument is located in a liminal border position, accentuated on a variety of levels. On the local geographic level, it stands between the town cemetery of Portbou and the railroad station. Politically, socially, and culturally, it stands between France and Spain, between the then Nazi-occupied region and what was perceived to be the gateway to freedom. On a more mystical plane, it stands between the jagged cliffs, the heavens above and the depths of the sea below. The monument's formal composition is fittingly "passage-oriented": the stark natural rust steel walls form a concealed shaft that opens up to the sky only once one reaches the uncovered final section that extends to the sheet of glass with its inscription. Similarly, the sea is concealed until one starts down the flight of steps. A clear link may be made between the steel and glass composition of the monument and that of the Parisian arcades whose architectural and cultural composition occupied much of Benjamin's thought in his *Passagen-Werk*. And yet there is a also a striking void – the empty space that makes up the body of the monument's interior – that may, if we are to take the lead of other contemporary architects such as Daniel Libeskind, have to do with the absence of those who constitute the imagined community of the nameless.[77]

Benjamin – who in his historical theses, written just shortly before his suicide in 1940, almost uncannily noted that "even the dead will not be safe from the enemy if he wins" (GS I-2, 695; I 255) – was never accorded a proper burial. "We have nothing but one more death without burial among so many others," remarks the French scholar Pierre Missac in his recent, aptly titled *Walter Benjamin's Passages*: "no name on a common grave, even for someone who, while alive, provided a name for the nameless."[78] While Karavan's monument has been likened to Maya Lin's *Vietnam Veterans Memorial*, it is certainly not the "national healing shrine" that the Vietman memorial has come to represent; and here, of course, we are not only dealing with the named (as is the case with the Vietman memorial), but precisely with the nameless.[79] In 1979, in the immediate wake of the Franco era, the city of Portbou mounted a plaque on the cemetery wall as "an initial token of remembrance." Karavan's monument then came as a continuation of the commitment expressed by the city of Portbou to preserving the memory of Walter Benjamin. However, it is not a monument designed to mourn Benjamin; in fact, the monument's construction defies traditional Jewish mourning, as it does not offer a level space like a tombstone on which to place stones of remembrance. It is in this regard an antimonument, or a countermonument, in the sense that the memory of Benjamin is not glorified as in the traditional monuments to fallen heroes.[80] Benjamin himself was critical of the "culture of commemoration" that dominated late nineteenth-century and early twentieth-century Europe. In his Moscow diary of 1926–27, for example, he noted: "There is . . . hardly a square in Europe whose secret structure was not profaned and impaired . . . by the introduction of a monument."[81] Karavan's monument is not placed in the center of the town – as a traditional European monument – nor is it, for that matter, in any place of obvious prominence. Instead, it is on the borders, subtly situated in the indeterminate site of Benjamin's death.

With regard to the subtlety and ambiguity of the monument, the tie to Benjamin's own sense of memory must be drawn. What hope Benjamin expressed in his writings on memory was clearly utopian and messianic – the hope, as he put it, that at "every second of time was the strait gate through which the Messiah might enter" (GS I-2, 704; *Illuminations*, 264). Moreover, Benjamin's hope, felt even in moments of danger, was oriented to some extent toward a messianic return, a "coming community" as Giorgio Agamben has called it.[82] Similarly, the commemoration of the nameless in Karavan's monument has a clear "restorative" or redemptive bent: the lost community of the nameless who never received a proper burial can only be remembered via historical construction. And it is thus finally a means of preventing future generations from forgetting, a means of materializing and authenticating a story for future transmission.

# Epilogue:
# Beyond Symbiosis

At a 1983 symposium on Jews in modern German literature, the Germanist Hans Mayer posed what may be the single most loaded question for any discussion of German-Jewish modernism in the postwar period: "Was this Jewish-German symbiosis . . . ever anything more than Jewish hope, perhaps even Utopia?"[1] Challenging the efforts of some contemporary German critics to rewrite a tainted history in unduly affirmative terms, Mayer's question revisits a debate first opened in the early 1960s that has since achieved even greater resonance. At stake is how to conceive of a highly complex relationship, one in which optimistic beginnings were filled with promises that ultimately were not kept, but nonetheless brought with it a remarkably wide array of cultural production, the end of which was signaled by the catastrophic turn during the Third Reich.

The question, then, is whether one can regard the modern interaction of Jews and Germans – especially at the height of their "engagement" in the first decades of this century – as a "symbiosis," a mutually beneficial joint existence. Were these two groups members of a common community, or did this community, and all of its offshoots, exist only in each group's respective fantasies? In his famous polemic, "Against the Myth of German-Jewish Dialogue" (1962), Gershom Scholem has responded resoundingly in the negative: "The allegedly indestructible community of the German essence and the Jewish essence consisted, so long as these two essences really lived with each other, only of a chorus of Jewish voices and was, on the level of historical reality, never anything else than a fiction."[2] Scholem goes so far as to reject the presumption of a German-Jewish symbiosis as "blasphemy," thus leveling a devastating critique at what he views as a consistently one-sided effort, "even to the point of complete self-abnegation," on the part of the Jews. This perspective unmistakably recalls Moritz Goldstein's 1912 assertion of "unrequited love." Yet it is important to keep in mind that all post-Shoah assessments of German-Jewish relations are necessarily colored by that event.

To invoke the idea of a German-Jewish symbiosis today is to reconsider the problems inherent not only to the historical phenomenon itself, but also to contemporary historical analysis and memory. In the five decades since the Shoah, the relationship between Germans and Jews has certainly been wrought with more tension than it was prior to the rise of Nazism. As Max Horkheimer remarked in his "Über die deutschen Juden" ("On German Jews," 1961):

> The understanding for Jews in Germany today is at once difficult and easy. Difficult for many reasons, among them, because the German collective pride (*Kollektivstolz*) is more seriously damaged than most suspect. . . . Damaged pride means a wound in the collective no less than in the individual. The Jews, who were the victims, are connected with the memory of catastrophe: with the violence committed by the Germans and with that which was committed toward the Germans. Within the subconsciousness the roles [i.e., of Jews and of Germans] become reversed. Not the murderer, but rather the murdered is guilty.[3]

German national identity – in spite of, or rather because of, the near annihilation of European Jewry – continues to be bound up with Jewish identity. "After Auschwitz," remarks historian Dan Diner, "it is actually possible – what a sad irony – to speak of a 'German-Jewish symbiosis,' albeit a negative one. For both Jews and Germans, whether they like it or not, the aftermath of mass murder has been the starting point for self-understanding – a kind of communality of opposites. Once again, Germans and Jews have been brought together."[4]

In recent years, scholars have explored the degree to which the discourses of German identity and Jewish identity are interconnected – in terms of history, cultural memory, and political self-fashioning.[5] Much of the debate on *Vergangenheitsbewältigung*, or "coming to terms with the past," in Germany has made this its central focus. Discussions of the Holocaust, especially as they were articulated in the 1980s during the famous *Historikerstreit* (Historians' Debate), are not merely about Germany coming to grips with its scarred past, but once again about how to grasp the Jewish element running throughout its history, at least from Weimar to the present day.[6] In a sense, the Shoah has made and continues to make it harder than ever to ignore the links between these two cultures.

In approaching German-Jewish modernism from a post-Shoah standpoint, I am mindful of the implications that the symbiosis debate has on my work. However, my approach aims to move beyond the question of "symbiosis" per se, and into the discursive ties between Germans and Jews, between German modernism and Jewish modernism. It is my belief that any attempt either to affirm or to refute the notion of a German-Jewish symbiosis is a limited enterprise. It does little to unveil the deeper complexities of the cultural history.

Consider, for example, the case of Kafka. Conceivably, one might argue that Kafka represents German-Jewish symbiosis at its best. He wrote in German. He was Jewish. He drew inspiration from both worlds. Yet it is far more fruitful to explore the various extractions – both German and Jewish – incorporated into his writings, and how these interact with each other, than it would be to attempt a final judgment on Kafka's status as either a German or a Jewish modernist. Focusing on his preoccupation with Yiddish and Eastern Jewish lore by no means reduces the significance of his status as a German modernist. On the contrary, it enhances our understanding of both worlds, demonstrating on various levels that German modernism and Jewish modernism partook of a shared cultural realm.

All four of the cases addressed in this book are studies of German modernism, and yet they might just as easily be designated studies of Jewish modernism. It was the tension between the two – and constitutive of the two – that yielded the richness and heterogeneity of the modernist era. While it would no doubt be a crude exercise of revisionism to claim that *all* of German modernism was German-Jewish modernism, there are clearly moments, texts, ideas, and debates that suggest that it existed. German-Jewish modernism was an effort, perhaps in vain, on the part of Germans and Jews alike to understand themselves within the context of two colliding worlds. To simplify this struggle in terms of "symbiosis" or lack thereof is to rob the period of its due complexity.

# Abbreviations

| | |
|---|---|
| B | Franz Kafka, *Briefe* |
| C&S | Ferdinand Tönnies, *Community and Society* |
| CS | Franz Kafka, *Collected Stories* |
| D | ———, *Diaries* |
| DoA | Arnold Zweig, *Das ostjüdische Antlitz* |
| E | Franz Kafka, *Erzählungen* |
| GCD | Rainer Werner Fassbinder, *Garbage, the City and Death* |
| GS | Walter Benjamin, *Gesammelte Schriften* |
| H | Franz Kafka, *Hochzeitsvorbereitungen auf dem Lande* |
| I | Walter Benjamin, *Illuminations* |
| J | Gustav Janouch, *Conversations with Kafka* |
| L | Franz Kafka, *Letters to Friends, Family, and Editors* |
| LF | ———, *Letter to His Father* |
| LM | ———, *Letters to Milena* |
| M | ———, *Briefe an Milena* |
| PJ | Roman Vishniac, *Polish Jews* |
| R | Walter Benjamin, *Reflections* |
| RK | Mark Anderson, *Reading Kafka* |
| T | Franz Kafka, *Tagebücher* |

# Notes

### INTRODUCTION

1. For an illuminating discussion of Jewish (self-) representation in the modern world, see Garb, "Introduction."
2. See Steve Giles's overview in *Theorizing Modernism*, 171–86; cf. Bradbury and McFarlane, eds., *Modernism 1890–1930*; and Berman, *All That Is Solid*.
3. Bauman, "Parvenu and Pariah: The Heroes and Victims of Modernity," *Postmodernity and its Discontents*, 71. See also Bürger, *Theory of the Avant-Garde*, esp. Jochen Schulte-Sasse's "Foreword: Theory of Modernism versus Theory of the Avant-Garde," vii–xlvii; Herf, *Reactionary Modernism*; David Bathrick and Andreas Huyssen, "Modernism and the Experience of Modernity," *Modernity and the Text*, eds. Huyssen and Bathrick, 1–16; and Michaels, *Our America*.
4. Plessner, *Grenzen der Gemeinschaft*, 26. In his cultural history of German Jewry during the Weimar Republic, Michael Brenner views the turn toward community as a fundamental shift in Jewish self-understanding at the time. See his *The Renaissance of Jewish Culture in Weimar Germany*, esp. "Gemeinschaft and Gemeinde: The Ideological Transformation of the Jewish Community," 36–65.
5. See Gross, *The Past in Ruins*.
6. Peter Gay, *Weimar Culture*, esp. "The Hunger for Wholeness," 70–101. More recently, the literary critic Leon Wieseltier has remarked in a similar vein, "The lure of identity is the lure of wholeness. It proposes to bind up the parts and pieces of a life and transform them into a unity, into a life that adds up. This provides a mixture of psychological and aesthetic elation." *Against Identity*, 32.
7. For an excellent historical account of German-Jewish modernism in the Weimar Republic, see Michael Brenner, *The Renaissance of Jewish Culture in Weimar Germany*.
8. On the emancipation and self-cultivation of the Jews, particularly in Germany, see Mosse, *German Jews Beyond Judaism*. See also his *Germans and Jews*; Peter Gay, *Freud, Jews and other Germans*; Sorkin, *The Transformation*

*of German Jewry, 1780–1840*; Hertz, *Jewish High Society in Old Regime Berlin*; Kaplan, *The Making of the Jewish Middle Class*; Traverso, *The Jews and Germany*; and Michael Brenner, *The Renaissance of Jewish Culure in Weimar Germany*. On the Austro-Hungarian variant, see Rozenblit, *The Jews of Vienna, 1867–1914*; Beller, *Vienna and the Jews, 1867–1938*; and Wistrich, *The Jews of Vienna in the Age of Franz Joseph*. On the Czech variant, see Gary B. Cohen, *The Politics of Ethnic Survival*; Kieval, *The Making of Czech Jewry*; and Iggers, ed., *The Jews of Bohemia and Moravia*. For a recent critique of the historiographical trends in scholarship on German Jewry, see Moyn, "German Jewry and the Question of Identity."

9. Michael A. Mayer advances a similar line of argument in his introduction to *Jewish Identity in the Modern World*. According to Mayer, the wide-reaching impact of the Enlightenment, antisemitism, and Zionism "compelled Jews to rethink and reevaluate their Jewish self-definition and the role of Jewishness in their lives" (8).

10. The generation to which I am referring is comprised mainly of Jews who came of age (and whose Jewishness became a concern) in the years just prior to the First World War. In terms of the key figures treated in this study, Kafka was born in 1883, Arnold Zweig in 1887, and Walter Benjamin in 1892. As for the impact that the *Ostjuden* had on German Jewry, the best historical account to date is Aschheim, *Brothers and Strangers*.

11. Rathenau, *Schriften*, 114.

12. Cited and translated in Gilman, *Freud, Race, and Gender*, 24. Emphasis added.

13. For all biographical and historical information on Tönnies, I am indebted to John Samples's critical introduction to the most recent English edition, *Community and Society*, xi–xxvi. For a more thorough discussion of Tönnies and his model of sociological thought, see Mitzman, *Sociology and Estrangement*, 39–131.

14. Tönnies first described his concepts as such in an article that appeared nearly a half a century following the original publication of *Gemeinshaft und Gesellschaft*. See "Gemeinschaft und Gesellschaft," *Handwörterbuch der deutschen Soziologie* (Stuttgart: Ferdinand Enke Verlag, 1931); this essay has been reprinted and translated in *Community and Society*, 237–59.

15. See Liebersohn, *Fate and Utopia in German Sociology*, 13. Emphasizing the superficial nature of *Gesellschaft*, David Frisby makes a similar point in *Fragments of Modernity*, 13. In regard to the question of authenticity in modern life, Tönnies seems to foreshadow the discussion that Walter Ben-

jamin provides in "Das Kunstwerk im Zeitalter seiner Reproduzierbarkeit" (1936) and "Der Erzähler" (1936).

16. See, for example, Plessner, *Grenzen der Gemeinschaft*; Karl Dunkmann, "Die Bedeutung der Kategorien Gemeinschaft und Gesellschaft für die Geisteswissenschaften," *Kölner Vierteljahrshefte für Soziologie* 5:1/2 (1925): 35ff.; Arje Berger, *Gemeinschaft und Gesellschaft in der Geistesgeschichte des Judentums*.

17. Peter Gay, *Weimar Culture*, 80. In his chapter on the "Hunger for Wholeness" in Weimar, Gay offers the following critique: "The complex of feelings and responses I have called 'the hunger for wholeness' turns out on examination to be a great regression born from a great fear: the fear of modernity. The abstractions that Tönnies and Hofmannsthal and the others manipulated – *Volk, Führer, Organismus, Reich, Entscheidung, Gemeinschaft* – reveal a desparate need for roots and for community, a vehement, often vicious repudiation of reason accompanied by the urge for direct action or for surrender to a charismatic leader. The hunger for wholeness was awash with hate; the political, and sometimes the private, world of its chief spokesmen was a paranoid world, filled with enemies: the dehumanizing machine, capitalist materialism, godless rationalism, rootless society, cosmopolitan Jews, and the great all-devouring monster, the city" (96).

18. Cf. Fritz Stern, *The Politics of Cultural Despair* and Herf, *Reactionary Modernism*.

19. Weber, "Science as Vocation" (1919), *Max Weber: Essays in Sociology*, 155.

20. Arendt, "The Jew as Pariah." As a means of legitimizing the inclusion of Charlie Chaplin among her cast of Jewish social pariahs, Arendt remarks, "even if not himself a Jew, he epitomized in an artistic form a character born of the Jewish pariah mentality" (69). See also her chapter "The Jews and Society" in *The Origins of Totalitarianism*, 54–88.

21. See Rabinbach, "1944: Hannah Arendt." According to Rabinbach, "Weber's 'story tellers, actors in a cultic masquerade, and gnostic intellectuals' [from his *Ancient Judaism*] prefigured Arendt's modern social pariah" (611). See also Enzo Traverso's discussion in his chapter "The Jew as Pariah," *The Jews and Germany*, 43–64.

22. Scholem, "With Gershom Scholem: An Interview," *On Jews and Judaism in Crisis*, 1.

23. In his reappraisal of the debate, written forty-five years after his controversial article appeared, Goldstein cites the reception of his article among the Nazis. An anonymously published tract titled *The Jews in Germany* (pub-

lished by the so-called "Institute for the Study of the Jewish Question") employs Goldstein's text for its own ideological purposes: by quoting selectively from his critique of German-Jewish assimilation, the Nazi text bolsters its propagandistic aim to distort the Jewish domination of German culture. Taking Goldstein's assertion that the Jews were the guardians of German "spiritual property" at face value, the prized citations confirm Nazi suspicions: "No one seriously questions the power which the Jews wield in the press. Especially reviewing, at any rate in the capitals and their influential papers, has become a virtual Jewish monopoly. The predominance of the Jewish element in the theatre is also well known: Almost all Berlin directors are Jews, the same is true perhaps of the majority of the actors. . . . A recent development is the fact that the study of German literature seems to be falling into Jewish hands. . . . Finally, not a few guardians of German art realize with anger, how many Jews there are among 'German poets'" (238). Goldstein himself viewed the article as a form of "confession," but of an entirely different sort. See Goldstein, "German Jewry's Dilemma," 236–54.

24. Goldstein, "Deutsch-jüdischer Parnaß"; English translation in Goldstein, "German Jewry's Dilemma," 237.

25. See, for example, Scholem's famous polemic, "Against the Myth of a German-Jewish Dialogue," *On Jews and Judaism in Crisis*, 61–70, as well as my epilogue to the present study, "Beyond Symbiosis."

26. See Aschheim, "1912: The publication of Moritz Goldstein's 'The German-Jewish Parnassus.'" This separatist view found an unlikely sympathizer in the American leader of black nationalism, Malcolm X. In his autobiography, he makes the following remark on what he sees as the unfortunate fate of German-Jewish assimilation: "[H]istory's most tragic result of a mixed, therefore diluted and weakened, ethnic identity has been experienced by a white ethnic group – the Jew in Germany. . . . He had made greater contributions to Germany than Germans themselves had. Jews had won over half of Germany's Nobel Prizes. Every culture in Germany was led by the Jew; he published the greatest newspaper. Jews were the greatest artists, the greatest poets, composers, stage directors. But those Jews made a fatal mistake – assimilating." See *The Autobiography of Malcolm X*, 277.

27. The quest for authenticity among newly awakened young German Jews manifested itself in a variety of ways (e.g., in language, the arts, politics, and spiritual life). See Michael Brenner's extensive discussion in part three ("In Search of Authenticity") of *The Renaissance of Jewish Culture in Weimar Germany*, 129–211. In view of contemporary debate on the cultural

question of authenticity, Leon Wieseltier has provocatively remarked, "Authenticity is a reactionary ideal. . . . It is the idolatry of origins" (*Against Identity*, 57). See also the classic study by Lionel Trilling, *Sincerity and Authenticity*, esp. 135–72.

28. See Rabinbach, "Between Enlightenment and Apocalypse."

29. Gustav Landauer, "Sind das Ketzergedanken?" *Vom Judentum*, 252.

30. See, for example, Hermann, "Zur Frage der Westjuden."

31. An important turning point in Jewish cultural affirmation at the beginning of the century was the establishment of the Buber-inspired periodical *Ost und West*. See the editorial statement introducing the first issue, "Ost und West," *Ost und West* 1.1 (1901): 2–3, and Buber's own contribution, "Jüdische Renaissance" (7ff.). On the greater significance of the journal and its history, see David A. Brenner, *Marketing Identities*.

32. In the second volume to his *Untergang des Abendlandes*, Spengler writes: "'Intellect,' '*Geist*,' 'esprit,' is the specific urban form of the understanding waking-consciousness. All art, all religion, and science, become slowly intellectuallized, alien to the land, incomprehensible to the peasant of the soul. With the Civilization set in the climacteric. The immemorially old roots of Being are dried up in the stone masses of its cities. And the free intellect – fateful word! – appears like a flame, mounts spendid into the air, and pitiably dies." Excerpted in Spengler, "The Soul of the City, 67–68.

33. Herf, *Reactionary Modernism*, 86. On Jünger's notion of the affinity between the "new community" and the urban landscape, Herf writes: "Ernst Jünger expressed a widely held right-wing view when he connected technology with the wartime *Gemeinschaft* rather than the fragmented, postwar *Gesellschaft*. When the right-wing literati idealized the lost communities of the past, they looked back to the modern battlefield and the trenches, not the preindustrial landscape" (24).

34. Jünger, "Großstadt und Land." Cited and translated in Herf, *Reactionary Modernism*, 86.

35. Only a year prior to Jünger's "Großstadt und Land," Adolf Hitler published *Mein Kampf*, in which he articulated his position on the urban problem as follows: "[O]ur cities of the present lack the outstanding symbol of the *national community* which . . . sees no symbol of itself in the cities. The inevitable result is a desolation whose practical effect is the total indifference of the big-city dweller to the destiny of his city. This, too, is the sign of our declining culture and our general collapse" (266; emphasis added).

36. Cited and translated in Herf, *Reactionary Modernism*, 86. See also Andreas

Huyssen, "Fortifying the Heart – Totally: Ernst Jünger's Armored Texts," *New German Critique* 59 (Spring/Summer 1993): 3–23.

37. Herf, *Reactionary Modernism*, 47. In his analysis of Jünger's "armored texts," Andreas Huyssen contends that the effect of his writing is "aesthetic reification: the armored text which corresponds directly to the fascist fantasy of the invincible armored body, whether it be that of the male, the Party, or the nation" ("Fortifying the Heart" 14).

38. Mosse, *Confronting the Nation*, 59.

39. In his article "Zion's Cities: Projections of Urbanism and German-Jewish Self-Consciousness, 1909–1933," Michael Berkowitz explores the Zionist conception of the urban community in Palestine. Focusing on the early examples of Haifa, Tel Aviv, and Jerusalem, Berkowitz highlights the connections between nationalism and urbanism: "The Zionists' fostering of 'Jewish cities' in Palestine allowed Jewry in Western Europe to see itself as a normal, rooted, genuine people, engaged in healthy national pursuits and propitiously wedded to modernity. . . . At any rate, images of Zionist cities helped a significant minority of German Jews to envisage a supplementary nationality and an alternative national community for themselves when they were increasingly excluded from the nation to which they believed themselves to belong" (121).

40. For statistics and other information on the rise of the German city in Weimar, see the recent study by Detlev Peukert, *The Weimar Republic*, 181 ff.

41. Theilhaber, *Der Untergang der deutschen Juden*. For information on Theilhaber, I am indebted to Mitchell Hart, *Social Science*. On the shared discourse of race and nationalism, see Efron, *Defenders of the Race*, esp. 13–32 and 123–74.

42. Mosse, *Confronting the Nation*, 127.

43. Buber, "Die Erneuerung des Judentums," *Drei Reden über das Judentum*, 44ff; trans. as "Renewal of Judaism," in *On Judaism*, 37. Although Buber appeared to accentuate the central position of community in Jewish renewal around 1911, he also maintained a certain oscillatory stance on the matter. At the turn of the century he pointed to the need for Jews to rediscover *Gemeinschaft*, to return to their original communal ties, while at the same time he edited a book series in Frankfurt entitled *Die Gesellschaft*, publishing works by such figures as Werner Sombart, Georg Simmel, and Ferdinand Tönnies. In a 1923 lecture in Zurich, Buber finally returned to the question of founding a community in the Western city, altering his initial position: "We cannot leave the city to take refuge in the village. The village is still close to the primitive community. The city is the form that cor-

responds to differentiation. We can no longer turn back the clock on the city, we must overcome (*überwinden*) the city itself" (cited in Löwy, *Redemption & Utopia*, 55).

44. Baeck, "Kulturzusammenhänge," 81; translation mine. See also his later essay, "Gemeinde in der Großstadt," in which he examines the possibilities for maintaining "community" amidst the forces of cultural fragmentation in the big city.

45. On the origin of the *Zivilisation-Kultur* dichotomy, see Elias, *Über den Prozeß der Zivilisation*, vol. 1.

46. Investigating the "constant transformation" of cultural identities, the social critic Stuart Hall has remarked: "Far from being grounded in the mere recovery of the past, which is waiting to be found, and which when found, will secure our sense of ourselves into eternity, identities are the names we give to the different ways we are positioned by, and position ourselves within, the narratives of the past." See Hall, "Cultural Identity and Cinematic Representation," 70.

### 1. IN SEARCH OF LANGUAGE

1. Havel, "On Kafka."

2. Havel, "On Kafka." Following a similar line of argument, Theodor Adorno has noted that the Kafka reader often encounters a sense of déja vu, an uncanny familiarity with his work. "The realm of the déjà vu," Adorno asserts, "is populated by doubles, *revenants*, buffoons, Hasidic dancers, boys who ape their teachers and then suddenly appear ancient, archaic." See Adorno, "Notes on Kafka," 253.

3. Franz Kafka, "Der Fahrgast" (E31). In English, see Kafka, "On the Tram," (CS 388). Christoph Stölzl has interpreted this passage as representative of the crisis of Judaism and modernity in which "the fragmented Jewish individualist experience[s] himself as an abstract vessel." See his "Kafka: Jew, Anti-Semite, Zionist," 58.

4. See Beck, *Kafka and the Yiddish Theater*, ix ff. Although Beck's study represents a major contribution to Kafka research and is in many ways highly useful for scholars interested in Kafka's relationship to the Yiddish Theater, her readings of the Yiddish plays inscribed in Kafka's work are in some instances overdetermined. It is less my concern here to examine the appropriations of the actual plays than to explore the perceptions of a *Sprachgemeinschaft* that Kafka developed during his contact with the Yiddish Theater and its players.

5. See Goldstücker, "Kafkas Werk," 165.

6. Robertson, "'Antizionismus, Zionismus,'" 27. See also his sustained treatment of Kafka's views on Judaism and Jewish culture in *Kafka: Judaism, Politics, and Literature.*

7. Hartmut Binder, "Rede über die jiddische Sprache," *Kafka-Handbuch*, vol. 2, 504.

8. In his survey of fin-de-siècle Prague, Klaus Wagenbach cites a telling statement by one of Kafka's contemporaries, the writer Johannes Urzidil: "Czechs, Germans, Jews, and the supranational Austrian nobles had created a vitally productive world that was always ready to explode." This explosive quality of Prague is often portrayed in Kafka's fictional and nonfictional works alike. See Wagenbach, "Prague at the Turn of the Century," 31.

9. See Tramer, "Prague – City of Three Peoples." I am indebted to Tramer for the statistics cited above as well as for information about Kafka's Prague. See also Robertson, *Kafka: Judaism, Politics, and Literature*, 1–37; Kieval, *The Making of Czech Jewry*, 10–17 and 36–63; Gary B. Cohen, "Jews in German Society"; Kestenberg-Gladstein, "The Jews Between Czechs and Germans"; Stölzl, *Kafkas böses Böhmen*; and Wagenbach, *Kafkas Prag.*

10. Felix Weltsch, "The Rise and Fall of the Jewish-German Symbiosis," 255. Subsequent references to Weltsch will be cited parenthetically as "Rise and Fall" within the text.

11. In his 1917 essay on the German literary and cultural scene of Prague, the (gentile) writer Paul Leppin declares the net result of Jewish predominance in the German art, theater, media, and literature of the city "eine jüdische Kolonie" ("a Jewish colony"). He contends that the participation among Jews in these areas is more than 90 percent, calling into question the notion of a true "cultural symbiosis." See his "Die jüdische Kolonie."

12. Weltsch expounds upon this problem as follows: "In a city, once known as 'Mother in Israel' and once a centre of Jewish intellectual life, there hardly remained anything left of Jewish knowledge. The number of observant Jews had shrunk to a small circle. . . . Prague Jewry was more remote from Judaism than its co-religionists in Germany. The reason was undoubtedly its rapid and uninhibited entry into the world of German culture. . . . The process was so fast and it encompassed intellectual life so thoroughly that in a very short time, perhaps in one generation, the religious life of the vast majority of the Jews was almost completely devitalized" ("Rise and Fall," 259).

13. Cited in Pazi, "Franz Kafka, Max Brod und der 'Prager Kreis,'" 77.

14. First published in 1911, these lectures became an immediate bestseller and were considered required reading for young Jews throughout German-

speaking Central Europe. See Robert Weltsch's introduction to Buber, *Der Jude und sein Judentum*, xiii–xl. On the greater impact of Buber's lectures, see Maurice Friedman's chapter, "The Prague Bar Kochbans and the 'Speeches on Judaism,'" in his *Martin Buber's Life and Work*, 124–47.

15. Cited and translated in Kieval, *The Making of Czech Jewry*, 128. In light of Kafka's position, the importance of this letter is, as Marthe Robert has argued, that it "goes straight to the core of the young Kafka's personal Jewish question and of the depressing situation confronting him." That is, Kafka faced the divisions among the Prague Jewish community that separated the liberal German patriots from the Zionists, and thus he constantly felt compelled to ask himself where his Jewishness fit in. See Robert, *As Lonely as Franz Kafka*, 211.

16. Buber, "Judaism and the Jews," *On Judaism*, 16 – trans. rev. Cf. Buber, *Der Jude und sein Judentum*, 13. On Buber's significance for Prague Zionism, see Kieval, *The Making of Czech Jewry*, 124–53.

17. Numerous Kafka scholars, including Hartmut Binder, Ritchie Robertson, and Klaus Wagenbach have affirmed the likelihood that Kafka attended these lectures. In one of his letters to his fiancée Felice Bauer, Kafka also explicitly mentions that he had personally heard Buber speak. See his letter of 16 January 1913 in Kafka, *Briefe an Felice*; in English, *Letters to Felice*, 157.

18. Robert Weltsch notes that the rebellion among the young Jews in Prague, especially the "rebellion of the sons," represented a "critique of empirical Judaism par excellence." They were, as he claims, very much attuned to the "vulgarity and hypocrisy" that characterized the Judaism practiced by the bourgeois liberal Jews of their parents' generation. See his "Die schleichende Krise der jüdischen Identität," 20. See also his early treatise, "Die Jugend des jüdischen Prag" of 1917, in which he launches a sharp critique against the lost Jewish roots of the fathers. This essay is contained in the Prague anthology of the same year, *Das jüdische Prag*, 17–18.

19. The name *Bar Kochba*, presumably a reference to the 1897 play by Czech playwright Jaroslav Vrchlicky, recalls the Jewish revolt against Rome in 132 C.E. On the rise of Zionism in Prague, see Kieval, *The Making of Czech Jewry*, 93–123; Tramer, "Prague – City of Three Peoples," 306ff.; Kestenberg-Gladstein, "The Jews Between Czechs and Germans," 59–61; Pawel, "Der Prager Zionismus zu Kafkas Zeit"; Böhm, "Wandlungen im Zionismus"; and Friedrich Mautner, "Der Prager Zionismus."

20. The Prague Zionist weekly, *Die Selbstwehr*, published its rendition of Ahad Ha'am in an editorial of 6 January 1911: "What we want: that is the preservation of the present and the future of the Jewish people [*Volk*]; that is the

battle against the 'un-Jewish' [*das Unjüdische*] in Judaism, against all displaced tendencies within the Jewish community [*Gemeinschaft*]; that is the invigoration of the idea of Jewishness [*die Belebung der jüdischen Idee*] that sustains our people." Cited in Binder, ed., *Kafka Handbuch*, vol. 1, 371.

21. M. Friedman, *Martin Buber's Life and Work*, 126–27.

22. Kohn, "Gleitwort," v. Kohn specifies in his preface that while the political convictions of the contributors may differ to some degree, all of the authors consider themselves conscious members of the Jewish *Volksgemeinschaft*. In his historical account of the Jewish Question, Alex Bein argues that the *Bar Kochba* anthology represents "the best expression of the profound transformation" among German-speaking Central Europe's Jewish intelligentsia. See his *The Jewish Question*, 691. See also Andreas Herzog, "'Vom Judentum.'"

23. Binder, "Franz Kafka und die Wochenschrift 'Selbstwehr.'" Binder provides an excellent survey of the paper's history and its relation to Kafka's personal development of Jewish self-awareness. Much of the information provided in my brief discussion of the *Selbstwehr* has been adopted from Binder's more thorough treatment. All subsequent references to Binder's essay shall be made parenthetically as "Wochenschrift" and incorporated into the text.

24. According to Binder's convincing account, Kafka read the paper regularly from 1917 onward. Binder substantiates this claim by way of detailed examinations of Kafka's letters to Max Brod during his travels to Zürau in September of 1917, Kafka's discussions with his Hebrew teacher Friedrich Thieberger in 1919, and the numerous letters and notes from the years 1919 leading up until his death in 1924 ("Wochenschrift," 287).

25. Brod, "Zum Problem der Gemeinschaft," 10; and *Franz Kafkas Glauben und Lehre* (1948), in *Über Franz Kafka*, 247–48.

26. Brod, "Unsere Literaten und die Gemeinschaft," 463–64.

27. Christoph Stölzl offers a fair assessment of Kafka's Zionism: "He was a Zionist insofar as he felt a strong bond, even a blood brotherhood, with Eastern European Jewry; and according to reports of his later life, this feeling of kinship became increasingly evident over time. But unlike his friend Max Brod, Kafka was unable to draw nationalistic conclusions from this feeling." See his "Kafka: Jew, Anti-Semite, Zionist," 78.

28. Max Brod reports a similar situation in his own diary entry of 23 August 1913: "Afternoon with Kafka. Bathing, rowing. Conversations about feelings of community. Kafka says he has none, because his strength just about

suffices for himself alone." See *Über Franz Kafka*, 100; in English, *Franz Kafka: A Biography*, 113.

29. Urzidil, "Two Recollections," 60.

30. In his analysis of this phenomenon, Giuliano Baioni writes: "In only a few decades the assimilated Jew had góne from the medieval ghetto to modern industrial society, and the consequent disorientation made him the paradigm of a crisis in European consciousness. He, more than any other, was condemned to a laborious search for his cultural memory and the meaning of his superseded historical tradition – in other words, to reestablish the continuity between national culture and bureaucratic modernity" (Baioni, "Zionism, Literature, and the Yiddish Theater," in 101).

31. Since Janouch's work originally appeared in Czech, and was subsequently translated into German and English, I provide no references to the original. For a fascinating comparison to Kafka's memories of the Prague ghetto, see Perutz, *Nachts unter der steinernen Brücke*.

32. In a letter to his lover, the Czech translator Milena Jesenská, Kafka postulates: "Writing letters is actually an intercourse with a ghost and by no means just with the ghost of the addressee but also with one's own ghost, which secretly evolves inside the letter one is writing or even in a whole series of letters, where one letter corroborates another can refer to it as witness" (M 260; LM 223). At times both his experiences with writing and Judaism – especially East European Judaism – function for Kafka as a ghostly enterprise, a spiritual meditation on past ages and on past traditions.

33. Clement Greenberg attributes a special role to the repository of Jewish memory in Kafka's Prague: "There was the Jewry of that city, and its past, and the larger past of all Central and East European Jewry. Kafka carried with him a kind of 'racial' memory of that past. Though he was an emancipated Jew, he was still its product and after-effect." See Greenberg, "The Jewishness of Franz Kafka," 320. On Kafka and the golem, see Urzidil, "Two Memories," 63ff.; and Felstiner, "Kafka and the Golem." On Kafka's affinity with kabbalistic discourse, see Alter, "Kafka as Kabbalist" and Grötzinger, *Kafka und Kabbalah*.

34. "In terms of Judaism," notes Walter Sokel, "this conflict [between past and present] corresponds to the contrast between the Eastern Jew with his still prevailing ties with the ancient tribal religion and the emancipated Western Jew who is cut adrift from his former moorings, deeply unsure and exposed to destruction." See Sokel, "Franz Kafka as a Jew," 233. Walter Jens joins Sokel in his reading of the contrast between the Eastern and Western European Jews in Kafka, suggesting however that Kafka's encounter with the

*Ostjuden* is more than anything a confrontation with his own past. It represents, according to Jens, "a re-remembering [*Wiedererinnern*] in the Proustian sense, a 'Madeleine' experience of the highest order. Among the Yiddish actors – and nowhere else – Kafka had the feeling of not being 'alone with himself,' but rather in the deeper sense, of being 'among others.' Here Jews acted as Jews." Jens, "Franz Kafka," 276. See also his earlier discussion of Kafka's Jewishness, "Ein Jude namens Kafka."

35. On Herrmann Kafka's background, see Northey, "Die Kafkas" and *Kafkas Mischpoche*.

36. Brod, *Über Franz Kafka*, 246. On Kafka's general perception of Western Jewry, see Milfull, "'Weder Katze noch Lamm?'" and "Franz Kafka – The Jewish Context."

37. Cf. Robert Weltsch, "Die Jugend des jüdischen Prag," 17ff. According to Weltsch, the losses of a spiritual home [*geistige Heimat*] in Judaism and of the "invigorating power of the *Gemeinschaft*" were due in large measure to the neglect of the fathers.

38. See Mark Anderson's excellent discussion of the connection between *mauscheln* and Josephine's mouse vernacular in *Kafka's Clothes*, 194–216. "Although etymologically related to the names Mauschel, Moishele, and Moses," explains Anderson, "the verb *mauscheln* – to speak German 'like a Jew' – can be interpreted as Kafka's fictional version of *Mauscheldeutsch* and, perhaps, as a figure for his own Jewish-German language. If so, the *Volk* referred to in the story would not be the Jewish people generally, as commentators have often assumed, but the German-Jewish people as a particular moment in history, that is, the generation of 'Western Jews' between emancipation and Zionism to which Kafka felt he belonged" (205–6).

39. Kafka spent the last six years of his life learning Hebrew, another "authentic" Jewish language. For a discussion of the impact of Hebrew on Kafka's work, see Alter, *Necessary Angels*, 27–63. See also the personal reflections of Kafka's Hebrew teacher, Puah Ben-Tovim, "Ich war Kafkas Hebräischlehrerin."

40. Cf. Kafka's descriptions of Frau Tschissik's art and her beauty in his diary entries of 5 and 7 November 1911.

41. In his illuminating discussion of Kafka's "Josephine" and "Jewish" music, Mark Anderson cites a critical passage from Richard Wagner's polemic of 1850, "Das Judentum in der Musik" ("Judaism in Music"), which treats the same problem of language as viewed from a German, distinctly anti-Jewish, perspective: "The Jew speaks the language of the country in which he

has lived from generation to generation, but he speaks it as a foreigner" (Anderson, *Kafka's Clothes*, 197). Less than ten years after Kafka's death, when German modernism and the linguistic debates surrounding it acquired a new, vociferous political and racial inflection, the Nazi-inspired *Deutsche Studentenschaft* circulated a pamphlet containing the following words: "The Jew can only think in Jewish [*jüdisch denken*]. If he writes in German, he lies. . . . Jewish works appear in the Hebew language. If they appear in German, they are to be characterized as translations." Cited in Schöne, "'Diese nach dem jüdischen Vorbild erbaute Arche,'" 350.

42. Such general statements as "would like to know Yiddish literature" (T 66; D 70) to the more specific listings of his various Yiddish and general Jewish studies fill the pages of his diaries during this time. In a Yiddish article on his Prague experiences, written on the occasion of Max Brod's fiftieth birthday, Löwy notes, "The exotic and religious qualities of Eastern Jewry excited and attracted the Prague writers [i.e., Kafka and Brod]." See Djak Levi (a.k.a. Yitzhak Löwy), "Tvey Prager Dikhter" ("Two Prague Writers"), *Literarische Bleter* 34 (1934): 557–58; English translation in Beck, *Kafka and the Yiddish Theater*, 222. Cf. *Kafka-Handbuch*, vol. 1, 390–95.

43. See Sander Gilman's informative chapter, "On Difference, Language, and Mice," in *Franz Kafka, the Jewish Patient*, 1–40. On the relation between Kafka's animal figures and Jews (especially Eastern Jews), see also Robertson, *Kafka: Judaism, Politics, and Literature*, 164ff and 275ff.; Felix Weltsch, "The Rise and Fall of the Jewish-German Symbiosis," 268ff.; and Binder, "Franz Kafka and the Weekly Paper 'Selbstwehr,'" 144ff.

44. Graetz's infamous phrase is cited in Birnbaum, "Sprachadel," 84. Traverso has recently noted that Graetz was so repulsed by Yiddish that he even objected to a Yiddish translation of his *History of the Jews*. See *The Jews & Germany*, 18.

45. Benjamin, "Franz Kafka", (I 132).

46. Bergmann, "Franz Kafka und die Hunde," 4; Harshav, *The Meaning of Yiddish*, 115–16.

47. Baioni, "Zionism, Literature, and the Yiddish Theater," 105.

48. Traverso, *The Jews & Germany*, 68.

49. On Kafka's perceptions of the Eastern Jews, Felix Weltsch writes: "Admittedly, in Kafka's encounter with the Jews of Eastern Europe a strange, shy love for Frau Tschisik [sic], one of the actresses, played a certain part. So also did the 'sympathy,' as he himself said, with the actors, and especially with Löwy. But the essential was still his experience of a people that through its homogeneity, tradition and sheer numbers led a life in com-

mon that Kafka the Jew lacked. The experience gave him the positive side to the negative picture; it revealed what he constantly missed in his own existence as an assimilated Jew and German writer, lacking full historical consciousness" ("Rise and Fall," 272). For a discussion of the larger implications of Kafka's encounters with the Yiddish actors on the communal level, see Pan, "Kafka as a Populist."

50. Bergmann, *Jawne und Jerusalem*, 29. See also his "Schulzeit und Studium."

51. Harshav, *The Meaning of Yiddish*, 3–4. "This popular nickname of the Yiddish language [*mame-loshn*]," he continues, "is diametrically opposed to the sociological term used in modern Yiddish, the cold, Germanizing, *muter-shprakh*, 'mother-tongue'" (4).

52. Diamant, "Mein Leben mit Franz Kafka," 185.

53. In his biography of Kafka, Ernst Pawel makes a similar claim: "What he sought in Judaism was not faith so much as a *living community*, one of which he could himself be a living part. And therein resided the seductive magic of Yitzhak Levi [sic] and his players: eight messengers from the world in which his own father had himself been a son, kindred spirits to a spirit that was stirring within him, *speaking his own lost language, rooted and secure in their unassailable identity as Jews, Jewish in the way the Czechs were Czech, the Germans German – and he himself was nothing.*" See Pawel, *The Nightmare of Reason*, 240; emphasis added. The idea of a *Gemeinschaft* in Yiddish – both the actors and the language – might also be seen in Kafka's notion of "eine kleine Literatur" ("a minor literature"), which in his eyes is composed of such communal traits (cf. T 154–55; D 150–51). See also Gilles Deleuze and Félix Guattari, *Kafka: Toward a Minor Literature.*

54. Kafka, "Rede über die jiddische Sprache," (H 306–9); in English, "An Introductory Talk on the Yiddish Language," trans. Mark Anderson (RK 263–66).

55. The reasons for Baum's rejections are not stated. What is important, however, is that Kafka initially shows a great deal of discomfort in taking on this responsibility. He explains in his diary entry of 25 February that he dedicated an entire evening to changing Baum's mind, only to discover a special-delivery postcard the following day reneging on their tentative agreement for Baum to reclaim his responsibility.

56. In his attempts to strengthen his knowledge of Jewish history and literature, Kafka records in his diaries his readings of Heinrich Graetz's three-volume *Geschichte des Judentums* (*History of the Jews*, 1888–89), Meyer Isser Pinès's *L'Histoire da la littérature Judéo-Allemande* (*History of Yiddish Literature*, 1911) and Jakob Fromer's *Der Organismus des Judentums* (*The Organ-*

*ism of Jewry*, 1909), all between November 1911 and January 1912. His notes on the Yiddish literary tradition, as learned from Pinès, are included in the English edition of his diaries only (D 173–76). On Kafka's conception of Yiddish, see Cooper, *Kafka and Language*, esp. the chapter entitled "Jargon: Kafka's Search for Roots," 40–59. Cf. Gilman, *Franz Kafka, the Jewish Patient*, 27ff.

57. See Birnbaum, *Ausgewählte Schriften zur jüdischen Frage*. See also Fishman, *Ideology, Society and Language*, esp. chapters 3 and 4. For a discussion of Birnbaum's influence on Kafka, see Baioni, "Zionism, Literature, and the Yiddish Theater," 97ff. On the more general trend in modern linguistic nationalism – and the place of Yiddish within this trend – see Hobsbawm, *Nations and Nationalism Since 1780*, 110–11; and Benedict Anderson, *Imagined Communities*, esp. 141–54.

58. A statement attributed to Birnbaum's lecture in Prague expresses the underlying thrust of his position on the *Ostjuden* and their language: "The Eastern European Jews are unified, convivial and vital human beings." Cited in *Kafka-Handbuch*, vol. I, 292.

59. Birnbaum, "Sprachadel," 85–86.

60. See Kaufmann et al., "Zum Programm der Freistatt," 3. On Kaufmann's influence as editor and advocate of Yiddish, see Max Mayer, "A German Jew Goes East," 349; and Myers, "'Distant Relatives Happening into the Same Inn,'" 79–82. For a passionate defense of Yiddish by an Eastern Jew, contained in Kaufmann's journal, see Schalit, "Uebersicht über die jiddische Literatur," 176–80. For a further defense, albeit more tempered, by a Western Jew, see Calvary, "Jiddisch." On the debates concerning Yiddish among German Jews in general, see Gilman, *Jewish Self-Hatred*; Grossman, *Language and Control*; and Bechtel, "Cultural Transfers Between *Ostjuden* and *Westjuden*."

61. Schalit, "Uebersicht über die jiddische Literatur," 180.

62. The review is reprinted in translation, in Beck, *Kafka and the Yiddish Theater*, 227.

63. Felix Weltsch, "Franz Kafka gestorben."

64. On the larger debates concerning Jewish writing in "Jewish languages," see Michael Brenner's chapter, "Authenticity Revisited," in *The Renaissance of Jewish Culture in Weimar Germany*, 185–211.

## 2. THE IMAGINED COMMUNITY

1. Vishniac, *Polish Jews*. For a broader selection of Vishniac's work, see his extensive photo-anthology, *A Vanished World*.

2. Since the focus of this chapter is on the *Shtetl-Gemeinschaft* as viewed by German Jews, I am mainly concerned with the predominant perceptions of traditional/communal Jewish life in the East. It should be noted, however, that the Jewish *Haskalah* (Enlightenment) had reached the East by the end of the nineteenth century and that there was, in turn, a growing population of "modernized" Jews, mostly living in the larger cities. The Yiddish national poet I. L. Peretz recounts the moment that the modern Yiddish playwright Abraham Goldfaden cried out, "It's a new day! We Jews should be out in the street!" Peretz explains that in the East, Jews and Gentiles were largely "of two different worlds," yet they had also in small measure begun to grow together. To this he adds a final note: "I fell victim to the Enlightenment." See Peretz, *My Memoirs*, 309, 325. On the broader intellectual currents of Jewish Eastern Europe, see Dawidowicz., ed., *The Golden Tradition*. For a review of some of the literature on Western and Eastern Jews, see also Hamerow, "Cravat Jews and Caftan Jews."

3. On the remarkably wide reception and profound influence of Buber's Hasidic writings, see Mendes-Flohr, "Fin de Siècle Orientalism." See also David A. Brenner's fascinating survey of the early German-Jewish monthly, *Ost und West*, founded in 1901 (edited by Buber, Max Nordau, and others) and deeply concerned with Eastern Jewish culture: *Marketing Identities*.

4. Zipperstein, "The Shtetl Revisited," *Shtetl Life*," 19.

5. See, for example, Eliasberg, ed. and trans., *Ostjüdische Erzähler*. This collection, adorned with a classical etching of an Eastern Jew by Hermann Struck, contains stories by Sholom Aleichem, I. L. Peretz, and other greats of modern Yiddish literature. Aside from Eliasberg's collection, there were numerous Eastern Jewish titles published by the Jüdischer Verlag in Berlin. For a review of titles from the early 1920s, see Döblin, "Alfred Döblin über ostjüdische Dichtung." Döblin concludes his review with a favorable reference to the timeliness of Arnold Zweig's *Das ostjüdische Antlitz*.

6. There were several prewar journeys made by Western Jews to the East. Kafka's contemporary Hugo Bergmann was among the early travelers, as was Judah L. Magnes, the San Francisco-born rabbi. In a letter to his family from 1902, written while studying in Germany, Magnes expresses the spirit of the early pilgimages to the "authentic" Jews of the East: "I shall make a *Judenreise*, i.e. I shall visit Galicia, and by touring on foot for about two months I think I shall become acquainted with my brethren." Cited in

Goren, "Judah L. Magnes' Trip to Przedborz," 164. See also Max Mayer, "A German Jew Goes East."

7. For a thorough account of the greater historical context and the wide scope of literary and cultural production, see Aschheim, *Brothers and Strangers*. See also the more recent essay by Myers, "'Distant Relatives Happening onto the Same Inn.'"

8. Aschheim, *Brothers and Strangers*, 142. Cf. Zechlin, *Die deutsche Politik und die Juden*. For a particularly poignant example of wartime hopes, see Buber, "Die Losung."

9. "Appell an die deutschen Juden zur Verteidigung des Vaterlandes," *Jüdische Rundschau* XIX, Nr. 32 (7 August 1914): 343. Rpt. in Reinharz, ed., *Dokumente zur Geschichte*, 145–46. On Zionist support of the war, see Poppel, *Zionism in Germany 1897–1933*, 79ff. See also Mosse, "The Jews and the German War Experience 1914–1918."

10. In consultation with the statistics presented in Jakob Segall's work of 1922, *Die deutschen Juden als Soldaten im Krieg 1914–18*, Saul Friedländer points out that, despite the Weimar cries of Jewish betrayal and conspiracy (e.g., the widespread *Dolchstoß* legend), nearly the same proportion of Jews fought for Germany as non-Jews (17.3% of all Jews to 18.73% of all non-Jews). See his "Die politischen Veränderungen der Kriegszeit," 38, n. 28. Up to this day, a tour of Berlin's *Weißensee* Jewish cemetery reveals the vast participation among Jews in the First World War – the pride in serving as a soldier stands out prominently on numerous Jewish soldiers' epitaphs.

11. Mosse, "The Jews and the German War Experience, 1914–1918," 3, 5. Mosse states that "most German Jews succumbed to the almost irresistible temptation to share the full German war experience" (25). On the notion of the "spirit of 1914," see Fussell, *The Great War and Modern Memory*.

12. See, for example, Gronemann, *Hawdoloh und Zapfenstreich*, 60–61, 143ff. Saul Friedländer suggests that there was a general atmosphere, albeit short-lived, of *Gemeinschaftsgefühl* (communal feeling) among the German and Jewish soldiers. See his "Die politischen Veränderungen der Kriegszeit und ihre Auswirkungen auf die Judenfrage," 31.

13. "Das Wilnaer Ghetto," *Der Israelit* 58.26 (28 June 1917): 9–10; cited in Aschheim, *Brothers and Strangers*, 143.

14. See Treitschke, "Unsere Aussichten" (1879), 116; and Franzos, *Aus Halb-Asien*. On the discourse of orientalism and the role of the Eastern Jew, see Mendes-Flohr, "Fin de Siècle Orientalism."

15. Aschheim, *Brothers and Strangers*, 148.

16. Friedländer, "Die politischen Veränderungen der Kriegszeit und ihre Auswirkungen auf die Judenfrage," 34. Cf. Aschheim, "The East European Jew and German Jewish Identity," 14.

17. See Robert Weltsch, "Die schleichende Krise der jüdischen Identität," 16. Weltsch asserts that a number of Jewish soldiers in the First World War experienced embarrassment and degradation when, at the shows of the officer's theater on the front, they were to observe "Jewish" ("often obscene") cabaret numbers acted out by gentile soldiers. See also Hamerow, "Cravat Jews and Caftan Jews," which concurs that the parodied Eastern Jew "was a stock figure in a vaudeville sketch, with his sing-song speech, incongruous dress, excited gesticulation, dishonest trickery" (35).

18. Aschheim, *Brothers and Strangers*, 139. The result, writes Aschheim, was that "German Jews were forced to confront the problem of Eastern Jews [i.e., the so-called *Ostjudenfrage*]. Their responses to the challenge not only mirrored their changing feelings and attitudes towards the Ostjuden but also provided a sensitive measure of their own self-conceptions, their understanding of the relation between *Deutschtum* and *Judentum*, between being German and being Jewish" (141). In his survey of German Zionism, Poppel similarly underscores the importance of the contact between German-Jewish soldiers and the Eastern Jewish population: "Heretofore these *Ostjuden* had been encountered only as uprooted immigrants trying to make their way in Germany. But now German Jews had the opportunity to discover the integral and vibrant world of East European Jewish culture. For some the experience only confirmed their former negative judgment. But others, by far the majority, 'were gripped by the strength and warmth, by the piety and idealism that they discovered underneath the crust of need and poverty.' Here was a living Jewish *community* whose vitality could only serve to demonstrate to German Jewry how much it had lost in the process of assimilation." *Zionism in Germany 1897–1933*, 78; emphasis added.

19. Arnold Zweig, who along with a host of other German and German-Jewish writers, intellectuals, and politicians, participated in the debates on East European Jewry, notes the interdependence of *Ostjuden* and German Jews in his article, "Außenpolitik und Ostjudenfrage." Zweig argues that whenever the *Ostjuden* are blamed, the German Jews are implicated in this attack. They are, in short, seen as accomplices in the alleged crimes of the *Ostjuden* (51).

20. Birnbaum, *Was sind Ostjuden? Zur ersten Information*, 14–15. On the general stakes of the *Ostjudenfrage*, see my discussion in chapter 3. See also Volkov, "The Dynamics of Dissimilation."

21. Fritz, *Die Ostjudenfrage.* See also the German-Jewish opposition to the *Ostjuden* in Naumann, *Vom nationaldeutschen Juden.* According to Naumann, the Jews of the East maintain "moral views of half-Asia [*Halbasiens*] foreign to the German spirit" and therefore pose a threat to the well-being of the nation. "The national German Jew," he concludes, "is too much of a German to desire exceptional treatment for the benefit of the Jews, who are among these damaging creatures" (22).

22. Wassermann, *Mein Weg als Deutscher und Jude*, 113. For a critical Eastern Jewish perspective on this matter, see Deutscher, *The Non-Jewish Jew*, 46–47: "To someone of my background, the fashionable longing of the Western Jew for a return to the sixteenth century, a return which is supposed to help him in recovering, or re-discovering, his Jewish cultural identity, seems unreal and Kafkaesque."

23. Excerpts from the document are cited and translated in Angress, "The German Army's 'Judenzählung' of 1916," 117. Angress gives a detailed account of the measure, which, in his final estimation, "was a symptom, a warning sign that antisemitism in Germany was alive and well, especially in times of stress and national reverses" (135).

24. Michael Brenner, "1916: The German army orders a census of Jewish soldiers" 349.

25. Zweig, Letter of 15 February 1917 to Martin Buber, rpt. in Wenzel, ed., *Arnold Zweig*, 74.

26. Zweig, Letter of 27 August 1914 to Helene Weyl, Arnold-Zweig-Archiv, Berlin (East); rpt. in Wenzel, *Arnold Zweig*, 62–63. As a literary testimony to Zweig's wartime enthusiasm, see his collection of short fiction, *Die Bestie* (*The Beast*, 1914). Cf. Hermand, *Arnold Zweig*, esp. "Das Erlebnis des Ersten Weltkriegs (1914–18)," 25–36. I am indebted to Hermand for much of the information provided on Zweig's wartime service.

27. Zweig, "Zum Problem des jüdischen Dichters in Deutschland." Zweig argued that Jewish writers such as Wasserman and Buber belong among the contemporary greats of German literature – and, furthermore, that as Jews, they had made the German literary and cultural concerns into their own.

28. This is precisely the point of departure for the study conducted by the American Jewish Committee in the same year. See *The Jews in the Eastern War Zone* (New York: American Jewish Committee, 1916), 7ff.

29. The text, which was later published in *Die Schaubühne* 13.5 (February 1917): 115–17, has been reprinted in Wenzel, *Arnold Zweig*, 555–57. Cf. Zweig, "Die Judenzählung," in Ludger Heid and Julius H. Schoeps, eds., *Juden in*

*Deutschland: Von der Aufklärung bis zur Gegenwart* (Munich: Piper, 1994) 224–27.

30. Zweig, "Judenzählung vor Verdun," 117. See also Jost Hermand's excellent discussion of Zweig's Jewishness in *Engagement als Lebensform*, 11–34.

31. On Struck's position at Ober-Ost, see Gronemann, *Hawdoloh und Zapfenstreich*, 12–16. Also, see Struck's early contribution to the *Skizzen Mappe der 'Kownoer Zeitung'*, in particular, issue number 12 (30 April 1916), in which his illustrations of the Eastern Jews appear together with the lead article "Die Entwicklung des Ostjudentums." At Ober-Ost, Zweig also came into contact with Gronemann, Richard Dehmel, and Herbert Eulenberg. There they formed what Gronemann ironically refers to as the "Klub ehmaliger Intellektuellen" ("Club of Former Intellectuals"). See Gronemann, *Hawdoloh and Zapfenstreich*, 20ff. For a more detailed portrait of Struck's life, see the memoirs of his brother-in-law, Henry Pachter, *Weimar Etudes*, 203–7.

32. See Zweig's review of Struck's first volume of etchings of Eastern Jews, "Strucks 'Ostjuden,'" 2. Zweig is most impressed by Struck's impassioned portraits of Jewish life in the East, his "infinite familiarity" with the "law of harmony," and the political function his art has for a better undertanding of the *Ostjuden*.

33. Zweig, Letter of 13 May 1918 to Martin Buber, in Buber, *Briefwechsel aus sieben Jahrzehnten*, vol. 1, 534.

34. Bernd Hüppauf introduces this point in his essay, "Ende der Hoffnung – Anfang der Illusionen? Der Erste Weltkrieg in den Schriften deutscher Juden," 204–205. See also the comments by Walter Preuss, who like Zweig, finds a similar (self-)discovery in the Eastern Jews. "Here, in Tomaszow, it first dawned on me how different Jewish reality in Poland appeared than we Western Jews had arrogantly imagined it to be: how much more natural the social structure was than in Germany, where Jewry [*Judenheit*] consisted merely of the bourgeoisie and intellectuals, how much more Jewish and more tradition-based it still was." Cited in Adler-Rudel, *Ostjuden in Deutschland 1918–1933*, 50–51.

35. On the notion of community among the Hasidim, Buber writes, "Hasidism derives its uniqueness and greatness not from a doctrine but from an attitude; it is an attitude that promotes community and is by nature dependent on community." Buber, *The Origin and Meaning of Hasidism*, 24.

36. Zweig's attempt to present a corrective to the misconceptions of Eastern Jewry might also be seen in the context of other – largely Zionist – attempts to fashion more positive images of the *Ostjuden*. In an article pub-

lished in the *Jüdische Turn- und Sportzeitung* of 1920, Fritz Scherbel reports on the Eastern Jewish wrestling champion, Stanislaus Czyganiewicz, the son of a Galician orthodox family who won the world championship in 1906. Scherbel suggests that Zbysko (as the wrestler is affectionately called) should stand as a role model, proving to a Western audience that a Galician Jew can achieve the "highest athletic title." See Scherbel, "Ein ost-jüdischer Weltmeister," 14.

37. Cf. Bayerdörfer, "Das Bild des Ostjuden," 231. On the Zionists' strategies for a more idealized artistic representation of their cause and their people, see Berkowitz, *Zionist Culture and West European Jewry Before the First World War*, esp. chapter 5 ("Art and Zionist Popular Culture"), 119–43.

38. See Wiznitzer, *Arnold Zweig*, 17ff. On the broader significance of Zweig's Jewishness for his literary career, see also Carmely, *Das Identitätsproblem jüdischer Autoren*; and, with particular attention to his famed novel, *Der Streit um den Sergeanten Grischa* (*The Case of Sergeant Grischa*, 1927), Jörg Schönert, "'. . . mehr als die Juden weiß von Gott und der Welt doch niemand.'"

39. See Zweig's "Zum Problem des jüdischen Dichters in Deutschland"; "Über jüdische Legenden"; and "Die Demokratie und die Seele des Juden." On Zweig's early Jewish preoccupations, see also Müller, "'Zum Problem des jüdischen Dichters in Deutschland.'" With regard to Zweig's encounters with Zionism, Jost Hermand also points to the fact that Beatrice Zweig, the cousin and later wife of Arnold, shared with him her more extensive knowledge of Zionism during these early years. See Hermand, *Arnold Zweig*, 16.

40. Hermand, "Arnold Zweigs Judentum," 78. The contemporary Polish-Jewish critic Marcel Reich-Ranicki similarly argues that "during the Weimar Republic, much more than before the war, Zweig stands under the influence of Judaism." See his *Deutsche Literatur in West und Ost*, 316. For a selection of Zweig's contributions to the Jewish press around the time of the publication of *Das ostjüdische Antlitz*, see *Jüdischer Ausdruckswille*, 41ff.

41. Cf. Zweig, "Die revolutionäre Jugend des Ostens." For this reference, I am indebted to Alt, "Zu Arnold Zweigs 'Das ostjüdische Antlitz,'" 185.

42. Zweig, *Das ostjüdische Antlitz* (DoA), 9.

43. Zweig first makes this point in his review of Struck's lithographs, "Strucks 'Ostjuden'" (2), and then once more in the preface to the first editon (DoA 10). See also the introduction to Joseph Roth's *Juden auf Wanderschaft* of 1927, which likewise pleas for a more sympathetic understanding of the *Ostjuden* among Western Jews: "The author harbors the foolish hope that

there are still readers before whom Eastern Jews need not be defended: readers who have respect for pain, human greatness, and the dirt that accompanies suffering wherever it goes; Western Europeans who are not proud of their clean mattress, who feel that there would be much for them to gain from the East, and who perhaps know that Galicia, Russia, Lithuania, and Romania bring forth great men and great ideas; but also people who are (in their sense) useful, who uphold and help to further the established framework of Western civilization – not just the pickpockets, who the vilest product of Western European society, the local news report, likes to term 'guests from the East.'" Roth, *Juden auf Wanderschaft*, 7.

44. Goldstein, "Arnold Zweig," 249.

45. The "human transformation" that Zweig mentions here is ascribed by Arie Wolf to the affirmative position that Zweig takes vis-à-vis the *Ostjuden*, which although previously a part of Zweig's Zionist sensibilities, is first realized in his encounters in the East. See Wolf, "Arnold Zweigs Ostjudenbild," 19.

46. See Heine, "Über Polen" (1923). While Heine is far more critical of the Eastern Jews than Zweig, he too follows the discursive line of East-West, traditional-modern, religious-secular opposition in his sketch. And in spite of his sometimes acerbic critique, Heine also arrives at a final assessment that rates the lifestyle of Polish Jews above that of modernized Jews in the West.

47. Zweig, "Strucks 'Ostjuden,'" 2.

48. A reproduction of the etching is contained in Berkowitz, *Zionist Culture*, 133. Berkowitz asserts that Struck's rendition of Herzl "proved to be the most popular and enduring single image of Zionism from 1897 to 1914" (131).

49. Berkowitz, *Zionist Culture*, 135.

50. Helzel, "Introduction," *Shtetl Life*, 13. With regard to the German-Jewish context, Steven Aschheim rightly claims that "the representation of the *Ostjude* was designed to give the German Jew a new and different picture of himself." To this, he adds, "Of course, this celebration of the ghetto [and, by way of extension, the shtetl] tells us more about the ideological predicament and proclivities of these German Jews than it illuminates the realities of ghetto culture." See Aschheim, "The East European Jew and German Jewish Identity," 19–20.

51. See Harshav, *The Meaning of Yiddish*, 153ff. Following the viewing of a Yiddish Theater performance of the *Dybbuk*, Zweig offered his moving account: "Jews, coming right out of Chagall's pictures, painted like the dance

masks of wild tribes, in costumes of South Seas' people . . . were jumping, walking, contorting themselves." Cited in Bechtel, "1922: *Milgroym*," 422.

52. Herzog and Zborowski, "Preface," *Life is With The People*, 22–23. Many critics have considered this work the main landmark in postwar shtetl sentimentalism. See, for instance, Ruth Gay, "Inventing the Shtetl." According to Gay, Zborowski and Herzog "provided just the myth that was needed" to satisfy the wishes of a Western Jewish (in Gay's case, American) audience (330). See also Joachim Neugroschel's introduction to *The Shtetl*. Finally, see Barbara Kirshenblatt-Gimblett's new critical introduction to the 1995 Schocken reprint of *Life is With People*, ix–xlvii.

53. Zipperstein, *The Shtetl Revisited*," 22.

54. Irving Howe and Eliezer Greenberg, "Introduction," *A Treasury of Yiddish Stories*, eds. Howe and Greenberg (New York: Schocken, 1973), 4. Howe's account of the "world of the East European Jews," while certainly compelling, is not altogether devoid of the romantic impulse. "For several hundred years," he writes, "there existed in Europe – mainly in Russia, Poland, Rumania, and Galicia – a culture probably without parallel in Western history. Bound together by the firmest spiritual ties, by a common if fluid language, and by a sense of destiny that often meant a sharing of martyrdom, the Jews of Eastern Europe were a kind of nation, yet without nationhood; a people, yet persistently denied the dignity of being people. Theirs was both a community and society: internally a community, a spiritual kingdom; and externally a society in peril, a society on the margin. The result was an experience highly unified, singular, and contiguous. Though the forces of disintegration that afflicted the West were destined to penetrate the ghetto as well, they came later and had far less impact. The world of the East European Jews showed severe signs of internal stagnation, but its recent destruction came not from within but from without" (3).

55. Hugo Bergmann criticizes the so-called "Parole der Haskalah" ("slogan of Haskalah") in his essay, "Der jüdische Nationalismus nach dem Kriege," 18. In his survey of Yiddish literature, the Eastern Jew Moses Schalit makes a programmatic statement, responding directly to the Haskalah principle: "Jewish life should be Jewish! Jewish at home and outside, in one's production and thought, in one's education and deeds." See Schalit, "Uebersicht über die jiddische Literatur," 180.

56. Döblin, *Journey to Poland*, 50. For additional historical commentaries on the uniqueness of the Eastern Jews, see also Birnbaum, *Was sind Ostjuden?*, 15; and Böhm, "Wandlungen im Zionismus," 139–54.

57. In his review of Döblin's *Reise in Polen*, Joseph Roth asserts that a more fitting title for Döblin's work would have been "Reise zu den Juden" ("Journey to the Jews"). See Roth, "Döblin im Osten." On the broader trend among German Jews to "travel to the Jews," see Gilman, "The Rediscovery of Eastern Jews: German Jews in the East, 1890–1918"; the important section, titled "The Invention of the Eastern Jew," in Gilman's *Jewish Self-Hatred*, 270–86; and Michael Brenner, *The Renaissance of Jewish Culture in Weimar Germany*, 142–48.

58. In his article, "The East European Jew and German Jewish Identity," Steven Aschheim cites two fascinating examples of German-speaking assimilated Jews (Ahron Marcus and Jiri Langer) who not only turned to the *Ostjuden* for spiritual sustenance, but also for an actual model for "becoming" *Ostjuden*. As he explains, "In the full anthropological sense of the word both went 'native' by leaving their familiar bourgeois world and totally immersing themselves in the life of the Eastern ghettos" (20–21). This sort of "ethnic crossdressing" was of course an unusually extreme response, though also quite revealing for its extremism: indeed, in these cases the Western Jews took their reliance on the *Ostjuden* for a means of self-understanding one step further. It wasn't simply to travel to the Eastern Jews and observe them from a distance, but to become Eastern Jews.

59. See Kafka's commentary on the Kol Nidre (the night preceding Yom Kippur, the Day of Atonement) service in his *Tagebücher, 1910–1923*, 54. In *Reise in Polen*, Döblin makes observations similar to Zweig: "Amid the utter hush of the assembly, the cantor intones the ancient Kol Nidre prayer. He is squat, has a white beard, a white coat, a prayer shawl over it. . . . The cantor has begun very softly. He chants the same prayer once again, louder. And now, for a third time, in a full lamenting voice. . . . This chant ushers in the evening, intensely and powerfully. . . . Then comes a passage that forms the climax of the evening. . . . And what I then hear, what he then sings is an echo of this wailing and yammering that I heard at the cemetery this morning. But now it's in the chant. . . . He truly weeps, he truly sobs. Sobbing has become singing. Singing borne by sobbing. The song sinks into its primal element" (*Reise in Polen*, 93–94; *Journey to Poland*, 67). Even Sammy Gronnemann, who otherwise focuses more on the ironies of life at Ober-Ost, when addressing prayer, becomes quite sentimental. See *Hawdoloh und Zapfenstreich*, 63–77.

60. Arthur Thilo Alt argues that "pan-Jewish renewal" is Zweig's ultimate goal in *Das ostjüdische Antlitz*. In this process of renewal the *Ostjuden* are

thought to play an exemplary role. See Alt, "Zu Arnold Zweigs 'Das ostjüdische Antlitz,'" 174.

61. Letter of 13 May 1918 to Martin Buber, *Briefwechsel*, 534.

62. Five years later, Zweig's publication of *Das neue Kanaan* would develop further his notions of a utopian Zionism, as expressed in a more skeletal form in *Das ostjüdische Antlitz*. Cf. Thielking, *Auf dem Irrweg ins "Neue Kanaan"?*; Wiznitzer, *Arnold Zweig*, 31–33; Wolf, "Arnold Zweigs Ostjudenbild," 24–25; and Kahn, "Arnold Zweig." True to the mythical ideal of *Gemeinschaft*, Zweig first searched for a utopian community – in part, modeled after the shtetl – in Palestine and then, after Israeli independence, in the German Democratic Republic. Though beyond the immediate scope of this chapter, the continuity in communal idealism in Zweig might serve as yet another case illustrating the multifaceted character of *Gemeinschaft* in its various uses among German Jews.

63. Zweig, "Grabrede auf Spartakus."

64. Benedict Anderson, *Imagined Communities*, 7.

65. Goldstein, "Arnold Zweig," 249.

66. See Zucker, "Mythen der Gegenwart."

67. Zucker finally suggests, in his consistently ironic tone, that he hopes it was the intention of both artists "to present more than a holiday sermon in a small Zionist newspaper" (465).

68. The romantic and mythical qualities of *Das ostjüdische Antlitz* seemed to have remained with Zweig, at least for part of his life. When asked in 1925 what he considered the Jewishness in his soul and his work, Zweig responded by contrasting the Appolonian character of his Germanness with the Dionysian character of his Jewishness: the language and lessons of Lessing, Kleist, and Büchner with the riches of his sense of home (*Beheimatung*), familiarity, and belonging. See "Das Jüdische in meinem Wesen und Schaffen," 1.

69. Zweig, "Nachwort," *Herrkunft und Zukunft*, 225.

### 3. WEIMAR CINEMA, THE CITY, AND THE JEW

1. Fassbinder, *Der Müll, die Stadt und der Tod*, 15; in English, *Garbage, the City and Death* (GCD) in Fassbinder, *Plays*, 161–89; here 170 (trans. rev.). All subsequent references to GCD will be taken from this translation, while page numbers as well as notice of my own occasional revisions to Denis Calandra's translation will appear parenthetically within the text.

2. In his essay "Über einige Motive in Baudelaire" (1939), Walter Benjamin writes, "Fear, revulsion, and horror were the emotions which the big-city

crowd aroused in those who first saw it." GS I-2, 629; in English, "On Some Motifs in Baudelaire," 174.

3. On "Jewish" capitalism, see Sombart, *Die Juden und das Wirtschaftsleben*. On "Jewish" race "science," see, most notably, Arthur de Gobineau, *Essai sur l'inégalité des races humaines*; and Chamberlain, *Die Grundlagen des neunzehnten Jahrhunderts*.

4. For information on the Fassbinder controversy, I am indebted to Denis Calandra's critical introduction, "The Antitheater of R. W. Fassbinder," *Works*, 9–17; here 12. The statement from the *FAZ* article comes from the journalist and Hitler biographer Joachim Fest, the B'nai Brith statement from E. L. Ehrlich. In the wake of the controversy, the Suhrkamp publishing house withdrew its collection of Fassbinder's plays that had included *Der Müll, die Stadt und der Tod*; cf. Fassbinder, *Stücke* 3. On the controversy, the two best collections are Kiderlen, ed., *Deutsch-jüdische Normalität . . . Fassbinders Sprengsätze*; and Lichtenstein, ed., *Die Fassbinder-Kontroverse oder Das Ende der Schonzeit*. In English, see Markovits et al., "Rainer Werner Fassbinder's *Garbage, the City, and Death*"; Wistrich, "The Fassbinder Controversy"; and, most recently, Markovits and Noveck, "1985: Rainer Werner Fassbinder's play *Garbage, the City and Death*, produced in Frankfurt, marks a key year of remembrance in Germany."

5. Marx defines the Jew within the terms of modernity, i.e., within the discourse of capitalism: "What is the worldly basis of Judaism? Practical necessity, selfishness. What is the worldly culture of the Jew? Commerce. What is his worldly God? Money." Marx, *Zur Judenfrage* (Berlin, 1844); excerpted and translated in Mendes-Flohr and Reinharz, eds., *The Jew in the Modern World*, 266.

6. In his account of the controversy, Robert Wistrich writes, "*Garbage*, for all its failings, does hold up a kind of distorting mirror to a disturbing and unhealthy reality of postwar German-Jewish existence" ("The Fassbinder Controversy," 127). I would argue that the "distorting mirror" that Fassbinder's play invokes also has an undeniable bearing on the problems of "German-Jewish existence," however historically unique, at the beginning of this century.

7. Cited in Fassbinder, *Plays*, 13.

8. Seyla Benhabib advances this argument in her contribution to a roundtable discussion on the "affair" held, in the wake of Reagan's Bitburg visit, at Harvard University's Center for European Studies on 17 December 1985. "Fassbinder's play," she concludes, "has become a metaphor for German identity after 40 years, expressed in the desire of large numbers of West

Germans to be able to speak not only about themselves, but about others, the Jews, without being suffocated by the censure of guilt and the past. It has also become a metaphor for the right of the Jews in Germany to determine how one will speak and write about them, and how they view themselves. As such, the debate has extended far beyond the question of how they are viewed by an avant-garde artist with good intentions." See Markovits et al., "Rainer Werner Fassbinder's *Garbage, the City, and Death*," 19.

9. For an earlier, much condensed version of the following film analysis, see my "October 29, 1920: Paul Wegener's *Der Golem: Wie er in die Welt kam* debuts in Berlin."

10. Kracauer, "Kult der Zerstreuung," *Das Ornament der Masse*, 311–17; in English, "Cult of Distraction," trans. Thomas Y. Levin, *New German Critique* 40 (Winter 1987): 95.

11. In a lecture given on 24 April 1916, "Neue Kinoziele" ["New Goals for the Cinema"], Paul Wegener spoke of film as a "Theater des kleinen Mannes" ["theater for the little man"], a place where the masses congregate in the anonymity of the darkness of the cinema house. See excerpts from this lecture in Greve et al., eds., *Hätte ich das Kino!*; 117–18.

12. Kracauer, *From Caligari to Hitler*, 28. Kracauer points out that Wegener's sensational imagination made him "a natural ally for the Nazis, for whom he was to write, in 1933, the official screen play on Horst Wessel" (29).

13. Earlier adaptations of the theme can be found in the works of such authors as Theodor Storm (1851), Wolf Pascheles (1853), and Nathan Grün (1885). For a detailed list of the various renditions of the golem myth in art, literature, music, and popular culture, see Bilsky, ed., *Golem! Danger, Deliverance and Art*, 112–21; Rybár, "Golem; or Myths and Legends of the Prague Ghetto"; and specifically on the production of Wegener's golem-films, see the insightful essay by Elfriede Ledig, "Making Movie Myths," as well as her more extensive, *Paul Wegeners Golem-Filme*.

14. I use the term "circulation of social energy" advisedly, appropriating it here as defined by Stephen Greenblatt in his *Shakespearean Negotiations*. Primarily focused on the "the signs of contingent social practices," Greenblatt's notion of "social energy" asks "how collective beliefs and experience were shaped, moved from one medium to another, concentrated in manageable aesthetic form, offered for consumption" (5).

15. Citations of the intertitles and inserts from Wegener's 1920 film are taken from his novelistic script, *Der Golem: Wie er in die Welt kam*, here 13 (translations are my own). In addition to Wegener's work, I have consulted the English translation in *Masterworks of the German Cinema*, ed. Roger Man-

vell (New York: Harper & Row, 1973), 19–51; here 20. All subsequent references to Wegener's script will be provided parenthetically within the text.

16. In his essay on early Weimar cinema, Thomas Elsaesser suggests that silent film's predilection for ancient settings serves both to "represent" and "disguise" such conflict. See his "Social Mobility and the Fantastic.

17. Scholem, "The Golem of Prague" 337. Cf. Scholem's earlier, more extensive survey of the Golem myth, "Die Vorstellung vom Golem in ihren tellurischen und magischen Beziehungen." On the mechanization of man, see also Rabinbach, *The Human Motor*.

18. For a brief discussion of the golem, the medieval ghetto, and urbanism, see Wolitz, "The Golem (1920)." "The city," writes Wolitz, "the central image of modernity for so much expressionist cinema, emerges in this film as the massive Golem itself, unnatural, unformed, incomplete, alone. The ghetto is the synecdoche of the city. Exotic, fascinating, it symbolically becomes modern urban life" (392). Looking at the golem myth from the standpoint of the 1980s, the Yiddish author and Nobel laureate Isaac Bashevis Singer asks, "What are the computers and robots of our time if not golems?" (Bilski, *Golem*, 6).

19. In his text, Wegener refers to Loew as both "Wunderrabbi" and "Meister." See Wegener, *Der Golem*, 7.

20. On Rathenau and the problem of Jewish participation in German politics around 1920, see Felix, *Walther Rathenau and the Weimar Republic*; Loewenberg, "Walther Rathenau and Henry Kissinger"; and Barnouw, *Weimar Intellectuals and the Threat of Modernity*, 44–77.

21. Benjamin, *Das Passagen-Werk* [N2a, 3] in *Gesammelte Schriften*, vol. V-1, 576–77; for an English translation, see "N [Theoretics of Knowledge; Theory of Progress]," *The Philosophical Forum* XV:1–2 (Fall–Winter 1983–84): 1–19; here 7. In the same essay from which I adopt the epigraph opening this chapter, "Cultural Identity and Cinematic Representation," the British critic Stuart Hall suggests that cultural identity is as much "a matter of 'becoming' as well as of 'being'. It belongs to the future as much as to the past" (70).

22. Although never constituting more than one percent of the general population, the near half-million Jews of Germany largely resided in such big cities as Berlin, Frankfurt, Leipzig, and Munich. In 1920s Berlin, of the some 173,000 Jews, approximately one-fourth were *Ostjuden*. These figures are significant only insofar as Jewishness was often defined in terms of Eastern Jewish physiognomy and physical traits. Statistical tables listing these,

as well as other, figures are provided in Adler-Rudel, *Ostjuden in Deutsch-land*, 164–65.

23. Wegener, "Schauspielerei und Film," originally published on the opening day of his first golem-film at the Union-Theater Kurfürstendamm in the *Berliner Tageblatt* (15 January 1915); excerpts reprinted in Greve, *Hätte ich das Kino*, 116.

24. Kracauer, "Die Photographie," *Frankfurter Zeitung* (28 October 1927); rpt. in *Das Ornament der Masse*, 39; in English, "Photography," trans. Thomas Y. Levin, *Critical Inquiry* 19:3 (Spring 1993): 436 (trans. rev.).

25. The relationship between power and aesthetics in cinema implicit here has since occupied a central position in the discussion of Walter Benjamin's well-known essay "The Work of Art in the Age of Mechanical Reproduction" and ensuing debates on the "aestheticization of politics." See, for example, Martin Jay, "'The Aesthetic Ideology' as Ideology," 71–83.

26. For an illuminating discussion of the Jew's power over the aesthetic spectacle, indeed over the cinematic apparatus – here in reference to Fritz Lang's *Siegfried* (1924) – see Levin, *Richard Wagner, Fritz Lang, and the Nibelungen*, 123–29.

27. On the figure of Ahasverus in German culture, see Rose, *German Question/ Jewish Question*, esp. 23–43. See also the Herzl-inspired Austrian film of 1920, *The Wandering Jew* (dir. Rudolph and Joseph Schildkraut).

28. Although I do not deal with this aspect in greater detail, the Faustian element of Wegener's film highlights a number of provocative issues, e.g., the projection of "German" myth onto the Jew and the resultant intersection of myth and modernity. For a more thorough discussion of *Faust* and modernity, see Marshall Berman's chapter, "Goethe's *Faust*: The Tragedy of Development" in *All That Is Solid Melts into Air*, 37–86.

29. Commenting on film and its impact on identity formation, Stuart Hall has noted, "The past speaks to us. It is always constructed through memory, fantasy, narrative and myth" ("Cultural Identity and Cinematic Representation," 72).

30. Based on Hugo Bettauer's novel of the same name, Breslauer's film offers a unique take on the matter. After the Jews are expelled from the city (Vienna), all forms of cultural, social, and economic exchange come to a halt: the banks collapse, the theaters close, the coffee-house culture can no longer sustain itself, and the newspapers deteriorate. The Jews, according to Breslauer's version, must therefore be asked to return to the city in order to reinvigorate its dying state. Indeed, this subtle critique of antisemitism makes Breslauer's film a fascinating example, albeit one from outside

Weimar's film industry. On Bettauer's novel, see Traverso, *The Jews & Germany*, xx–xxi.

31. For the reference to the biblical passages and the treatment of the *Bilderverbot*, I am indebted to Gertrud Koch's discussion in her recent work, *Die Einstellung ist die Einstellung*, esp. her chapter "Mimesis und Bilderverbot in Adorno's Ästhetik," 16–29. In addition to the recurrent biblical commandment, Koch also cites talmudic and kabbalistic meditations on the problem of Divine creation: "All faces are allowed to be represented – with the exception of the human countenance," Koch states from the Talmud, following with the kabbalistic position of the *Book of Zohar*, "for the human countenance has the power over all things" (23).

32. Adorno, *Ästhetische Theorie*, 106.; in English, *Aesthetic Theory*, 106. On Jews and the *Bilderverbot*, see Russell A. Berman "Citizenship, Conversion, and Representation: Moritz Oppenheim's *Return of the Volunteer*," *Cultural Studies of Modern Germany*, 52ff.

33. Horkheimer and Adorno, *Dialektik der Aufklärung*, 199; in English, *Dialectic of Enlightenment*, 189.

34. Wegener, "Die Zukunft des Films" ("The Future of Film," 1920). See also Wegener's lecture of 1917, "Von den künsterlischen Möglichkeiten des Wandelbildes," contained in the Archiv der Stiftung Deutsche Kinemathek, Berlin.

35. Similar to the film-within-a-film confusion in Wegener's *Golem* (i.e., the cinematic "show" by Rabbi Loew before the court), Porter's film exhibits the inability of the spectator to distinguish between film and reality. This self-reflexive technique of the metacinema not only calls attention to the role of the spectator but also questions "the cinematic illusion," an urgent concern for both Wegener and Porter. Cf. Hansen, *Babel and Babylon*, 25ff. I am indebted to David J. Levin for bringing this connection to my attention. See his *Richard Wagner, Fritz Lang, and the Nibelungen*, 122–23.

36. In a Zionist tract of 1920 on the Eastern Jews, the problem of Jewish identification and mythical exaggeration becomes clear: "Nowhere in politics and economic life is there as great a danger that typological myths will develop as where Eastern European conditions are concerned. This has produced a tangled skein of distortions and lies about the numerically weak and insignificant immigration of Eastern Jews. The systematic incitement by certain parties was responsible for this, and as a result even many German men who care about truthfulness, justice, and humaneness have let themselves be led astray." *Die Einwanderung der Ostjuden in Deutschland*, cited and trans. in Bein, *The Jewish Question*, 708. On the Jewish response

to cinematic representation, see Brod, "Zum Problem der Gemeinschaft," 8–10. Brod fears what he calls the *Scheingemeinschaften* (illusory communities) of the cinema and the lack of authenticity that such representational modes convey. In addition to Brod, there were numerous prominent Jewish figures, including Felix Theilhaber, who responded negatively to the cinema. See Theilhaber, "Randbemerkungen eines Gesundheitsfanatikers," 7–10.

37. On the cultural logic of Jewish "uncanniness," see Shapiro, "The Uncanny Jew."

38. Zweig, "Zum Problem des jüdischen Dichters in Deutschland." Years later, from Parisian exile, Zweig returns to the topic of Jewish urban identity in his article, "Ueber Asphaltliteratur." Zweig explains that throughout recent history the German reactionary has always played out the contradiction between the rural countryside and the big cities. Referred to as "Montmartre-Zigeuner," "Berliner Elendsmaler," and "Asphaltliteraten," the Jew is equated with the degenerate city. Zweig retorts with a counter-argument: "The big cities are the battle fields of the spirit," the testing ground for "the most diverse currents of the new" and the site where modern "taste is formed."

39. Cf. chapter 2 of the present study.

40. Sander L. Gilman refers to the debates as such, pointing to the critical stakes: "assimilation or preservation of Eastern Jewry in the expanded German Reich." See his essay, "The Rediscovery of the Eastern Jews," 357. See also the lecture by Rabbi Felix Goldmann, *Die Stellung des deutschen Rabbiners zur Ostjudenfrage*, in which he claims that nearly all parties of German political life addressed the question with great zeal and yet without any resolve. "Today," he writes in 1916, "Eastern Judaism [*Ostjudenheit*] is the sensation of the day" (4).

41. Adolf Friedemann, *Wir und die Ostjuden*, 1; see also his "Die Bedeutung der Ostjuden für Deutschland."

42. Friedemann employs the concept *Volksgemeinschaft* in its normative usage, emphasizing the autonomy of Jewish tradition – the *Tracht* (costume), *Sprache* (language), and *Lebenserfahrung* (cultural, or ethnic, experience) – that the *Ostjuden* enjoy (1).

43. Cf. Herf, *Reactionary Modernism*.

44. Goldmann, *Die Stellung des deutschen Rabbiners zur Ostjudenfrage*, 34.

45. Scholem, *Von Berlin nach Jerusalem*, 60; in English, *From Berlin to Jerusalem*, 44.

46. On the origins of this shift in Jewish identity formation, see Massing, *Rehearsal to Destruction*.

47. See, for example, Fritz, *Die Ostjudenfrage*. Using the work of such Zionist social scientists as Arthur Ruppin and Felix Theilhaber, Fritz warned that the threat of the Eastern Jewish migration was more dangerous than any migration in the history of mankind. Therefore, according to Fritz, the racial preservation [*Rassenpflege*] of the German *Volk* was imperative.

48. Scholem, "On the Social Psychology of the Jews in Germany," 22. See also Reichmann, "Der Bewußtseinswandel der deutschen Juden."

49. See, e.g., Mühsam, "Zur Judenfrage," an essay which appeared against the backdrop of the German Worker's Party twenty-five point party platform and the German publication of the *Protocols of the Elders of Zion*. At the same time, reassessments of the *Ostjudenfrage* also appeared. See, e.g., Kaufmann and Senator, *Die Einwanderung der Ostjuden in Deutschland*; *Was Wird aus den Ostjuden?*; Nathan, ed., *Ostjuden in Deutschland*; *Die Ostjuden in Deutschland*; Brodritz, *Zum Ostjudenproblem*. Eduard Fuchs, the so-called "collector" (Benjamin), published an extensive anthology of international caricatures of Jews that extend from the Middle Ages to the German and Austrian election campaign posters of 1920. See his *Juden in der Karikatur*.

50. These figures are cited in Aschheim, *Brothers and Strangers*, 215–16. According to Adler-Rudel, in 1910 in Berlin alone there were approximately 22,000 *Ostjuden*, a figure that increased to just under 44,000 by 1925. *Ostjuden in Deutschland*, 164–65.

51. Lukács, "Gedanken zu einer Ästhetik des Kinos" (1913), 146.

52. *Der Kinematograph* 721 (1920); excerpts reprinted in Greve, *Hätte ich das Kino!* 120.

53. Finkielkraut, *The Imaginary Jew*, 15.

54. In an essay on Poelzig's film sets for *The Golem*, Wolfgang Pehnt asserts that the ghetto buildings not only invoke a certain corporality in themselves, but also "appeal to the spectator's own bodily senses, as if the drama of Rabbi Löw [sic] and his creation, the collapse of the royal palace and the burning of the ghetto take place not in some external location, but in the labyrinth of the human body itself." See his "La porta sul prodigioso," 85.

55. Joseph Roth, "Flüchtlinge aus dem Osten," *Neue Berliner Zeitung* 20 October 1920, rpt. in Bienert, ed., *Joseph Roth in Berlin*, 78.

56. For a discussion of the Jew's alleged physical and physiognomic connection to the city, see Gilman, *The Jew's Body*, 31ff., 48–49. On the broader reactionary discursive link of Jews to the city, see Herf, *Reactionary Modern-*

*ism*, esp. 130–51. This lineage of a declared Jewish-urban affinity reaches further back than Sombart's work of the 1910s, recalling such figures as Julius Langbehn, whose enormous best-seller of 1890, *Rembrandt als Erzieher*, asserted the Jewishness of Berlin. On Langbehn, see Stern, *The Politics of Cultural Despair*, 97–180.

57. Andrej, "Ein Gespräch mit Paul Wegener," 2.

58. For a survey of the history and culture of Berlin's *Scheunenviertel*, see Geisel, ed., *Im Scheunenviertel*. See also Brian Ladd's discussion of the district in his *Ghosts of Berlin*, esp. 110–15.

59. In his biography of Poelzig, Theodor Heuss writes, "At the time, during the age of silent film, he used the crudely sarcastic word that at least the buildings should *mauschel* [i.e., speak Yiddish] – an imagined gaiety runs through the entire gloomy and dull world." Heuss, *Hans Poelzig*, 69–70. This statement is also referred to in the recent publication of a special issue of the Goethe-Institute journal *Sequenz* on the *Golem*. According to Peter Schott's "Arbeitsanleitungen, Lösungen und Antworten," Poelzig "wanted to build Gothic buildings that spoke Yiddish." *Sequenz: Film und Pädagogik* 7 [Special Issue: *Der Golem*] (1994): 77.

60. Andrej, "Ein Gespräch," 2.

61. Lester D. Friedman, "The Edge of Knowledge," 53.

62. Eisner, *The Haunted Screen*, 23. Siegfried Kracauer's discussion of the street in his final film work, *Theory of Film*, also remarks on this relationship, although he fully omits any reference to Jewish specificity: "The street in the extended sense of the word is not only the arena of fleeting impressions and chance encounters but a place where the flow of life is bound to assert itself. Again one will have to think mainly of the city with its ever-moving anonymous crowds. The kaleidoscopic sights mingle with unidentified shapes and fragmentary visual complexes and cancel each other out, thereby preventing the onlooker from following up any of the innumerable suggestions they offer. What appear to him are not so much sharp-contoured individuals engaged in this or that definable pursuit as loose throngs of sketchy, indeterminate figures. Each has a story, yet the story is not given" (72).

63. Paul Westheim's review, "Eine Filmstadt von Poelzig, 1920," originally appeared in *Das Kunstblatt* 4 (1920): 325; rpt. in Greve, *Hätte ich das Kino!*, 120.

64. In his unpublished memoirs, the co-director and special effects technician Carl Boese suggests that the architectural composition of the film was to produce "an entirely new face," one that reflects the mystique of the mate-

rial. See excerpts from his *Erinnerungen an die Entstehung*. This original text is contained in the Archiv der Stiftung Deutsche Kinemathek in Berlin. Wolfgang Pehnt has likewise noted the physical quality of the film sets: "With their protruding gables, crooked bow-windows, twisting tiled-roofs and precarious towers, the buildings Poelzig created . . . themselves performed almost like actors" (83–85).

65. Meyrink, *The Golem*, 15.
66. Vidler, *The Architectural Uncanny*, 27. See also Vidler's essay on filmic space in modernist cinema, "The Explosion of Space." In his lecture, "The Visibility of the Jew in the Diaspora: Body Imagery in its Cultural Context," Sander L. Gilman points out that Jews have often been seen as "black" and "swarthy," as diseased and sexually abnormal. *B. G. Rudolph Lecture in Judaic Studies, Syracuse University* (10 October 1991): 1–41; see also his *The Jew's Body*, in which Gilman offers an extensive analysis of the diverse representations of Jewish physiognomy.
67. Dinter, *Die Sünde wider das Blut*, 186. See also Jay Geller's highly informative essay on Dinter, "Blood Sin," 21–48. On the Nazi representation of Jewish sexuality, see Showalter, *Little Man, What Now?*, 86–108.
68. On the question of antisemitism in *Nosferatu*, see Hoberman, *Bridge of Light*, 61 ff.; Kaes, "Film der Weimarer Republik, 52ff.; Roiphe and Cooper, "Batman and the Jewish Question"; Gelder, *Reading the Vampire*, 13–17; and Tatar, *Lustmord*, 57–64.
69. Hitler, *Parteiprogramm der NSDAP*.
70. Dawidowicz, *The War Against the Jews*, 19. The year 1920 marks not only Hitler's conception of German racial politics, but also the publication of the German edition of the *Protocols of the Elders of Zion*, the czarist forged booklet forecasting Jewish world domination. First appearing in Russia at the turn of the century, the *Protocols* document the alleged meetings of Jewish internationalists conspiring to take over the world. On the history and reception of the Protocols, see Cohn, *Warrant for Genocide*; and Segel, *A Lie and a Libel*. Also of interest is the publication of Henry Ford, *The International Jew: The World's Foremost Problem* in 1920; rpt. as *The Jewish Question*. In addition to his enormous success in Germany in the 1920s, Ford played an instrumental role in promoting the image of Jewish world conspiracy. Not only did he regard the major European cities as "Jew cities," but also in 1920 he declared the Jew "the enigma of the world" (20). See his article of 24 July 1920, "An Introduction to the 'Jewish Protocols'" (46–55), in which he claims the veracity of what he calls "the theory of Jewish World Power."

71. Cited and trans. in Kershaw, *Hitler*, 26.

72. Andrej, "Ein Gespräch," 2.

73. According to the advertisements in the *Film-Kurier*, Wegener's *Golem* played in Berlin's Ufa-theaters continuously for two straight months, clearly indicating a successful record.

74. Cf. Kracauer, *From Caligari to Hitler*, 6–8, 272. On the sharp limitations of Kracauer's thesis and the historical context in which he advances it, see my "Investigations of Character."

### 4. CULTURE IN RUINS

1. Honneth, "A Communicative Disclosure of the Past," 83.

2. On the reception of Benjamin and the divergent strategies of his commentators, see Garber, *Rezeption und Rettung*; Wolff, "Memoirs and Micrologies"; Wolin, "Introduction" (1994), *Walter Benjamin*; and Steiner, "The Remembrancer." Opening with an anecdote on Gershom Scholem's idealized seven-point list of "minimal prerequisites for those aspiring to read Walter Benjamin seriously" (e.g., vast knowledge of the German language and culture, a solid background in Judaism, Marxism, Romanticism, etc.), Steiner goes on to explain the "tedious nullity" of the majority of the "Walter Benjamin industry" critics. "It is because," he suggests, "they seek to enlist Benjamin in their own causes; it is because they batten on this most guarded and subtle of spirits without reticence of apprehension, without disinterestedness" (37).

3. A small, and by no means exhaustive, sampling of German and English volumes on Benjamin's literary, philosophical, and cultural impact includes: Unseld, ed., *Zur Aktualität Walter Benjamins*; Smith, ed., *On Walter Benjamin*; Nägele, ed., *Benjamin's Ground*; Bolz and Witt, eds., *Passagen: Walter Benjamins Urgeschichte*; Ingrid and Konrad Scheurmann, eds., *Für Walter Benjamin*; Benjamin and Osborne, eds., *Walter Benjamin's Philosophy*; Ferris, ed., *Walter Benjamin*; Fischer, ed., *'With a Sharpened Axe of Reason'*; Steinberg, ed., *Walter Benjamin and the Demands of History*.

4. Rabinbach, "Introduction," ix.

5. On the importance of the urban metropolis for Benjamin's sense of self and for his general worldview, see Gilloch, *Myth and Metropolis*, esp. his second chapter titled "Urban Memories," 55–92.

6. Habermas, *The Philosophical Discourse of Modernity*, 12.

7. Emil Benjamin was certainly not alone in this trend among assimilated German Jews to embrace *Deutschtum*. More prominent examples include Hermann Kafka, father of Franz, and Arthur Scholem, father of Gershom.

We know of Hermann Kafka's assimilatory impulses from the numerous biographical accounts by Max Brod and others and from Kafka's illustrious *Brief an den Vater* (*Letter to His Father*) of 1919. On Arthur Scholem's attitude towards assimilation, see Biale, *Gershom Scholem*, 9ff. See also Alter, *Necessary Angels*, in which he reads the fathers as representatives of the bourgeois *Gesellschaft* and the target of the sons' anti-assimilationist responses (31–32).

8. This term comes from Anson Rabinbach's excellent essay, "Between Enlightenment and Apocalypse." See also Löwy, *Redemption and Utopia*, esp. his chapter titled "Pariahs, Rebels and Romantics," 27–46. Löwy cites a revealing statement by Leo Löwenthal, describing this turn among the young Jews of Benjamin's generation: "My family household, as it were, was the symbol of everything I did not want – shoddy liberalism, shoddy Aufklärung, and double standards" (33).

9. Benjamin, *Briefe*, vol. 1, 425 (hereafter cited in the text as *Briefe* with reference to the volume and page number [e.g., *Briefe* I, 425]); translated in English as *The Correspondence of Walter Benjamin*, 300 (hereafter cited in the text as *Correspondence*).

10. While all of these phases are of critical importance, I mainly focus on the first two and, in subsequent sections, more specifically on the final phase. The third phase receives the least amount of attention, as it has already been extensively treated by Benjamin scholars (e.g., Rose and Wohlfarth) and tends, in my judgment, to obfuscate more than illuminate the problem of Judaism in Benjamin. I am more concerned with the actual concrete responses by Benjamin to Jewish culture and politics than with the covert presence of Jewish tradition in his work. Benjamin's discussion of Judaism and Jewishness in general – and not his implicit appropriations of these traditions – are as much illuminations of his broader positions on modernism as are his writings on modernism latent discussions of Judaism. It is precisely this relationship that occupies the center of my discussion.

11. Yerushalmi, *Zakhor*, xv; emphasis added. See also Yerushalmi's further analysis of the Passover ritual, illustrating the structural core of the Seder: "The entire Seder is a symbolic enactment of an historical scenario whose three great acts structure the Haggadah that is read aloud: slavery – deliverance – ultimate redemption" (44).

12. In Kafka's *Brief an den Vater*, one finds a striking parallel to Benjamin's critique of the Pessach ritual. According to Kafka, his family Seder "increasingly became more of comedy with fits of laughter" (H 145).

13. Scholem, *From Berlin to Jerusalem*, 55. For a detailed account of Benjamin's early debates on Judaism, see Smith, "'Das Jüdische versteht sich von selbst,'" 318–36; see also Rabinbach, "Between Enlightenment and Apocalypse."

14. Under the pseudonym Franz Quintin, Ludwig Strauß published his response to Goldstein in the August issue of the *Kunstwart*. See his "Sprechsaal. Aussprache zur Judenfrage," *Der Kunstwart* 25: 22 (August 1912): 243 ff; rpt. in part in Puttnies and Smith, eds., *Benjaminiana*, 45. Benjamin's letter of 11 September 1912, in which he addresses the *Kunstwart*-debate, is originally contained in the Jerusalem Nachlaß of Ludwig Strauß; rpt. in *Benjaminiana*, 46–48. On the greater impact of the "German-Jewish Parnassus" debate on Benjamin's life and work, see Wohlfarth, "'Männer aus der Fremde.'"

15. Indeed, it was only on a summer trip to Stopmünde in August 1912 that Benjamin noted, "for the first time I have been confronted with Zionism and Zionist activity as a possibility and hence perhaps a duty" (*Briefe* I, 44; *Correspondence*, 17).

16. See also Puttnies and Smith, eds., *Benjaminiana*, 51. Oddly enough, the same passage from Benjamin's letter to Strauß has been printed incompletely: "Mein entscheidendes geistiges Erlebnis hatte ich, bevor jemals das Judentum mir wichtig geworden war."

17. Janouch, *Conversations with Kafka*, 155.

18. On the Youth Movement, see Laqueur, "The German Youth Movement"; his booklength study, *Young Germany*; Mosse, *Germans and Jews*, 77–116; and Stachura, *The German Youth Movement*.

19. The Enlightenment component of Benjamin's stance on Judaism is rendered most poignantly in a somewhat abstract piece written in October 1912 in response to his ongoing discussion with Strauß. See his "Dialog über die Religiosität der Gegenwart" ("Dialogue on the Religiosity of the Present," GS II-1, 16–35), a more esoteric commentary on the role of religion in the modern world. See also his earliest reflections – almost in the form of a parable – on religion in "Drei Religionssucher" ("Three Searchers for Religion," 1910), orginally printed in *Der Anfang* 20 (August 1910): 38ff; rpt. in GS II-3, 892–94. In the reminiscences of Kurt Tuchler, Benjamin's other main interlocutor on Zionism and the German Youth Movement, Tuchler notes how in 1912 he attempted to bring Benjamin closer to Zionism (even suggesting membership in a Zionist fraternity), while Benjamin in turn attempted to introduce the Youth Movement to him. "It was truly a struggle [*ein Ringen*] around our mutually, deeply grounded views, yet also around

the *right* path of life." See his letter of 26 February to Gerschom Scholem, rpt. in Puttnies and Smith, eds., *Benjaminiana*, 40–41 (cf. GS II-3, 836).

20. Only a few years later, in the company of Scholem, Benjamin would ridicule Buber by asking Scholem if he had already "had his Jewish experience." Cf. Scholem's unpublished diary entry from 23–24 August 1916 in Puttnies and Smith, eds., *Benjaminiana*, 59.

21. In May of 1915, after Wyneken had published his essay in support of the war, "Jugend und Krieg" ("Youth and War," 1914), Benjamin "totally and unconditionally" dissociated himself from the man who ostensibly first introduced him to "the life of the mind." See his letter of 9 May 1915 to Wyneken (*Briefe* I, 120–22; *Correspondence*, 75–76). On the antisemitic trend within the Youth Movement, see Laqueur, *Young Germany*, 74–83.

22. Nora, "Between Memory and History," 8, 16. See also Nora's *Annales* group colleague Jacques Le Goff's recent work, *History and Memory*, in which he too declares the Jews "the people of memory par excellence" (69).

23. It is this form of cultural or "spiritual Zionism," as it is sometimes called, that offers a degree of appeal for Benjamin, who like Ahad Ha'am sees the inner transformation of cultural Zionism as far more viable than emigration to Palestine. On the tradition of cultural Zionism, see Laqueur, *A History of Zionism*, 162ff.

24. This arguably over-zealous statement by Benjamin, likely attributed to his early contact with Scholem, is later echoed in a similar remark made in his correspondence with the Swiss editor Max Rychner. In March of 1931, Benjamin writes of the theological "essence" of his work: "I have never been able to think and research otherwise than, if I may say so, in a theological sense – namely in accordance with the talmudic theory of 49 levels of meaning in each passage of the Torah" (*Briefe* I, 524; *Correspondence*, 372).

25. See Rose, "Walter Benjamin out of the Sources of Judaism"; Wohlfarth, "On Some Jewish Motifs in Walter Benjamin."

26. Bloch, "Recollections of Walter Benjamin," 339.

27. Wohlfarth, "'Der Umgekehrte Turmbau zu Babel,'" 103. Wohlfarth likens Benjamin's sense of Judaism to his notion of aura, thereby taking Scholem's more concrete reading of Judaism in Benjamin to task: "According to Scholem, Benjamin's relationship to Marxism was an illegitimate one. Yet it was no more and no less illegitimate than was his liaison to Judaism [Judentum]. Judaism, too, he brushed against the grain, and as a result he was made into a Jew among the Jews. He stood even closer to Judaism, the more it appeared that he was distancing himself from it. It is no coincidence that this paradoxical fusion of closeness and distance reminds us of

his famous definition of aura. For if Benjamin's own aura is unmistakably Jewish, then Judaism often remains present in his thought only – but still nonetheless – as an aura" (102–3).

28. Bernd Witte makes a similar claim in his biography *Walter Benjamin*, 82–83.

29. Cf. Susan A. Handelman's recent book on Benjamin, Scholem, and Levinas, which includes a chapter drawing on the words of the Baal Shem: "Memory is the Secret of Redemption: Messianism and Modernity," *Fragments of Redemption*, 149–73. Though the functions of Jewish memory in a post-Shoah world have changed, the urgency has not vanished with the end of Jewish "exile" and the creation of the national state. In fact, today this exact epigraph from Baal Shem Tov stands prominently above the entrance to the Yad Vashem Holocaust Memorial Museum in Jerusalem, Israel.

30. For an excellent discussion of the relationship between Jewish history and Jewish memory, see Yosef Hayim Yerushalmi's seminal work, *Zakhor*. On the Jewish commandment, see also Assmann, "Die Katastrophe des Vergessens."

31. Benjamin, "Über den Begriff der Geschichte," GS I:2, 704; English translation by Harry Zohn, "Theses on the Philosophy of History," (I 264).

32. Benjamin's notion of Judaism, particularly in his later years, increasingly bears redemptive strains of messianism. Indebted to such thinkers as Ernst Bloch and Franz Rosenzweig, Benjamin's brand of Jewish messianism is fueled by the desire to transcend the stagnant era of modern historicism and "progress," whereby a romantic anticapitalist realm is reached; here Benjamin maintains a highly utopian, radically apocalyptic sense of Judaism. As Anson Rabinbach has pointed out, there is an element in Benjamin's messianism that "involves a quantum leap from the present to future, from exile to freedom. This leap necessarily brings with it the complete destruction and negation of the old order. Messianism is thus bound up with both violence and catastrophe" ("Between Enlightenment and Apocalypse," 86). Benjamin's messianic proclivities gauge the imminent catastrophe while maintaining the unfailing hope of *tikkun*. Michael Löwy, in *Redemption and Utopia*, has noted that for Benjamin, there is a similar need to turn against the capitalist heritage of his parents and towards a more radical spiritualism. According to Löwy, Benjamin stands on the threshold of the tradition of Jewish libertarian thought in Central Europe. In Benjamin's writings, Löwy asserts, one finds "the burning spiritual flame of the work: the revolutionary redemption of mankind" (126).

33. Adorno, "Vorwort," *Briefe* 14; in English, "Benjamin the Letter Writer," 329.
34. On this dialectic of tradition and modernity, see McCole, *Walter Benjamin and the Antinomies of Tradition*.
35. Steiner, "The Remembrancer," 38.
36. See Gross, *The Past in Ruins*.
37. Adorno, *Minima Moralia*, 199–200. Michael Löwy considers this statement as defining an entire generation of the "defeated of history" to which Benjamin belonged: Kafka, Landauer, Rosenzweig, Lukács, Bloch, et al. See Löwy, *Redemption & Utopia*.
38. Each of the three concepts has a particular character in its German usage: *Eingedenken*, literally "the memory of one," is generally associated with personal memory, as in autobiography; *Erinnerung* and the infinitive *Erinnern* signify the act of remembering or the processes of memory, as in the French *mémoire*; and *Gedächtnis*, as the repository of memory, bears a more collective and communal inflection. While Benjamin uses all three of these concepts in their respective forms, they are often used in a more idiosyncratic fashion, in some cases even interchangeably. Where appropriate, I will attempt to distinguish the differences among these usages. On Benjamin's notion of *Erinnerung*, see Folkers, "Die gerettete Geschichte." For a brief survey of Benjamin's concept of *Eingedenken*, see Moses, "Zu Benjamins Begriff des Eingedenkens." Martin Jay also draws this distinction among Benjamin's concepts in his essay, "Experience Without a Subject." Finally, see the recent discussion by John Pizer, "Reconstellating the Shards of the Text." Pizer goes so far as to assert, "Only in 'Eingedenken' does Benjamin articulate a technique for envisioning hope and salvation" (287). Hope and the faith in a redemptive moment do, however, appear throughout much of Benjamin's general discussion of memory and collection.
39. Jürgen Habermas takes note of the power of memory in Benjamin: "Here [in Benjamin's philosophy of history] the liberating power of memory is supposed not to foster a dissolution of the power of the past over the present, as was from Hegel down to Freud, but to contribute to the dissolution of guilt on the part of the present with respect to the past" (*Philosophical Discourse of Modernity*, 15).
40. Wolin, *Walter Benjamin*, xlix.
41. Moses, "Zu Benjamins Begriff des Eingedenkens," 100. See also his more extensive discussion, "The Theological-Political Model of History."
42. Benedict Anderson, *Imagined Communities*, 204. See also Jonathan Boyarin's study on Jewish memory, *Storm from Paradise*, in which he states,

adding to Anderson, "Jews have always, it seems, used narrative to recreate their shared identities across time" (xvii). Benjamin's predilection for storytelling as a source of identity construction can also be observed in his radio plays (GS VII), written and broadcast during the same time in which he wrote his *Berliner Kindheit*. On the radio plays, see Mehlman, *Walter Benjamin for Children*.

43. For a more thorough discussion of the Benjamin-Brecht dispute, see Moses, "Brecht und Benjamin als Kafka-Interpreten."

44. On Tönnies's model of thought, in particular his *Gemeinschaft-Gesellschaft* dichotomy, see my discussion in the introduction. In his essay "A Communicative Disclosure of the Past," Axel Honneth also calls attention to this relationship between Tönnies's thought and Benjamin: "The image [of storytelling] he employs – a somewhat nostalgic one, and obviously influenced by Tönnies – assumes that, in premodern times, the integration of the social community still came about by handing down narratives in which experiences that shaped life-histories were passed on from generation to generation in a coded form; under conditions of increasing industrialization, such narrative processes of socialization are replaced by unilateral information circulated by media – that is, information about occurrences that are merely registered as 'sensations'" (88).

45. Jay, "Experience Without a Subject," 146.

46. In *Walter Benjamin and the Antinomies of Tradition*, John McCole perceptively notes that during the 1930s, when Benjamin was in his worst economic, political, and pychological state, his writings consistently focused on memory and its relation to tradition and experience. See, in particular, his introductory chapter (1–34) and chapter six, "Benjamin and Proust: Remembering" (253–79).

47. Although this issue lies beyond the scope of my discussion, it is worth considering the conservative strains of nostalgia in Benjamin. As Richard Wolin points out, "There is considerable nostalgia in his [Benjamin's] tone when he speaks wistfully of the decline of the integrated fabric of experience which was characteristic of communal social life; and redeeming aspects of modernity are nowhere to be found. Moreover, the sets of antitheses which form the methodological basis of the essay – story and novel, community and society, tradition and modernity – only reinforce the impression that the author seeks to establish an abstract opposition between past and present, compelling the reader to choose between one and the other – when in reality a choice so simple does not in fact exist" (226).

48. Baudelaire, *The Prose Poems*, 44.

49. Scholem, *Walter Benjamin: The Story of a Friendship*, 190; emphasis added.
50. I have revised E. Jephcott's translation to bring to bear the original arche-ological connotations of the ruins of old cities (cf. *Berliner Chronik*, GS VI, 486–87).
51. Arendt, "Walter Benjamin: 1892–1940" (I 42).
52. First published in the issue of 17 July 1931 (cf. GS IV:1, 388–96; "Unpacking my Library" [I 59–67]).
53. From his correspondence with Scholem, we also know of Benjamin's in-tent in 1934 to publish a review essay of *Die Geschichte des deutschen Buchhandels* (*The History of German Bookselling*) in a journal entitled *Die Sammlung*, one of the many small but not altogether insignificant projects that never came to fruition (cf. letter of 3 March 1934).
54. In his letters from exile, we learn the absolutely essential and even existen-tial value of his library, as Benjamin continually attempts to smuggle out parts of it from Germany, later stored at Brecht's summer house in Den-mark, his sister Dora's apartment, and the various apartments he inhabited in Paris. See, in particular, his correspondence with Scholem after 1932. On the bibliophile tradition among German Jews of Benjamin's generation, see Homeyer, *Deutsche Juden als Bibliophilen*. See also Holdengräber, "Un-packing Benjamin's Library."
55. On the motif of the *chiffonier* and Benjamin's concept of collection, see Wohlfarth, "Et Cetera?"
56. Adorno, "A Portrait of Walter Benjamin," 236. I have borrowed the term "memory-artist" (*Gedächtniskünster*) from Roland Kany, *Mnemosyne als Programm*, 215.
57. Habermas, "Consciousness-raising or Rescuing Critique," 101.
58. On the cultural practice of collecting, see Cahn, "Das Schwanken zwischen Abfall und Wert"; Holdengräber, "Between the Profane and the Redemp-tive"; and Steinberg, *Walter Benjamin and the Demands of History*, 88–118. See also Benjamin's own critical reflections in his essay "Eduard Fuchs, der Historiker und der Sammler" (GS II-2, 465–95).
59. Szondi, "Walter Benjamin's City Portraits," 28. "Memory, the staging of the past," remarks Susan Sontag, "turns the flow of events into tableaux. Benjamin is not trying to recover the past; but to understand it: to con-dense it into spatial forms, its premonitory structures." Sontag, "Under the Sign of Saturn," 116.
60. In February and March 1933 twelve episodes of Benjamin's memoirs ap-peared in the *Frankfurter Zeitung* under the title "Berliner Kindheit um 1900." Shortly thereafter he managed to publish another single episode

("Das Fieber") in the *Vossische Zeitung*. Finally, in August 1934, under the pseudonym Detlef Holz, Benjamin published yet another episode ("Blumeshof 12") in the *Frankfurter Zeitung*. On the evolution of the text and the different versions, see the editors' notes in GS IV-2, 964–86.

61. Adorno, "On the Question: 'What is German?,'" 126. Although Adorno makes this statement in reference to his own decision to return to the place of his childhood following the war, Benjamin's autobiography is most certainly bound up in a similar notion of restoration; moreover, he also returns to the place of his childhood, to the "sites of memory."

62. Scholem, "Walter Benjamin," 197; trans. rev. Scholem's thesis is further elaborated in the study by Friedrich Georg Friedmann, *Von Cohen zu Benjamin*.

63. For this reading, I am indebted to Jeffrey Mehlman who, in his analysis of the above cited passage, insists that "one is inclined to see in the need for a patron to escort him to the synagogue and the ultimate avoidance of attending the service prefigurations of failure to make the much anticipated trip (under Scholem's patronage) to Palestine." See his *Walter Benjamin for Children*, 70ff.

64. In his essay of 1936, "Der Erzähler" ("The Storyteller"), Benjamin writes: "Memory creates the chain of tradition that passes a happening from generation to generation" (GS II:2, 453; I 98). Similarly, Benjamin's childhood memoirs respond to the "chain of tradition" passed down to him.

65. Arendt, "Walter Benjamin: 1892–1940," 28–29; see also Gershom Scholem's far more affirmative reading: "How a child of that golden ghetto explores its length and breadth, how he shines the light of his imagination into all its corners as if it were the child's universe, was brought vividly to life by Benjamin." Scholem, "Walter Benjamin," 176.

66. On the Jewish antibourgeois movement, see Löwy, *Redemption and Utopia*; and Aschheim, *Culture and Catastrophe*, 31–44. On the urban affinity in Benjamin's writings, see Alexander Gelley, "City Texts: Kracauer and Benjamin," unpublished working paper, The Center for German and European Studies, University of California at Berkeley (European Society and Culture Research Group, June 1993); Lindner, *"Das Passagen-Werk"*; Kleinschmidt, "Die Stadt als Landschaft"; Weigel, *Body- and Image-Space*, esp. 109–127; and Graeme Gilloch, *Myth and Metropolis*.

67. Cf. Stüssi, *Erinnerung an die Zukunft*.

68. See Alter, "On Walter Benjamin": "His sense of homesickness, cultural, and ultimately, theological, makes more intelligible his attachment to Marxist messianism, to Zionism, to the Jewish past, and to the 19th cen-

tury" (93); see also Alter's more recent considerations in "Modernism and Nostalgia." On the motif of departure (*Abschied*) in *Berliner Kindheit*, see Thiekötter, "Ausgraben und Erinnern." Thiekötter argues that Benjamin's childhood memories are saturated with references to departure: the departure from the bourgeois security of his family home, the departure from Berlin as a refugee, and finally the departure from life via suicide. "However, the shadows that finally consumed him were first and foremost a result of his birth: that he was born a Jew" (36).

69. See Agamben, *The Coming Community*, 53ff.

70. Peter Szondi's thesis in "Hoffnung im Vergangenen" is that in Benjamin's childhood memoirs, the search for a "lost past" finds its correlate in the search for a "lost future"; to be sure, the path to the past transforms into a path to the future (92). See also Fischer, "Ethnicity and the Post-Modern Arts of Memory": "What thus seem initially to be individualistic autobiographical searchings turn out to be revelations of traditions, re-collections of disseminated identities and of the divine sparks from the breaking of the vessels. These are the Pythagorean arts of memory: retrospection to gain a vision of the future" (198).

71. Cf. McCole, *Walter Benjamin and the Antinomies of Tradition*, 304–308.

72. Szondi, "Hope in the Past," 501.

73. Witte, "Bilder der Endzeit." In his obituary for Benjamin, originally published *Die Tat* 5:246 (18 October 1940): 5 ff., Hans Mayer asks whether Benjamin's death signals "the collapse of a culture to which Benjamin felt deeply connected." See his *Der Zeitgenosse Walter Benjamin*, 83. Mayer points out that Benjamin's death is but one of the many deaths of German modernist authors and critics: Joseph Roth, Ernst Toller, Walter Hasenclever, Ernst Weiss, among others.

74. Peter Suhrkamp's statement first appeared in a 1951 *Spiegel* article on "the year's best- and worst-selling German books." Cited in Smith, *On Walter Benjamin*, 2.

75. Stern, "The Man With Qualities," 38.

76. Karavan, "Dani Karavan on the 'Passages' Memorial to Walter Benjamin," 255, 263. See also Konrad Scheurmann, "Borders, Thresholds, Passages"; and Konrad and Ingrid Scheurmann, eds., *Dani Karavan: Hommage an Walter Benjamin*.

77. See Huyssen, "Monuments and Holocaust Memory in a Media Age" in *Twilight Memories*; and Geyer and Hansen, "German-Jewish Memory and National Consciousness."

78. Missac, *Walter Benjamin's Passages*, 10.

79. Michèle C. Cone draws the connection to Maya Lin in "Memorial to Walter Benjamin," 17. For a fascinating discussion of the Vietnam Veteran's Memorial, see Berdahl, "Voices at the Wall."

80. On the function and critical use of monuments, in particular Holocaust monuments, see Young, *The Texture of Memory*. See also Gillis, ed., *Commemorations*; and, for a brief overview, Phillips, "Making Memories."

81. Benjamin, *Moscow Diary*, 65.

82. See Agamben, *The Coming Community*, 53ff.

EPILOGUE

1. Hans Mayer, "Das Gedächtnis und die Geschichte," 22.

2. Scholem, "Against the Myth of the German-Jewish Dialogue" (1962), *On Jews and Judaism in Crisis*, 63.

3. Horkheimer, "Über die deutschen Juden," 144–45.

4. Diner, "Negative Symbiosis," 251. See also Zipes, "Preliminary Diagnosis," *The Operated Jew*, 1–46, esp. 9–10; and Rabinbach, "Introduction: Reflections on Germans and Jews since Auschwitz," *Germans and Jews Since the Holocaust*, 3–24.

5. See, most recently, Herf, *Divided Memory*; and Markovits and Reich, *The German Predicament*.

6. See Maier, *The Unmasterable Past*; and Aschheim, *Culture and Catastrophe*.

# Works Cited

Adler-Rudel, S. *Ostjuden in Deutschland 1918–1933*. Tübingen: J. C. B. Mohr, 1959.

Adorno, Theodor W. "Auf die Frage: 'Was ist deutsch?'" *Stichworte: Kritische Modelle 2*. Frankfurt a. M.: Suhrkamp, 1969. 102–12. English: "On the Question: 'What is German?'" Trans. Thomas Y. Levin. *New German Critique* 36 (Fall 1985): 121–31.

———. *Ästhetische Theorie*. Frankfurt a. M.: Suhrkamp, 1973. English: *Aesthetic Theory*. Trans. C. Lenhardt. London: Routledge & Kegan Paul, 1984.

———. "Aufzeichnungen zu Kafka." *Prismen: Kulturkritik und Gesellschaft*. Frankfurt a. M.: Suhrkamp, 1977. 302–42. English: "Notes on Kafka." Trans. Samuel and Shierry Weber. *Prisms*. Cambridge, Mass.: MIT, 1981. 245–72.

———. "Charakteristik Walter Benjamins." *Prismen: Kulturkritik und Gesellschaft*. Frankfurt a. M.: Suhrkamp, 1977. 234–49. English: "A Portrait of Walter Benjamin." Trans. Samuel and Shierry Weber. *Prisms*. Cambridge, Mass.: MIT, 1981. 227–41.

———. *Minima Moralia: Fragmente aus einem beschädigten Leben*. Frankfurt a. M.: Suhrkamp, 1951.

———. "Vorwort." *Briefe* 14–21. English: "Benjamin the Letter Writer." Trans. Howard Stern. Smith 329–37.

Agamben, Giorgio. *The Coming Community*. Trans. Michael Hardt. 1990. Minneapolis: U of Minnesota P, 1993.

Alt, Arthur Thilo. "Zu Arnold Zweigs 'Das ostjüdische Antlitz.'" Midgley et al. 171–86.

Alter, Robert. "Kafka as Kabbalist." *Salmagundi* 98–99 (Spring–Summer 1993): 86–99.

———. "Modernism and Nostalgia." *Partisan Review* 60.3 (Summer 1993): 388–402.

———. *Necessary Angels: Tradition and Modernity in Kafka, Benjamin, and Scholem*. Cambridge, Mass.: Harvard UP, 1991.

## Works Cited

————. "On Walter Benjamin." *Commentary* 48 (1963): 86–93.

Anderson, Benedict. *Imagined Communities*. Rev. ed. London: Verso, 1991.

Anderson, Mark. *Kafka's Clothes: Ornament and Aestheticism in the Habsburg Fin de Siècle*. Oxford: Clarendon, 1992.

————, ed. *Reading Kafka: Prague, Politics and the Fin de Siècle*. New York: Schocken, 1989.

Andrej. "Ein Gespräch mit Paul Wegener." *Film Kurier* 2.244 (29 October 1920): 2.

Angress, Werner T. "The German Army's 'Judenzählung' of 1916: Genesis – Consequences – Significance." *Leo Baeck Institute Year Book* 23 (1978): 117–37.

Arendt, Hannah. "The Jew as Pariah: A Hidden Tradition." *The Jew as Pariah: Jewish Identity and Politics in the Modern Age*. Ed. Ron H. Feldman. New York: Grove, 1978. 67–90.

————. *The Origins of Totalitarianism*. San Diego: Harcourt, Brace, 1973.

————. "Walter Benjamin: 1892–1940." W. Benjamin, *Illuminations* 1–55.

Aschheim, Steven E. *Culture and Catastrophe: German and Jewish Confrontations with National Socialism and Other Crises*. New York: New York UP, 1996.

————. *Brothers and Strangers: The East European Jew in German and German Jewish Consciousness 1800–1923*. Madison: U of Wisconsin P, 1982.

————. "1912: The publication of Moritz Goldstein's 'The German-Jewish Parnassus' sparks debate over assimilation, German culture, and the 'Jewish spirit.'" Gilman and Zipes 299–305.

————. "The East European Jew and German Jewish Identity." *Studies in Contemporary Jewry* 1 (1984): 3–25.

Assmann, Aleida, and Dietrich Harth, eds. *Mnemosyne: Formen und Funktionen der kulturellen Erinnerung*. Frankfurt a. M.: Fischer, 1991.

Assmann, Jan. "Die Katastrophe des Vergessens: Das Deuteronium als Paradigma kultureller Mnemotechnik." Assmann and Harth 337–55.

Baeck, Leo. "Gemeinde in der Großstadt." *Der Morgen* 5 (1929): 583–90.

————. "Kulturzusammenhänge." *Der Morgen* 1 (April 1925): 72–83.

Baioni, Giuliano. "Zionism, Literature, and the Yiddish Theater." Trans. Mark Anderson. Anderson 95–115.

Barnouw, Dagmar. *Weimar Intellectuals and the Threat of Modernity*. Bloomington: Indiana UP, 1988.

Baudelaire, Charles. *The Prose Poems and La Fanfarlo*. Trans. Rosemary Lloyd. New York: Oxford UP, 1991.

# Works Cited

Bauman, Zygmunt. *Postmodernity and its Discontents*. New York: New York UP, 1997.

Bayerdörfer, Hans-Peter. "Das Bild des Ostjuden in der deutschen Literatur." *Juden und Judentum in der Literatur*. Eds. Herbert A. Strauss and Christhard Hoffmann. Munich: dtv, 1985. 211–36.

Bechtel, Delphine. "Cultural Transfers Between *Ostjuden* and *Westjuden*: German-Jewish Intellectuals and Yiddish Culture, 1897–1930." *Leo Baeck Institute Year Book* 42 (1997): 67–83.

———. "1922: *Milgroym*, A Yiddish Magazine of Arts and Letters is founded in Berlin by Mark Wishnitzer." Gilman and Zipes 420–26.

Beck, Evelyn Torton. *Kafka and the Yiddish Theater: Its Impact on His Work*. Madison: U of Wisconsin P, 1971.

Bein, Alex. *The Jewish Question: Biography of a World Problem*. Trans. Harry Zohn. Rutherford, N.J.: Fairleigh Dickinson UP, 1990.

Beller, Steven. *Vienna and the Jews, 1867–1938: A Cultural History*. New York: Cambridge UP, 1989.

Bender, Thomas. *Community and Social Change in America*. 1978. Baltimore: Johns Hopkins UP, 1982.

Benjamin, Andrew, and Peter Osborne, eds. *Walter Benjamin's Philosophy*. New York: Routledge, 1994.

Benjamin, Walter. *Briefe*. 2 vols. Ed. Gershom Scholem and Theodor W. Adorno. Frankfurt a. M.: Suhrkamp, 1966. English: *The Correspondence of Walter Benjamin*. Trans. Manfred R. and Evelyn M. Jacobsen. Chicago: U of Chicago P, 1994.

———. *Gesammelte Schriften*. 7 vols. Eds. Rolf Tiedemann et al. Frankfurt a. M.: Suhrkamp, 1991.

———. *Illuminations*. Trans. Harry Zohn. Ed. Hannah Arendt. New York: Schocken, 1969.

———. *Moscow Diary*. Trans. Richard Sieburth. Ed. Gary Smith. Cambridge, Mass.: Harvard UP, 1986.

———. *Reflections*. Trans. Edmund Jephcott. Ed. Peter Demetz. 1978. New York: Schocken, 1986.

Ben-Tovim, Puah. "Ich war Kafkas Hebräischlehrerin." Koch 165–67.

Berdahl, Daphne. "Voices at the Wall: Discourses of Self, History and National Identity at the Vietnam Veterans Memorial." *History & Memory* 6.2 (Fall/ Winter 1994): 88–124.

## Works Cited

Berger, Arje. *Gemeinschaft und Gesellschaft in der Geistesgeschichte des Judentums.* Berlin: Fürst, 1936.

Bergmann, Hugo. "Franz Kafka und die Hunde." *Mitteilungsblatt des Irgun Olei* 43–35 (3 September 1972): 4.

———. *Jawne und Jerusalem: Gesammelte Aufsätze.* Berlin: Jüdischer Verlag, 1919.

———. "Schulzeit und Studium." *Koch* 13–24.

Berkowitz, Michael. *Zionist Culture and West European Jewry Before the First World War.* New York: Cambridge UP, 1993.

———. "Zion's Cities: Projections of Urbanism and German-Jewish Self-Consciousness, 1909–1933." *Leo Baeck Institute Year Book* 42 (1997): III–21.

Berman, Marshall. *All That Is Solid Melts into Air: The Experience of Modernity.* 1982. New York: Penguin, 1988.

Berman, Russell A. *Cultural Studies of Modern Germany: History, Representation, & Nationhood.* Madison: U of Wisconsin P, 1993.

Biale, David. *Gershom Scholem: Kabbalah and Counter History.* 2nd ed. Cambridge, Mass.: Harvard UP, 1982.

Bienert, Michael, ed. *Joseph Roth in Berlin.* Cologne: Kiepenheuer & Witsch, 1996.

Bilsky, Emily D., ed. *Golem! Danger, Deliverance and Art.* New York: The Jewish Museum, 1988.

Binder, Harmut. "Franz Kafka und die Wochenschrift 'Selbstwehr.'" *Deutsche Vierteljahrsschrift* 41.2 (1967): 283–304. English: "Franz Kafka and the Weekly Paper 'Selbstwehr.'" *Leo Baeck Institute Year Book* 12 (1967): 135–48.

———, ed. *Kafka Handbuch.* 2 vols. Stuttgart: Kröner, 1979.

———. *Motiv und Gestaltung bei Franz Kafka.* Bonn: Bouvier, 1966.

Birnbaum, Nathan. *Ausgewählte Schriften zur jüdischen Frage.* 2 Vols. Czernowitz: Birnbaum, 1910.

———. "Sprachadel: Zur jüdischen Sprachenfrage." *Die Freistatt: Alljüdische Revue* 1.1 (April 1913): 83–88.

———. *Was sind Ostjuden? Zur ersten Information.* Vienna: R. Löwit, 1916.

Bloch, Ernst. "Erinnerungen an Walter Benjamin." *Der Monat* 18.216 (September 1966): 38–41. English: "Recollections of Walter Benjamin." Trans. Michael W. Jennings. *Smith* 338–45.

Boese, Carl. *Erinnerungen an die Entstehung und an die Aufnahmen eines der berühmtesten Stummfilme: DER GOLEM. Jüdische Lebenswelten im Deutschen*

## Works Cited

*Film*. Eds. Erika Gregor et al. Berlin: Freunde der deutschen Kinemathek, 1993.

Böhm, Adolf. "Wandlungen im Zionismus." *Vom Judentum* 139–54.

Bolz, Norbert and Bernd Witte, eds. *Passagen: Walter Benjamins Urgeschichte des XIX. Jahrhunderts.* Munich: Wilhelm Fink, 1991.

Boyarin, Jonathan. *Storm from Paradise: The Politics of Jewish Memory.* Minneapolis: U of Minnesota P, 1992.

Bradbury, Malcom, and James McFarlane, eds. *Modernism 1890–1930.* New York: Penguin, 1976.

Brenner, David A. *Marketing Identities: The Invention of Jewish Ethnicity in* Ost und West. Detroit: Wayne State UP, 1998.

Brenner, Michael. "1916: The German army order a census of Jewish soldiers, and Martin Buber launches his cultural magazine *Der Jude.*" Gilman and Zipes 348–54.

———. *The Renaissance of Jewish Culture in Weimar Germany.* New Haven: Yale UP, 1996.

Brod, Max. *Franz Kafka: A Biography.* Trans. G. Humphreys Roberts and Richard Winston. 1937. New York: Schocken, 1963.

———. *Über Franz Kafka.* 1974. Frankfurt a. M.: Fischer, 1993.

———. "Unsere Literaten und die Gemeinschaft." *Der Jude* 1 (1916–1917): 457ff.

———. "Zum Problem der Gemeinschaft." Kaznelson 8–10.

Brodritz, Julius, *Zum Ostjudenproblem.* Berlin, Rudolf Mosse, n.d.

Bronsen, David, ed. *Jews and Germans from 1860 to 1933: The Problematic Symbiosis.* Heidelberg: Carl Winter, 1979.

Buber, Martin. *Briefwechsel aus sieben Jahrzehnten.* Ed. Grete Schaeder. Vol. 1: 1897–1918. Gerlingen: Lambert Schneider, 1972.

———. *Der Jude und sein Judentum.* Gerlingen: Lambert Schneider, 1993.

———. "Die Losung." *Der Jude* 1 (1916/17): 1–3.

———. *Drei Reden über das Judentum.* 2nd ed. Berlin: Schocken, 1932.

———. *On Judaism.* Ed. Nahum N. Glatzer. New York: Schocken, 1967.

———. *The Origin and Meaning of Hasidism.* Ed. and trans. Maurice Friedman. New York: Horizon, 1960.

*Buchlicht Männlein und Engel der Geschichte: Walter Benjamin, Theoretiker der Moderne.* Ed. Werkbund-Archiv. Gießen: Anabas, 1990.

Bürger, Peter. *Theory of the Avant-Garde.* Trans. Michael Shaw. Minneapolis: U of Minnesota P, 1984.

# Works Cited

Cahn, Michael. "Das Schwanken zwischen Abfall und Wert: Zur kulturellen Hermeneutik des Sammlers." *Merkur* 45.8 (August 1991): 674–90.

Calvary, Moses. "Jiddisch." *Der Jude* 1 (1916–1917): 25–32.

Carmely, Klara Pomeranz. *Das Identitätsproblem jüdischer Autoren im deutschen Sprachraum: Von der Jahrhundertwende bis zu Hitler.* Königstein/Ts.: Scriptor, 1981.

Chamberlain, Houston Stewart. *Die Grundlagen des neunzehnten Jahrhunderts.* Munich: F. Bruckmann, 1899.

Claussen, Detlev, ed. *Vom Judenhaß zum Antisemitismus.* Darmstadt: Sammlung Luchterhand, 1987.

Cohen, Arthur A., ed. *The Jew: Essays from Martin Buber's Journal "Der Jude,"* *1916–1928.* Trans. Joachim Neugroschel. Birmingham: U of Alabama P, 1980.

Cohen, Gary B. "Jews in German Society: Prague, 1860–1914." *Central European History* 10.1 (March 1977): 28–54.

——. *The Politics of Ethnic Survival: Germans in Prague, 1861–1914.* Princeton: Princeton UP, 1981.

Cohn, Norman. *Warrant for Genocide: World Conspiracy and the Protocols of Zion.* New York: Harper & Row, 1967.

Cone, Michèle C. "Memorial to Walter Benjamin" *Sculpture* (March-April 1995): 16–17.

Cooper, Gabriele von Natzmer. *Kafka and Language.* Riverside, Calif.: Ariadne, 1991.

Cuddihy, John Murray. *The Ordeal of Civility: Freud, Marx, Lévi Strauss, and the Jewish Struggle with Modernity.* Boston: Beacon, 1987.

Dawidowicz, Lucy S., ed. *The Golden Tradition: Jewish Life and Thought in Eastern Europe.* New York: Schocken, 1967.

——. *The War Against the Jews.* New York: Bantam, 1975.

Deleuze, Gilles and Félix Guattari. *Kafka: Toward a Minor Literature.* 1975. Minneapolis: U of Minnesota P, 1986.

Deutscher, Isaac. *The Non-Jewish Jew.* New York: Oxford UP, 1968.

Diamant, Dora. "Mein Leben mit Franz Kafka." Koch 174–85.

*Die Ostjuden in Deutschland.* Berlin: Philo, 1924.

Diner, Dan. "Negative Symbiose – Deutsche und Juden nach Auschwitz." *Jüdisches Leben in Deutschland seit 1945.* Eds. Micha Brumlik et al. Frankfurt a. M.: Athenäum, 1988. 243–57. English: "Negative Symbiosis: Germans and

## Works Cited

Jews After Auschwitz." *Reworking the Past: Hitler, the Holocaust, and the Historians' Debate*. Ed. Peter Baldwin. Boston: Beacon, 1990. 251–61.

Dinter, Artur. *Die Sünde Wider das Blut*. 12th ed. Leipzig: Mathes und Throst, 1920.

Döblin, Alfred. "Alfred Döblin über ostjüdische Dichtung." *Das jüdische Echo* 38 (1924): 285–87.

———. *Reise in Polen*. 1926. Olten: Walter-Verlag, 1968. English: *Journey to Poland*. Trans. Joachim Neugroschel. Ed. Heinz Graber. New York: Paragon House, 1991.

Efron, John. *Defenders of the Race: Jewish Doctors & Race Science in Fin-de-siècle Europe*. New Haven: Yale UP, 1994.

Eisner, Lotte. *The Haunted Screen*. Trans. Roger Greaves. 1952. Berkeley: U of California P, 1973.

Elias, Norbert. *Über den Prozeß der Zivilisation*. 2 vols. Frankfurt a. M.: Suhrkamp, 1976.

Eliasberg, Alexander, ed. and trans. *Ostjüdische Erzähler*. Weimar: Gustav Kiepenheuer, 1916.

Elsaesser, Thomas. "Social Mobility and the Fantastic: German Silent Cinema." *Wide Angle* 5.2 (1982): 14–25.

Fassbinder, Rainer Werner. *Der Müll, die Stadt, und der Tod*. 1975. Frankfurt a. M.: Verlag der Autoren, 1981.

———. *Plays*. Ed. and trans. Denis Calandra. New York: PAJ Publications, 1985.

———. *Stücke 3*. Frankfurt a. M.: Suhrkamp, 1976.

Felix, David. *Walther Rathenau and the Weimar Republic: The Politics of Reparations*. Baltimore: Johns Hopkins UP, 1971.

Felstiner, John. "Kafka and the Golem: Translating Paul Celan." *Prooftexts* 6.2 (May 1986): 172–83.

Ferris, David, ed. *Walter Benjamin: Theoretical Questions*. Stanford: Stanford UP, 1996.

Finkielkraut, Alain. *The Imaginary Jew*. Trans. Kevin O'Neill and David Suchoff. Lincoln: U of Nebraska P, 1994.

Fischer, Gerhard, ed. *'With a Sharpened Axe of Reason': Approaches to Walter Benjamin*. Oxford: Berg, 1996.

Fischer, Michal M. J. "Ethnicity and the Post-Modern Arts of Memory." *Writ-*

*ing Culture: The Poetics and Politics of Ethnography*. Eds. James Clifford and George E. Marcus. Berkeley: U of California P, 1986. 194–233.

Fishman, Joshua A. *Ideology, Society and Language: The Odyssey of Nathan Birnbaum*. Ann Arbor, Mich.: Karoma, 1987.

Folkers, Horst. "Die gerettete Geschichte: Ein Hinweis auf Walter Benjamins Begriff der Erinnerung." Assmann and Harth 363–77.

Ford, Henry. *The Jewish Question: A Selection of Articles (1920–1922)*. Paris: Editions R.I.S.S., 1931.

Franzos, Karl Emil. *Aus Halb-Asien: Culturbilder aus Galizien, der Bukowina, Südrussland und Rumänien*. 2nd ed. 1876. Leipzig: Breitkopf and Hartel, 1883.

Friedemann, Adolf. "Die Bedeutung der Ostjuden in Deutschland." *Süddeutsche Monatshefte* (February 1916): 674–81.

———. *Wir und die Ostjuden*. Berlin: Julius Sittenfeld, 1916.

Friedländer, Saul. "Die politischen Veränderungen der Kriegszeit und ihre Auswirkungen auf die Judenfrage." Mosse 27–65.

Friedman, Lester D. "The Edge of Knowledge: Jews as Monsters/Jews as Victims." *Melus* 11.3 (Fall 1984): 49–62.

Friedman, Maurice. *Martin Buber's Life and Work: The Early Years, 1878–1923*. New York: Dutton, 1981.

Friedmann, Friedrich Georg. *Von Cohen zu Benjamin: Zum Problem deutschjüdischer Existenz*. Einsiedeln: Johannes Verlag, 1981.

Friedmann, Lazarus. *Die Emanzipation der Ostjuden und ihr Einfluß auf die Westjuden: Ein Wort zur rechten Zeit*. Frankfurt a. M.: J. Kaufmann, 1917.

Frisby, David. *Fragments of Modernity: Theories of Modernity in the Work of Simmel, Kracauer and Benjamin*. Cambridge, Mass.: MIT P, 1988.

Fritz, Georg. *Die Ostjudenfrage–Zionismus & Grenzschluß*. Munich: J. F. Lehmann, 1915.

Fuchs, Eduard. *Juden in der Karikatur*. Munich: Albert Langen, 1921.

Fussell, Paul. *The Great War and Modern Memory*. New York: Oxford UP, 1975.

Garb, Tamar. "Introduction: Modernity, Identity, Textuality." *The Jew in the Text: Modernity and the Construction of Identity*. London: Thames and Hudson, 1995. 20–30.

Garber, Klaus. *Rezeption und Rettung: Drei Studien zu Walter Benjamin*. Tübingen: Niemeyer, 1987.

Gay, Peter. *Freud, Jews and Other Germans: Masters and Victims in Modernist Culture*. New York: Oxford UP, 1978.

————. *Weimar Culture: The Outsider as Insider*. New York: Harper & Row, 1968.

Gay, Ruth. "Inventing the Shtetl." *The American Scholar* 53 (Summer 1984): 329–49.

Geisel, Eike, ed. *Im Scheunenviertel*. Berlin: Severin und Siedler, 1981.

Gelder, Ken. *Reading the Vampire*. New York: Routledge, 1994.

Geller, Jay. "Blood Sin: Syphilis and the Construction of Jewish Identity." *Faultline* 1 (1992): 21–48.

Geyer, Michael, and Miriam Hansen. "German-Jewish Memory and National Consciousness." *Holocaust Rembrance*. Ed. Geoffrey Hartman. Oxford: Blackwell, 1994, 175–90.

Giles, Steve, ed. *Theorizing Modernism: Essays in Critical Theory*. New York: Routledge, 1993.

Gillis, John R., ed. *Commemorations: The Politics of National Identity*. Princeton: Princeton UP, 1994.

Gilloch, Graeme. *Myth and Metropolis: Walter Benjamin and the City*. Oxford: Polity, 1996.

Gilman, Sander L. *Franz Kafka, the Jewish Patient*. New York: Routledge, 1995.

————. *Freud, Race, and Gender*. Princeton: Princeton UP, 1993.

————. *Inscribing the Other*. Lincoln: U of Nebraska P, 1991.

————. *Jewish Self-Hatred: Anti-Semitism and the Hidden Language of the Jews*. Baltimore: Johns Hopkins UP, 1986.

————. *The Jew's Body*. New York: Routledge, 1991.

————. "The Rediscovery of the Eastern Jews: German Jews in the East, 1890–1918." Bronsen 338–65.

Gilman, Sander L., and Jack Zipes, eds. *The Yale Companion to Jewish Writing and Thought in German Culture, 1096–1996*. New Haven: Yale UP, 1997.

Gobineau, Arthur de. *Essai sur l'inégalité des races humaines*. 1853–1855. Paris: Firmin-Didot, 1884.

Goldmann, Felix. *Die Stellung des deutschen Rabbiners zur Ostjudenfrage*. Frankfurt a. M.: J. Kauffmann, 1916.

Goldstein, Moritz. "Arnold Zweig." *Juden in der deutschen Literatur: Essays über zeitgenössische Schriftsteller*. Ed. Gustav Krojanker. Berlin: Welt-Verlag, 1922. 241–50.

————. "Deutsch-jüdischer Parnaß." *Der Kunstwart und Kulturwart* 25.11

## Works Cited

(March 1912): 281–94. Rpt. in Goldstein, *Berliner Jahre: Erinnerungen 1880–1933*. Munich: Verlag Dokumentation, 1977. 213–24.

———. "German Jewry's Dilemma: The Story of a Provocative Essay." *Leo Baeck Institute Year Book* 2 (1957): 236–54.

Goldstücker, Eduard. "Kafkas Werk in unserer Erfahrung." *Was Bleibt von Franz Kafka?* Ed. Wendelin Schmidt-Dengler. *Schriftenreihe der Kafka-Gesellschaft* 1. Vienna: Baumüller, 1985. 165–71.

Goren, A. "Judah L. Magnes' Trip to Przedborz." *Studies in Contemporary Jewry* I (1984): 163–75.

Greenberg, Clement. "The Jewishness of Franz Kafka." *Commentary* 19.4 (April 1955): 320–24.

Greenblatt, Stephen. *Shakespearean Negotiations: The Circulation of Social Energy in Renaissance England*. Berkeley: U of California P, 1988.

Greve, Ludwig, et al., eds. *Hätte ich das Kino! Die Schriftsteller und der Stummfilm*. Stuttgart: Ernst Klett, 1976.

Grimm, Gunter E., and Hans-Peter Bayerdörfer, eds. *Im Zeichen Hiobs: Jüdische Schriftsteller und deutsche Literatur im 20. Jahrhundert*. Königstein/Ts.: Athenäum, 1986.

Gronemann, Sammy. *Hawdoloh und Zapfenstreich: Erinnerungen an die ostjüdische Etappe, 1916–1918*. Berlin: Jüdischer Verlag, 1924.

Gross, David. *The Past in Ruins: Tradition and the Critique of Modernity*. Amherst: U of Massachussetts P, 1992.

Grossman, Jeffrey Alan. *Language and Control: Jews, Germans and the Discourse on Yiddish in German Literature from the Enlightenment to the Second Empire*. Rochester, N.Y.: Boydell and Brewer/U of Rochester P, forthcoming.

Grötzinger, Karl Erich. *Kafka und Kabbalah*. Frankfurt a. M.: Eichborn, 1992.

Habermas, Jürgen. "Bewußtmachende oder rettende Kritik–die Aktualität Walter Benjamins." *Zur Aktualität Walter Benjamins*. Ed. Siegfried Unseld. Frankfurt a. M.: Suhrkamp, 1970. 173–223. English: "Consciousness-raising or Rescuing Critique." Trans. Frederick Lawrence. Smith 90–128.

———. *Der philosophische Diskurs der Moderne*. Frankfurt a. M.: Suhrkamp, 1985. English: *The Philosophical Discourse of Modernity*. Trans. Fredrick Lawrence. Cambridge, Mass.: MIT P, 1987.

Hall, Stuart. "Cultural Identity and Cinematic Representation." *Framework* 36 (1989): 68–81.

# Works Cited

Hamerow, Theodore S. "Cravat Jews and Caftan Jews." *Commentary* 77.5 (May 1984): 29–38.

Handelman, Susan A. *Fragments of Redemption: Jewish Thought and Literary Theory in Benjamin, Scholem and Levinas.* Bloomington: Indiana UP, 1991.

Hansen, Miriam. *Babel and Babylon: Spectorship in American Silent Film.* Cambridge, Mass.: Harvard UP, 1991.

Harshav, Benjamin. *The Meaning of Yiddish.* Berkeley: U of California P, 1990.

Hart, Mitchell. *Social Science and the Politics of Jewish Identity.* Stanford: Stanford UP, 1999.

Haumann, Heiko. *Geschichte der Ostjuden.* Munich: dtv, 1990.

Havel, Václav. "On Kafka." *The New York Review of Books* 37.14 (27 September 1990): 19.

Heine, Heinrich. "Über Polen" (1923). *Werke.* Vol. 2. Ed. Wolfgang Preisendanz. Frankfurt a. M.: Insel, 1968. 63–88.

Helzel, Florence B., ed. *Shtetl Life.* Berkeley, Calif.: Judah L. Magnes Museum, 1993.

Herf, Jeffrey. *Divided Memory: The Nazi Past in the Two Germanys.* Cambridge, Mass.: Harvard UP, 1997.

———. *Reactionary Modernism: Technology, Culture, and Politics in Weimar and the Third Reich.* New York: Cambridge UP, 1984.

Hermand, Jost. *Arnold Zweig.* Reinbeck bei Hamburg: Rowohlt, 1990.

———. "Arnold Zweigs Judentum." *Jüdische Intelligenz in Deutschland.* Eds. Jost Hermand and Gert Mattenklott. Hamburg: Argument, 1988. 70–95.

———. *Engagement als Lebensform: Über Arnold Zweig* Berlin: Edition Stigma, 1992.

Hermann, Georg. "Zur Frage der Westjuden." *Neue jüdische Monatshefte* 3.19/20 (10/25 July 1919): 399–405.

Hertz, Deborah. *Jewish High Society in Old Regime Berlin.* New Haven: Yale UP, 1988.

Herzog, Andreas. "'Vom Judentum:' Anmerkungen zum Sammelband des Vereins 'Bar Kochba.'" Krolop and Zimmerman 45–58.

Herzog, Elizabeth, and Mark Zborowski. *Life is With the People: The Culture of the Shtetl.* 1952. New York: Schocken, 1962.

Heuss, Theodor. *Hans Poelzig: Das Lebensbild eines deutschen Baumeisters.* Tübingen: Ernst Wasmuth, 1948.

## Works Cited

Hitler, Adolf. *Das Parteiprogramm der NSDAP*. Ed. Alfred Rosenberg. 1922. Munich: F. Eher, 1941.

———. *Mein Kampf*. Trans. Ralph Manheim. 1925. Boston: Houghton Mifflin, 1971.

Hoberman, J. *Bridge of Light: Yiddish Film Between Two Worlds*. New York: Modern Museum of Art/Schocken, 1991.

Hobsbawm, E. J. *Nations and Nationalism Since 1780: Programme, Myth, Reality*. Cambridge: Cambridge UP, 1990.

Holdengräber, Paul. "Between the Profane and the Redemptive: The Collector as Possessor in Walter Benjamin's *Passagen-Werk*." *History & Memory* 4.2 (Fall/Winter 1992): 96–128.

———. "Unpacking Benjamin's Library: Biblomania in Dark Times." *The Library of Babel*. Ed. Todd Alden. Buffalo, N.Y.: The Arts Center, 1991, 13–25.

Homeyer, Fritz. *Deutsche Juden als Bibliophile und Antiquare*. Tübingen: J. C. B. Mohr, 1963.

Honneth, Axel. "A Communicative Disclosure of the Past: On the Relation Between Anthropology and Philosophy of History in Walter Benjamin." Trans. John Farrell. *New Formations* 20 (Summer 1993): 83–94.

Horkheimer, Max, and Theodor W. Adorno. *Dialektik der Aufklärung*. 1947. Frankfurt a. M.: Fischer, 1988. English: *Dialectic of Enlightenment*. Trans. John Cumming. New York: Seabury Press, 1972.

Horkheimer, Max. "Über die deutschen Juden." *Der Spannungsbogen: Festgabe für Paul Tillich zum 75. Geburtstag*. Stuttgart: Evangelisches Verlagswerk, 1961). 131–47.

Hüppauf, Bernd. "Ende der Hoffnung–Anfang der Illusionen? Der Erste Weltkrieg in den Schriften deutscher Juden." *Kontroversen, alte und neue. Akten des VII. Internationalen Germanisten-Kongresses*. Göttingen 1985, Vol. 5. Tübingen: Niemeyer, 1986. 196–207.

Huyssen, Andreas. *Twilight Memories: Marking Time in a Culture of Amnesia*. New York: Routledge, 1995.

Huyssen, Andreas, and David Bathrick, eds. *Modernity and the Text: Revisions of German Modernism*. New York: Columbia UP, 1989.

Iggers, Wilma Abeles, ed. *The Jews of Bohemia and Moravia: A Historical Reader*. Trans. Wilma Abeles Iggers et al. Detroit: Wayne State UP, 1992.

Isenberg, Noah. "Invesigations of Character: Jewish Exiles Face the 'German Question.'" *German Politics and Society* 13.3 (Fall 1995): 81–88.

# Works Cited

———. "October 29, 1920: Paul Wegener's *Der Golem: Wie er in die Welt kam* debuts in Berlin." Gilman and Zipes 384–89.

Janouch, Gustav. *Conversations with Kafka*. Trans. Goronwy Rees. 1968. London: Encounter, 1985.

Jay, Martin. "Experience Without a Subject: Walter Benjamin and the Novel." *New Formations* 20 (Summer 1993): 145–55.

———. "'The Aesthetic Ideology' as Ideology: Or What Does It Mean to Aestheticize Politics?" *Force Fields*. New York: Routledge, 1993. 71–83.

Jens, Walter. "Ein Jude namens Kafka." *Porträts deutsch-jüdischer Geistesgeschichte*. Ed. Thilo Koch. Cologne: M. DuMont, 1961. 179–203.

———. "Franz Kafka." *Es ist ein Weinen in der Welt: Hommage für deutsche Juden unseres Jahrhunderts*. Ed. Hans Jürgen Schultz. Stuttgart: Quell, 1990. 263–83.

*The Jews in the Eastern War Zone*. New York: American Jewish Committee, 1916.

Jünger, Ernst. "Großstadt und Land." *Deutsches Volkstum* 8 (1926): 577–81.

Kaes, Anton. "Film der Weimarer Republik: Motor der Moderne." *Geschichte des deutschen Films*. Eds. Wolfgang Jacobsen et al. Stuttgart: Metzler, 1993. 38–100.

Kafka, Franz. *Briefe*. Ed. Max Brod. Frankfurt a. M.: Fischer, 1958.

———. *Briefe an Felice*. Eds. Erich Heller and Jürgen Born. Frankfurt a. M.: Fischer, 1967. English: *Letters to Felice*. Trans. James Stern and Elisabeth Duckworth. New York: Schocken, 1973.

———. *Briefe an Milena*. Ed. Willy Haas. Frankfurt a. M.: Fischer, 1952. English: *Letters to Milena*. Trans. Philip Boehm. New York: Schocken, 1990.

———. *Erzählungen*. Ed. Max Brod. 1935. Frankfurt a. M.: Fischer, 1989. English: *The Complete Stories*. Trans. Willa and Edwin Muir. Ed. Nahum N. Glatzer. New York: Schocken, 1971.

———. *Hochzeitsvorbereitungen auf dem Lande und andere Prosa aus dem Nachlaß*. Ed. Max Brod. Frankfurt a. M.: Fischer, 1989.

———. *Letters to Friends, Family, and Editors*. Trans. Richard and Clara Winston. Ed. Max Brod. New York: Schocken, 1977.

———. *Letter to His Father*. Trans. Ernst Kaiser and Eithne Wilkens. New York: Schocken, 1966.

———. *Tagebücher, 1910–1923*. Ed. Max Brod. Frankfurt a. M.: Fischer, 1989. English: *Diaries*. Trans. Martin Greenberg et al. Ed. Max Brod. 1948. New York: Schocken, 1976.

# Works Cited

Kahn, Lothar. "Arnold Zweig: From Zionism to Marxism." *Mirrors of the Jewish Mind*. New York: Thomas Yoseloff, 1968. 194–209.

Kany, Roland. *Mnemosyne als Programm: Geschichte, Erinnerung und die Andacht zum Unbedeutenden im Werk von Usener, Warburg und Benjamin*. Tübingen: Niemeyer, 1987.

Kaplan, Marion A. *The Making of the Jewish Middle Class: Women, Family and Identity in Imperial Germany*. New York: Oxford UP, 1991.

Karavan, Dani. "Dani Karavan on the 'Passages' Memorial to Walter Benjamin: An Interview with Ingrid and Konrad Scheurmann." Scheurmann and Scheurmann 255–64.

Kaufmann, Fritz Mordechai, and Werner Senator. *Die Einwanderung der Ostjuden in Deutschland: Eine Gefahr oder ein sozialpolitisches Problem?* Berlin: Welt, 1920.

Kaufmann, Fritz Mordechai, et al. "Zum Programm der Freistatt." *Die Freistatt: Alljüdische Revue*. 1.1 (April 1913): 3–5.

Kaznelson, Siegmund, et al., eds. *Das jüdische Prag: Eine Sammelschrift*. Prague: Selbstwehr Verlag, 1917.

Kershaw, Ian. *Hitler*. London: Longman, 1991.

Kestenberg-Glatstein, Ruth. "The Jews Between Czechs and Germans in the Historic Lands, 1848–1918." *The Jews of Czechoslovakia*. Vol. 1. Philadelphia: Jewish Publication Society of America, 1968. 21–71.

Kiderlen, Elisabeth, ed. *Deutsch-jüdische Normalität . . . Fassbinders Sprengsätze*. Frankfurt a. M.: Pflasterstrand, 1985.

Kieval, Hillel. *The Making of Czech Jewry: National Conflict and Jewish Society in Bohemia, 1870–1918*. New York: Oxford UP, 1988.

Kleinschmidt, Sebastian. "Die Stadt als Landschaft." In Walter Benjamin. *Berolina*. East Berlin: Union, 1987. 199–205.

Koch, Gertrud. *Die Einstellung ist die Einstellung: Visuelle Konstruktionen des Judentums*. Frankfurt a. M.: Suhrkamp, 1992.

Koch, Hans-Gerd, ed. *"Als Kafka mir entgegenkam . . ." Erinnerungen an Franz Kafka*. Berlin: Wagenbach, 1995.

Kohn, Hans. "Gleitwort." *Vom Judentum* v–ix.

Konrad, George. "The Modernization of the Jews." Trans. James Andrew Tucker. *Partisan Review* 63.3 (1996): 571–79.

Kracauer, Siegfried. *Das Ornament der Masse*. Frankfurt a. M.: Suhrkamp, 1963.

## Works Cited

————. *From Caligari to Hitler: A Psychological Study of the German Film.* Princeton: Princeton UP, 1947.

————. *Theory of Film: The Redemption of Physical Reality.* New York: Oxford UP, 1960.

Krolop, Kurt, and Hans-Dieter Zimmermann, eds. *Kafka und Prag.* Berlin: Walter de Gruyter, 1994.

Ladd, Brian. *The Ghosts of Berlin: Confronting German History in the Urban Landscape.* Chicago: U of Chicago P, 1997.

Landauer, Gustav. "Ostjuden und deutsches Reich." *Der Jude* 2 (1916/17): 436–37.

Laqueur, Walter. *A History of Zionism.* 1972. New York: Schocken, 1976.

————. "The German Youth Movement and the 'Jewish Question.'" *Leo Baeck Institute Year Book* 6 (1961): 193–205.

————. *Young Germany: A History of the German Youth Movement.* New York: Basic Books, 1962.

Le Goff, Jacques. *History and Memory.* Trans. Steven Rendall and Elizabeth Claman. 1977–82. New York: Columbia UP, 1992.

Ledig, Elfriede. "Making Movie Myths: Paul Wegener's 'The Golem.'" Bilski 36–43.

————. *Paul Wegeners Golem-Filme im Kontext fantastischer Literatur.* Munich: Verlegergemeinschaft, 1989.

Leppin, Paul. "Die jüdische Kolonie." Kaznelson 5–6.

Levin, David J. *Richard Wagner, Fritz Lang, and the Nibelungen: The Dramaturgy of Disavowal.* Princeton: Princeton UP, 1998.

Lichtenstein, Heiner, ed. *Die Fassbinder-Kontroverse oder Das Ende der Schonzeit.* Königstein/Ts.: Athenäum, 1986.

Liebersohn, Harry. *Fate and Utopia in German Sociology, 1870–1923.* Cambridge, Mass.: MIT P, 1988.

Lindner, Burkhardt. "*Das Passagen-Werk*, die *Berliner Kindheit* und die Archäologie des 'Jüngstvergangenen.'" *Passagen: Walter Benjamins Urgeschichte des XIX. Jahrhunderts.* Eds. Norbert Bolz and Bernd Witte. Munich: Wilhelm Fink, 1991, 27–48.

Loewenberg, Peter. "Walther Rathenau and Henry Kissinger: The Jew as Modern Statesman in Two Political Cultures." *Leo Baeck Memorial Lecture* 24 (1980).

## Works Cited

Löwy, Michael. *Redemption and Utopia: Jewish Libertarian Thought in Central Europe.* Trans. Hope Heany. Stanford: Stanford UP, 1992.

Lukács, Georg. "Gedanken zu einer Ästhetik des Kinos" (1913). *Theorie des Kinos. Ideoligiekritik der Traumfabrik.* Ed. Karsten Witte. Frankfurt a. M.: Suhrkamp, 1972. 142–48.

Maier, Charles S. *The Unmasterable Past: History, Holocaust, and German National Identity.* Cambridge, Mass.: Harvard UP, 1988.

Markovits, Andrei S., et al. "Rainer Werner Fassbinder's *Garbage, the City, and Death*: Renewed Antagonisms in the Complex Relationship Between Jews and Germans in the Federal Republic of Germany." *New German Critique* 38 (Spring/Summer 1986): 3–27.

Markovits, Andrei S., and Beth Simone Noveck. "1985: Rainer Werner Fassbinder's play *Garbage, the City and Death,* produced in Frankfurt, marks a key year of remembrance in Germany." Gilman and Zipes 805–11.

Markovits, Andrei S., and Simon Reich. *The German Predicament: Memory and Power in the New Europe.* Ithaca, N.Y.: Cornell UP, 1997.

Massing, Paul. *Rehearsal to Destruction: A Study of Political Anti-Semitism in Imperial Germany.* New York: Harper, 1949.

Mattenklott, Gert. "Ostjuden in Berlin." *Die Reise nach Berlin.* Ed. Berliner Festspiele. Berlin: Siedler, 1988.

Maurer, Trude. *Ostjuden in Deutschland 1918–1933.* Hamburg: Hans Christians, 1986.

Mautner, Friedrich. "Der Prager Zionismus." Kaznelson 53.

Mayer, Hans. "Das Gedächtnis und die Geschichte: Gedanken beim Aufschreiben von Erinnerungen." Moses and Schöne 13–24.

———. *Der Zeitgenosse Walter Benjamin.* Frankfurt a. M.: Jüdischer Verlag, 1992.

Mayer, Max. "A German Jew Goes East." *Leo Baeck Institute Year Book* 3 (1958): 344–57.

Mayer, Michael A. *Jewish Identity in the Modern World.* Seattle: U of Washington P, 1990.

McCole, John. *Walter Benjamin and the Antinomies of Tradition.* Ithaca, N.Y.: Cornell UP, 1993.

Mehlman, Jeffrey. *Walter Benjamin for Children: An Essay on His Radio Years.* Chicago: U of Chicago P, 1993.

## Works Cited

Mendes-Flohr, Paul R. "Fin de Siècle Orientalism, the *Ostjuden*, and the Aesthetics of Jewish Self-Affirmation." *Divided Passions: Jewish Intellectuals and the Experience of Modernity.* Detroit: Wayne State UP, 1991. 77–132.

Mendes-Flohr, Paul R., and Jehuda Reinharz, eds. *The Jew in the Modern World.* New York: Oxford UP, 1980.

Meyrink, Gustav. *The Golem.* Trans. Madge Pemberton. New York: Dover, 1976.

Michaels, Walter Benn. *Our America: Nativism, Modernism, Pluralism.* Durham, N.C.: Duke UP, 1995.

Midgley, David et al., eds. *Arnold Zweig–Poetik, Judentum und Politik.* Bern et al.: Peter Lang, 1989.

Milfull, Helen. "Franz Kafka – The Jewish Context." *Leo Baeck Institute Year Book* 23 (1978): 227–38.

———. "'Weder Katze noch Lamm?' Kafkas Kritik des 'Westjüdischen.'" Grimm and Bayerdörfer 178–92.

Missac, Pierre. *Walter Benjamin's Passages.* Trans. Shierry Weber Nicholsen. Cambridge, Mass.: MIT P, 1995.

Mitzman, Arthur. *Sociology and Estrangement: Three Sociologists of Imperial Germany.* New York: Knopf, 1973.

Moses, Stéphane, and Albrecht Schöne, eds. *Juden in der deutschen Literatur.* Frankfurt a. M.: Suhrkamp, 1986.

Moses, Stéphane. "Brecht und Benjamin als Kafka-Interpreten." Moses and Schöne 237–56.

———. "The Theological-Political Model of History in the Thought of Walter Benjamin." *History & Memory* 2 (1989): 5–33.

———. "Zu Benjamins Begriff des Eingedenkens." *Buchlicht Männlein und Engel der Geschichte* 100–101.

Mosse, George L. *Confronting the Nation: Jewish and Western Nationalism.* Hanover, N.H.: Brandeis UP, 1993.

———. *German Jews Beyond Judaism.* Bloomington: Indiana UP, 1985.

———. *Germans and Jews: The Right, the Left, and the Search for a "Third Force" in pre-Nazi Germany.* New York: H. Fertig, 1970.

———. "The Jews and the German War Experience." *Leo Baeck Memorial Lecture* 21 (1977): 3–28.

Mosse, Werner E., ed. *Deutsches Judentum in Krieg und Revolution 1916–1923.* Tubingen: J. C. B. Mohr, 1971.

# Works Cited

Moyn, Samuel. "German Jewry and the Question of Identity: Historiography and Theory." *Leo Baeck Intitute Year Book* 41 (1996): 291–308.

Mühsam, Erich. "Zur Judenfrage." *Die Weltbühne* 16 (25 November 1920): 643–47.

Müller, Hans-Harald. "'Zum Problem des jüdischen Dichters in Deutschland': Arnold Zweigs Auseinandersetzungen mit dem Judentum 1910–1933." Midgley 155–70.

Myers, David N. "'Distant Relatives Happening into the Same Inn': The Meeting of East and West as Literary Theme and Cultural Ideal." *Jewish Social Studies* 1.2 (Winter 1995): 75–100.

Nägele, Rainer, ed. *Benjamin's Ground: New Readings of Walter Benjamin.* Detroit: Wayne State UP, 1988.

Nathan, Paul, ed. *Ostjuden in Deutschland.* Berlin: Philo, 1921.

Naumann, Max. *Vom nationaldeutschen Juden.* Berlin: Albert Goldschmidt, 1920.

Neugroschel, Joachim, ed. and trans. *The Shtetl.* Woodstock, N.Y.: Overlook Press, 1989.

Nora, Pierre. "Between Memory and History: Les Lieux de Mémoire." Trans. Marc Roudebush. *Representations* 26 (1989): 7–25.

Northey, Anthoney. "Die Kafkas: Juden? Christen? Tschechen? Deutsche?" Krolop and Zimmermann 11–32.

———. *Kafkas Mischpoche.* Berlin: Wagenbach, 1988. English: *Kafka's Relatives: Their Lives and His Writing.* New Haven: Yale UP, 1991.

"Ost und West." *Ost und West* 1.1 (1901): 2–3.

Pachter, Henry. *Weimar Etudes.* New York: Columbia UP, 1982.

Pan, David. "Kafka as a Populist: Re-reading 'In the Penal Colony.'" *Telos* 101 (Fall 1994): 3–40.

Pawel, Ernst. "Der Prager Zionismus zu Kafkas Zeit." Krolop and Zimmermann 33–43.

———. *The Nightmare of Reason: A Life of Franz Kafka.* New York: Vantage, 1984.

Pazi, Margarita. "Franz Kafka, Max Brod und der 'Prager Kreis.'" *Franz Kafka und das Judentum.* Eds. Karl Erich Grözinger et al. Frankfurt a. M.: Jüdischer Verlag bei Athenäum, 1987. 71–92.

Pehnt, Wolfgang. "La porta sul prodigioso: Le architetture di Hans Poelzig per il film 'Der Golem.'" *Domus* 22 (November 1987): 83–85.

# Works Cited

Peretz, I. L. *My Memoirs* (1913–15). Trans. Seymour Levitan. *The I. L. Peretz Reader*. Ed. Ruth Wisse. New York: Schocken, 1990. 265–359.

Perutz, Leo. *Nachts unter der steinernen Brücke: Ein Roman aus dem alten Prag*. Frankfurt a. M.: Frankfurter Verlaganstalt, 1953. English: *By Night Under the Stone Bridge*. Trans. Eric Mosbacher. New York: Arcade, 1989.

Peukert, Detlev J. K. *The Weimar Republic*. Trans. Richard Deveson. 1987. New York: Hill and Wang, 1993.

Phillips, Patricia C. "Making Memories." *Sculpture* 16.3 (March 1997): 22–27.

Pizer, John. "Reconstellating the Shards of the Text: On Walter Benjamin's German/Jewish Memory." *German Studies Review* 18.2 (May 1995): 275–90.

Plessner, Helmuth. *Grenzen der Gemeinschaft: Eine Kritik des sozialen Radikalismus*. Bonn: Friedrich Cohen, 1924.

Poppel, Stephen M. *Zionism in Germany 1897–1933: The Shaping of Jewish Identity*. Philadelphia: Jewish Publication Society of America, 1977.

Puttnies, Hans, and Gary Smith, eds. *Benjaminiana*. Gießen: Anabas, 1991.

Rabinbach, Anson. "Between Enlightenment and Apocalypse: Benjamin, Bloch and Modern Jewish Messianism." *New German Critique* 34 (Winter 1985): 78–124.

Rabinbach, Anson, and Jack Zipes, eds. *Germans and Jews Since the Holocaust: The Changing Situation in West Germany*. New York: Holmes & Meier, 1986.

———. "Introduction." *The Correspondence of Walter Benjamin and Gershom Scholem, 1932–1940*. Trans. Gary Smith and Andre Lefevre. Ed. Gershom Scholem. Cambridge, Mass.: Harvard UP, 1992. vii–xxxviii.

———. "1944: Hannah Arendt writes 'The Jew as Pariah: A Hidden Tradition,' in which she describes the forgotten tradition of Jewish 'conscious pariahs.'" Gilman and Zipes 605–613.

———. *The Human Motor: Energy, Fatigue, and the Origins of Modernity*. New York: Basic Books, 1990.

Rathenau, Walther. *Schriften*. Eds. Arnold Hartung et al. Berlin: Berlin Verlag, 1965.

Reichmann, Eva. "Der Bewußtseinwandel der deutschen Juden." Mosse (Werner) 511–612.

Reich-Ranicki, Marcel. *Deutsche Literatur in West und Ost*. Munich: Piper, 1963.

Reinharz, Jehuda, ed. *Dokumente zur Geschichte des deutschen Zionismus 1882–1933*. Tübingen: J. C. B. Mohr, 1981.

# Works Cited

Robert, Marthe. *As Lonely as Franz Kafka*. Trans. Ralph Manheim. 1979. New York: Schocken, 1986.

Robertson, Ritchie. "'Antizionismus, Zionismus': Kafka's Responses to Jewish Nationalism." *Paths and Labyrinths*. Eds. J. P. Stern and J. J. White. London: Institute for Germanic Studies, 1985. 25–42.

———. *Kafka: Judaism, Politics, and Literature*. Oxford: Clarendon, 1985.

Rozenblit, Marsha L. *The Jews of Vienna, 1867–1914: Assimilation and Identity*. Albany: SUNY P, 1983.

Roiphe, Rebecca and Daniel Cooper, "Batman and the Jewish Question." *The New York Times* 2 July 1992: A19.

Rose, Gillian. "Walter Benjamin out of the Sources of Judaism." *Judaism and Modernity*. Oxford: Basil Blackwell, 1993. 175–210.

Rose, Paul Lawrence. *German Question/Jewish Question: Revolutionary Antisemitism from Kant to Wagner*. Princeton: Princeton UP, 1990.

Roth, Joseph. "Döblin im Osten." *Frankfurter Zeitung* 31 January 1926.

———. *Juden auf Wanderschaft*. 1927. Cologne: Kiepenheuer and Witsch, 1976.

Rozenblit, Marsha L. *The Jews of Vienna, 1867–1914: Assimilation and Identity*. Albany: SUNY P, 1983.

Rybár, Ctibor. "Golem; or Myths and Legends of the Prague Ghetto." *Jewish Prague*. Prague: 1991. 217–26.

Schalit, Moses. "Uebersicht über die jiddische Literatur." *Die Freistatt* 1.1 (April 1913): 176–80.

Scheffauer, Hermann G. "The Vivyfying of Space" (1920). *Introduction to the Art of the Movies*. Ed. Lewis Jacobs. New York: Noonday Press, 1960.

Scherbel, Fritz. "Ein ost-jüdischer Weltmeister." *Jüdische Turn- und Sport-Zeitung* [*Ostjuden Sonderheft*] 21 January 1920: 14.

Scheurmann, Ingrid, and Konrad Scheurmann, eds. *Für Walter Benjamin*. Frankfurt a. M.: Suhrkamp, 1992. English: *For Walter Benjamin*. Trans. Timothy Nevill. Bonn: Inter Nationes, 1993.

Scheurmann, Konrad. "Borders, Thresholds, Passages: On Dani Karavan's Concept for a Memorial to Walter Benjamin." I. Scheurmann and K. Scheurmann 237–53.

Scheurmann, Konrad, and Ingrid Scheurmann, eds. *Dani Karavan: Hommage an Walter Benjamin. Der Gedenkort "Passagen" in Portbou*. Mainz: Philipp von Zabern, 1995.

# Works Cited

Scholem, Gershom. "Die Vorstellung vom Golem in ihren tellurischen und magischen Beziehungen." *Zur Kabbala und ihrer Symbolik.* Zurich: Rhein-Verlag, 1960.

———. *On Jews and Judaism in Crisis.* Ed. Werner J. Dannhauser. New York: Schocken, 1976.

———. "On the Social Psychology of the Jews in Germany: 1900–1933." Bronsen 9–32.

———. "The Golem of Prague and the Golem of Rehuvot." *The Messianic Idea in Judaism.* New York: Schocken, 1971.

———. *Von Berlin nach Jerusalem.* Frankfurt a. M.: Suhrkamp, 1977. English: *From Berlin to Jerusalem.* Trans. Harry Zohn. New York: Schocken, 1980.

———. "Walter Benjamin." *Judaica* II. Frankfurt a. M.: Suhrkamp, 1970. 193–226. English: "Walter Benjamin." Trans. Lux Furtmüller. *On Jews and Judaism in Crisis.* 172–97.

———. *Walter Benjamin–die Geschichte einer Freundschaft.* Frankfurt a. M.: Suhrkamp, 1975. English: *Walter Benjamin: The Story of a Friendship.* Trans. Harry Zohn. Philadelphia: Jewish Publication Society of America, 1981.

Schöne, Albrecht. "'Diese nach dem jüdischen Vorbild erbaute Arche': Walter Benjamins *Deutsche Menschen.*" Moses and Schöne 350–65.

Schönert, Jörg. "'. . . mehr als die Juden weiß von Gott und der Welt doch niemand': Zu Arnold Zweigs Roman *Der Streit um den Sergeanten Grischa.*" Grimm and Bayerdörfer 223–42.

Segel, Binjamin W. *A Lie and a Libel: The History of the "Protocols of the Elders of Zion."* Ed. and Trans. Richard S. Levy. 1926. Lincoln: U of Nebraska P, 1995.

Shapiro, Susan E. "The Uncanny Jew: A Brief History of an Image." *Judaism* 46.1 (Winter 1997): 63–78.

Showalter, Dennis E. *Little Man, What Now? "Der Stürmer" in the Weimar Republic.* New York: Archon, 1982.

Singer, Isaac Bashevis. "Forword." Bilski 6–9.

Smith, Gary, ed. *On Walter Benjamin.* Cambridge, Mass.: MIT P, 1988.

———. "'Das Jüdische versteht sich von selbst': Walter Benjamins frühe Auseinandersetzung mit dem Judentum." *Deutsche Vierteljahrsschrift* 65 (1991): 318–36.

Sokel, Walter. "Franz Kafka as a Jew." *Leo Baeck Institute Year Book* 18 (1973): 233–38.

## Works Cited

Sombart, Werner. *Die Juden und das Wirtschaftsleben*. Leipzig: Duncker & Humblot, 1913.

Sontag, Susan. "Under the Sign of Saturn." *Under the Sign of Saturn*. New York: Farrar, Straus, Giroux, 1980, 107–34.

Sorkin, David. *The Transformation of German Jewry, 1780–1840*. New York: Oxford UP, 1987.

Spengler, Oswald. "The Soul of the City." Trans. Charles Francis Atkinson. *Classic Essays on the Culture of Cities*. Ed. Richard Sennett. Englewood Cliffs, N.J.: Prentice Hall, 1969. 61–88.

Stachura, Peter D. *The German Youth Movement 1900–1945*. New York: St. Martin's, 1981.

Steinberg, Michael P., ed. *Walter Benjamin and the Demands of History*. Ithaca, N.Y.: Cornell UP, 1996.

Steiner, George. "The Rembrancer: Rescuing Walter Benjamin from his Acolytes." *Times Literary Supplement* 4723, 8 October 1993: 37–38.

Stern, David. "The Man With Qualities: The Incongruous Achievement of Walter Benjamin." *New Republic* 10 April 1995: 31–38.

Stern, Fritz. *The Politics of Cultural Despair: A Study in the Rise of the Germanic Ideology*. Berkeley: U of California P, 1961.

Stölzl, Christoph. *Kafkas böses Böhmen*. Munich: text + kritik, 1975.

———. "Kafka: Jew, Anti-Semite, Zionist." Trans. Elizabeth Bredeck. Anderson 53–79.

Strauß, Ludwig. "Ein Dokument der Assimilation." *Die Freistatt* 1.1 (April 1913): 13–19.

Stüssi, Anna. *Erinnerung an die Zukunft. Walter Benjamin's 'Berliner Kindheit um Neunzehnhundert.'* Göttingen: Vandenhoeck and Ruprecht, 1977.

Szondi, Peter. "Hoffnung im Vergangenen: Über Walter Benjamin." *Satz und Gegensatz*. Frankfurt a. M.: Suhrkamp, 1964. 79–97. English: "Hope in the Past: On Walter Benjamin." Trans. Harvey Mendelsohn. *Critical Inquiry* 4.3 (Spring 1978): 491–506.

———. "Nachwort." *Walter Benjamin, "Städtebilder."* Ed. Theodor W. Adorno. Frankfurt a. M.: Suhrkamp, 1963, 79–99. English: "Walter Benjamin's City Portraits." Trans. Harvey Mendelsohn. Smith 18–32.

Tal, Uriel. *Christians and Jews in Germany: Religion, Politics and Ideology in the Second Reich*. Trans. Noah Jonathan Jacobs. Ithaca, N.Y.: Cornell UP, 1975.

# Works Cited

Tatar, Maria. *Lustmord: Sexual Murder in Weimar Germany*. Princeton: Princeton UP, 1995.

Theilhaber, Felix. *Der Untergang der deutschen Juden*. 2nd. ed. Berlin: Jüdischer Verlag, 1921.

———. "Randbemerkungen eines Gesundheitsfanatikers." *Jüdische Turn- und Sportzeitung [Ostjuden Sonderheft]* 21 January 1920: 7–10.

Thiekötter, Angelika. "Ausgraben und Erinnern: Berliner Kindheit um Neunzehnhundert." *Buchlicht Männlein und Engel der Geschichte* 30–38.

Thielking, Sigrid. *Auf dem Irrweg ins 'Neue Kanaan?' Palästina und der Zionismus im Werk Arnold Zweigs vor dem Exil*. Frankfurt a. M. et al.: Peter Lang, 1990.

Tönnies, Ferdinand. *Gemeinschaft und Gesellschaft*. 1887. 8th ed. Darmstadt: Wissenschaftliche Buchgesellschaft, 1979. English: *Community and Society*. Trans. Charles P. Loomis. 1957. New Brunswick, N.J.: Transactions Books, 1988.

Tramer, Hans. "Prague–City of Three Peoples." *Leo Baeck Institute Year Book* 9 (1964): 305–339.

Traverso, Enzo. *The Jews & Germany: From the 'Judeo-German Symbiosis' to the Memory of Auschwitz*. Trans. Daniel Weissbort. Lincoln: U of Nebraska P, 1995.

Treitschke, Heinrich von. "Unsere Aussichten" (1879). *Vom Judenhaß zum Antisemitismus*. Ed. Detlev Claussen. Darmstadt: Sammlung Luchterhand, 1987. 110–16.

Trilling, Lionel. *Sincerity and Authenticity*. Cambridge, Mass.: Harvard UP, 1971.

Unseld, Siegfried, ed. *Zur Aktualität Walter Benjamins*. Frankfurt a. M.: Suhrkamp, 1970.

Urzidil, Johannes. "Two Recollections: Prague II June 1924 and The Golem." *The World of Franz Kafka*. Ed. J.P. Stern. New York: Holt, Rinehart, and Winston, 1980. 56–68.

Vidler, Anthony. "The Explosion of Space: Architecture and the Filmic Imaginary." *Assemblage* 21 (1993): 45–59.

———. *The Architectural Uncanny: Essays in the Modern Unhomely*. Cambridge, Mass.: MIT P, 1993.

Vishniac, Roman. *A Vanished World*. New York: Farrar, Straus & Giroux, 1983.

———. *Polish Jews*. New York: Schocken, 1949.

Volkov, Shulamit. "The Dynamics of Dissimilation: Ostjuden and German Jews." *The Jewish Response to German Culture: From the Enlightenment to the Second World War.* Eds. Jehuda Reinharz and Walter Schatzberg. Hannover, N.H.: UP of New England, 1985. 195–211.

*Vom Judentum: Ein Sammelbuch.* Ed. Verein jüdischer Hochschüler Bar Kochba. Leipzig: Kurt Wolff, 1913.

Wagenbach, Klaus. *Kafkas Prag.* Berlin: Wagenbach, 1993.

———. "Prague at the Turn of the Century." Trans. Warren Habib. Anderson 25–52.

*Was wird aus den Ostjuden? Eine kritische Auseinandersetzung zur Ostjudenfrage.* Ed. Deutschvölkischer Schutz- und Trutz-Bund. Hamburg: Deutschvölkische Verlagsanstalt, 1920.

Wassermann, Jakob. *Mein Weg als Deutscher und Jude.* 1920/21. Berlin: Nishen, 1987. English: *My Life as German and Jew.* Trans. S. N. Brainin. New York: Coward McCann, 1933.

Weber, Max. *Ancient Judaism.* Trans. Hans H. Gerth and Don Martindale. Glencoe, Ill.: Free Press, 1952.

———. *Max Weber: Essays in Sociology.* Trans. H. H. Gerth and C. Wright Mills. New York: Oxford UP, 1946.

Weigel, Sigrid. *Body- and Image-Space: Re-reading Walter Benjamin.* Trans. Georgina Paul et al. New York: Routledge, 1996.

Wegener, Paul. *Der Golem: Wie er in die Welt kam. Eine Geschichte in fünf Kapiteln.* Berlin: August Scherl, 1921.

———. "Die Zukunft des Films" (1920). *Stimmen eines Jahrhunderts 1888–1990: Deutsche Autobiographien, Tagebücher, Bilder und Briefe.* Ed. Andreas Lixl-Purcell. Fort Worth, Tex.: Holt, Rinehart and Winston, 1990.

———. "Neue Kinoziele" (1916). Greve 117–18.

———. "Schauspielerei und Film" (1915). Greve 116.

———. *The Golem.* Trans. Roger Manvell. *Masterworks of the German Cinema.* Ed. Roger Manvell. New York: Harper & Row, 1973.

Weltsch, Felix. "Franz Kafka gestorben." Koch 9–11.

———. "The Rise and Fall of the Jewish-German Symbiosis: The Case of Franz Kafka." *Leo Baeck Institute Year Book* 1 (1956): 255–76.

Weltsch, Robert. "Die Jugend des jüdischen Prag." Kaznelson 17–18.

———. "Die schleichende Krise der jüdischen Identität." *Die deutsche Judenfrage: Ein kritischer Rückblick.* Berlin: Jüdischer Verlag, 1981. 9–22.

# Works Cited

Wenzel, Georg, ed. *Arnold Zweig 1887–1968: Werk und Leben in Dokumenten und Bildern.* East Berlin: Aufbau, 1978.

Wertheimer, Jack. *Unwelcome Strangers: East European Jews in Imperial Germany.* New York: Oxford UP, 1987.

Westheim, Paul. "Eine Filmstadt von Poelzig, 1920." Greve 120.

Wieseltier, Leon. *Against Identity.* New York: William Drenttel, 1996.

Wistrich, Robert. "The Fassbinder Controversy." *Between Redemption and Perdition: Modern Antisemitism and Jewish Identity.* New York: Routledge, 1990. 121–29.

———. *The Jews of Vienna in the Age of Franz Joseph.* New York: Oxford UP, 1989.

Witte, Bernd. "Bilder der Endzeit: Zu einem authentischen Text der *Berliner Kindheit* von Walter Benjamin." *Deutsche Vierteljahrsschrift* 58 (1984): 570–92.

———. *Walter Benjamin.* Reinbeck bei Hamburg: Rohwohlt, 1985.

Wiznitzer, Manuel. *Arnold Zweig: Das Leben eines deutsch-jüdischen Schriftstellers.* Königstein/Ts.: Athenäum, 1983.

Wohlfarth, Irving. "Et Cetera? De l'historien comme chiffonier." *Walter Benjamin à Paris.* Ed. Heinz Wismann. Paris: Editions du Cerf, 1986. 596–609.

———. "'Männer aus der Fremde': Walter Benamin and the 'German-Jewish Parnassus.'" *New German Critique* 70 (Winter 1997): 3–85.

———. "On Some Motifs in Walter Benjamin." *Problems of Modernity: Adorno and Benjamin.* Ed. Andrew Benjamin. New York: Routledge, 1988. 157–216.

———. "'Der Umgekehrte Turnbau zu Babel': Die Idee des Judentums bei Walter Benjamin." *Buchlicht Männlein und Engel der Geschichte* 102–4.

Wolf, Arie. "Arnold Zweigs Ostjudenbild." *Bulletin des Leo Baeck Instituts* 67 (1984): 15–40.

Wolff, Janet. "Memoirs and Micrologies: Walter Benjamin, Feminism and Cultural Analysis." *New Formations* 20 (Summer 1993): 113–22.

Wolin, Richard. *Walter Benjamin: An Aesthetic of Redemption.* Berkeley: U of California P, 1994.

Wolitz, Seth. "The Golem (1920): An Expressionist Treatment." *Passion and Rebellion: The Expressionist Heritage.* Eds. Stephen Eric Bronner and Douglas Kellner. New York: Universe, 1983. 384–97.

X, Malcolm. *The Autobiography of Malcolm X.* 1964. New York: Ballantine, 1992.

Yerushalmi, Yosef Hayim. *Zakhor: Jewish History and Jewish Memory.* 1982. New York: Schocken, 1989.

## Works Cited

Young, James E. *The Texture of Memory: Holocaust Memorials and Meaning.* New Haven: Yale UP, 1993.

Zechlin, Egmont. *Die deutsche Politik und die Juden im Ersten Weltkrieg.* Göttingen: Vandenhoeck und Ruprecht, 1969.

Zipes, Jack, ed. and trans. *The Operated Jew: Two Tales of Anti-Semitism.* New York: Routledge, 1991.

Zipperstein, Steven J. "The Shtetl Revisited." Helzel 17–24.

Zucker, Paul. "Mythen der Gegenwart." *Der Jude* 7/8 (1923): 464–65.

Zweig, Arnold. "Außenpolitik und Ostjudenfrage." *Neue Jüdische Monatshefte* 4.11/12 (1919/20): 244–49. Rpt. Claussen 47–54.

———. "Das Jüdische in meinem Wesen und Schaffen." *Jüdische liberale Zeitung* 5.42, 16 October 1925: 1. Rpt. Claussen 21–22.

———. *Das ostjudische Antlitz.* 2nd ed. Berlin: Welt-Verlag, 1922.

———. *Die Bestie.* Munich: Langen, 1914.

———. "Die Demokratie und die Seele des Juden." *Vom Judentum* 210–35.

———. "Die revolutionäre Jugend des Ostens." *Der Jude* 7 (October 1919): 296–305.

———. "Grabrede auf Spartakus." *Die Weltbühne* 15.4 (January 1919): 76–78.

———. *Herrkunft und Zukunft.* Vienna: Phaidon, 1929.

———. *Jüdischer Ausdruckswille.* Ed. Detlev Claussen. Berlin: Aufbau, 1991.

———. "Judenzählung vor Verdun." *Die Schaubühne* 13.5 (February 1917): 115–17.

———. "Strucks 'Ostjuden.'" *Vossische Zeitung,* evening ed., 29 October 1918: 2.

———. "Über jüdische Legenden." *Mitteilungen des Verbandes der jüdischen Jugendvereine Deutschlands* (1914): 14–17.

———. "Ueber Asphaltliteratur." *Pariser Tageblatt* 22 July 1934.

———. "Zum Problem des jüdischen Dichters in Deutschland." *Die Freistatt: Alljüdische Revue* 1.5 (August 1913): 375–80. Rpt. Claussen 33–40.

# Index

In the *Texts and Contexts* series

*Affective Genealogies*
*Psychoanalysis, Postmodernism, and*
*the "Jewish Question" after*
*Auschwitz*
By Elizabeth J. Bellamy

*Sojourners*
*The Return of German Jews and*
*the Question of Identity*
By John Borneman and
Jeffrey M. Peck

*Serenity in Crisis*
*A Preface to Paul de Man,*
*1939–1960*
By Ortwin de Graef

*Titanic Light*
*Paul de Man's Post-Romanticism,*
*1960–1969*
By Ortwin de Graef

*The Future of a Negation*
*Reflections on the Question of*
*Genocide*
By Alain Finkielkraut
Translated by Mary Byrd Kelly

*The Imaginary Jew*
By Alain Finkielkraut
Translated by Kevin O'Neill and
David Suchoff

*The Wisdom of Love*
By Alain Finkielkraut
Translated by Kevin O'Neill and
David Suchoff

*The House of Joshua*
*Meditations on Family and Place*
By Mindy Thompson Fullilove

*Inscribing the Other*
By Sander L. Gilman

*Antisemitism, Misogyny, and the*
*Logic of Cultural Difference*
*Cesare Lombroso and Matilde Serao*
By Nancy A. Harrowitz

*Opera*
*Desire, Disease, Death*
By Linda Hutcheon and
Michael Hutcheon

*Between Redemption and Doom*
*The Strains of German-Jewish*
*Modernism*
By Noah Isenberg

*Poetic Process*
By W. G. Kudszus

*Keepers of the Motherland*
*German Texts by Jewish*
*Women Writers*
By Dagmar C. G. Lorenz

*Madness and Art*
*The Life and Works of Adolf Wölfli*
By Walter Morgenthaler
Translated and with an introduc-
tion by Aaron H. Esman in col-
laboration with Elka Spoerri

*Organic Memory*
*History and the Body in the Late*
*Nineteenth and Early Twentieth*
*Centuries*
By Laura Otis

*Crack Wars*
*Literature, Addiction, Mania*
By Avital Ronell